F. Falaise.
1981.

CONTROL AND POWER IN CENTRAL-LOCAL GOVERNMENT RELATIONS

Control and Power in Central-Local Government Relations

R. A. W. RHODES
University of Essex

Gower

Published by
Gower Publishing Company Limited
Westmead, Farnborough, Hants, England.

 British Library Cataloguing in Publication Data

Rhodes, R.A.W.
  Control and power in central-local government
  relations.
  1. Local government - Great Britain - State
  supervision
  I. Title
  354.41'083   JS3137

  ISBN 0-566-00333-3

PRINTED BY NENE LITHO

BOUND BY WEATHERBY WOOLNOUGH

Contents

Preface and Acknowledgements

This book attempts to provide a reinterpretation of central-local relations in Britain. To be precise, it has four objectives:

(i) To identify the strengths and weaknesses of the existing literature and to provide a bibliographical guide for both students and those who might wish to carry out research in the field in the future.

(ii) To demonstrate that a focus on the links between central departments and local authorities is restrictive. The subject needs to be redefined as 'intergovernmental relations' in order to encompass the range of relationships between the various units of government.

(iii) To develop a theory of intergovernmental relations which not only raises interesting questions about the specific topic but also relates the study of intergovernmental relations to broader issues in the study of British government.

(iv) To identify a coherent programme of future research.

The book has had a somewhat unusual history and a brief note on its conception and gestation will help to explain the form of its birth. Its conception lies in a commissioned paper for the Committee of Inquiry into Local Government Finance (Layfield) published in 1976. Subsequently, I presented papers on future research into central-local relations to the Social Science Research Council's (SSRC) Panel on Research into Local Government (April 1977) and to a Public Administration Committee Working Group on Research into Central-Local Relations (November 1977). In January 1978, I was invited to join the SSRC Panel on Central-Local Government Relationships and I was asked to produce a review of the existing literature on the subject and to develop the analytical framework outlined in the foregoing papers. My paper for the Panel was completed in May 1978 and the Panel's own report was produced in January 1979. The Panel's recommendations were accepted by the Research Initiatives Board of the SSRC and, as part of the continuing effort to stimulate research into central-local relations, the SSRC decided to sponsor the publication of a number of the papers commissioned by the Panel. This book is a revision of the full-length version of my paper for the Panel.

In revising the original paper, I have not attempted to provide a guide to recent changes in the system of central-local relations. Rather the emphasis has remained on reviewing existing literature and research and as yet here has been little research on current developments.

Accordingly, I have concentrated on providing a perspective for the <u>future</u> study of central-local relations and the <u>revisions</u> have taken the form of clarifying the argument and effecting a reduction in the length of the original SSRC paper.

I was greatly aided in the process of revisions by the critical comments of my colleagues on the Panel. Early drafts of various sections of the paper were presented to a number of conferences and seminars. I would like to thank the Department of Politics (Aberdeen); the Department of Politics (Strathclyde); the Royal Institute of Public Administration (Edinburgh and East of Scotland Branch); the Institute of Local Government Studies (Birmingham); the Local Politics Group of the Political Studies Association (Birmingham and London); and the participants of the Public Administration Committee Annual Conference (York) and the Policy Studies Conference (Birmingham) for their patient and friendly criticism.

A number of individuals have also commented, either in whole or in part, on various drafts. My thanks to Doug Pitt (Strathclyde), Barbara Webster (Inlogov), Ed Page (Strathclyde), Ken Benson (Missouri - Columbia), Mike Goldsmith (Salford) and Bob Goodin (Essex). The first draft was written whilst I was a member of the Department of Administration, University of Strathclyde, and I must thank Lewis Gunn for his help and support. At different times, Ed Page and Kevin Pudney expedited the compilation and checking of the bibliography and Brian Hardy provided invaluable assistance at every stage in the preparation of the final manuscript. Maureen Russell (Strathclyde), Pat Caplin (Essex) and Desne Harrington (Essex) have patiently typed and retyped the various drafts. Finally, George Jones (LSE) and John Stewart (Inlogov) have been endless sources of criticism and encouragement and I owe both of them a special debt of gratitude. As ever, the responsibility for the remaining shortcomings is mine alone.

The author and publisher would like to thank the following who kindly gave permission for quotations to be included from their publications: The Clarendon Press for R.J. May, <u>Federalism and Fiscal Adjustment</u>; <u>Town Planning Review</u> for R.A.W. Rhodes, 'Some Myths in Central-Local Relations'; G.W. Jones for <u>Responsibility and Government</u>; American Elsevier and <u>the European Journal of Political Research</u> for R.A.W. Rhodes, 'Understanding Intergovernmental Relations'.

Rod Rhodes
Colchester

March, 1980.

1 Introduction

The subject of central-local relations has been of
peripheral interest to social scientists. The topic has
been seen as within the province of Public Administration
with an attendant fixation on the legal-institutional
aspects of the relationship. Recently, this situation
has been changing. First, central government has become
increasingly concerned about its perceived inability to
control local authority expenditure. The most obvious
manifestation of this concern was the appointment and
report of the Committee of Inquiry into Local Government
Finance (Layfield). (1)   Second, there has been a growing realisation that, in spite of the many changes in the
system of central-local relations over the last decade
and a half, there have been virtually no academic studies
of either the changes or the way the system actually
works. (2)

One of the major objectives of this book is to take
stock of that research which has been published on
central-local relations and to identify some of the
possible directions for future research. The review
covers the post-war period but, and the qualification is
an important one, it is not limited to central-local
relations narrowly defined. Perhaps one of the major
problems associated with the study of central-local
relations is the pre-occupation with a narrow range of
issues. This book argues that central-local relations is
but one facet of a larger system of intergovernmental
relations which encompases both links between the United
Kingdom government and the so-called peripheral areas of
Scotland, Wales and Northern Ireland and the links
between the various central governments and other sub-
national units of government.

The scope of this review is broader, however, than the
system of intergovernmental relations in Britain. Not
only has the literature on central-local relations been
pre-occupied with a limited number of governmental
institutions but it has also demonstrated a marked
aversion to theory. It will be argued that the study of
intergovernmental relations is important not just because
it is currently deemed to be a policy problem but because
it can illuminate facets of modern government of concern
to social scientists. A number of theories of advanced
industrial society raise issues of direct relevance to the
study of central-local relations. The bulk of this

chapter will review, albeit briefly, some of those macro theories capable of informing the study of central-local relations. Subsequent chapters will review in more detail some of the theoretical work on interorganisational analysis and intergovernmental relations which modify these general considerations for application in specific contexts. And the argument linking these, at times, disparate contributions is that the study of intergovernmental relations can only develop if it becomes consciously theoretical and encompasses issues and problems traditionally ignored or eschewed in the literature on central-local relations.

The pleas for theory and for a wider definition of the subject matter than a focus on central-local relations are, of course, easy to make. The problems of developing such a theory are far greater. However, if this review is to identify future areas of research, it is essential to move beyond exhortation and provide a framework for the analysis of intergovernmental relations in Britain. In the absence of such a framework, there is a danger that one compiles a list or shopping-bag of 'interesting' projects. These projects can have no overall rationale and could bear little relationship to each other. A framework of analysis is essential if such fragmentation is to be avoided.

The justification for a theoretical framework does not lie, however, either in the inadequacies of previous work or in the need to identify a coherent group of projects. It lies in the ability of that framework to identify issues and problems previously ignored; to raise new questions; and to provide a distinctive reinterpretation of the subject. The 'power-dependence' model of intergovernmental relations developed in this book suggests that these relations are simultaneously rational, ambiguous and confused. In other words, the functional links between national and sub-national units of government are rational within a given policy area. Actors in the same policy area at different levels of government share common interests in the development of that policy area. However, the links between policy areas are ambiguous and, when the system is viewed as a whole, as is the case for public expenditure decisions, the pattern of relationships is confused. The framework presented in this book attempts to explain why the system is rational, ambiguous and confused. However, this statement anticipates future chapters. Recently, emphasis has been placed upon the problems associated with central-local relations, especially the failure of central government to control the level of local expenditure. (3) In these circumstances, it is particularly important to demonstrate that the study of intergovernmental relations can shed light on matters of more general concern in the social sciences.

THE CONTEXT OF INTERGOVERNMENTAL RELATIONS:
some theoretical issues

Phrases such as 'the contract state', 'the new industrial state', 'turbulent environments' and 'organised social complexity' occur with increasing frequency in both academic and more popular literature along with expressions of concern about the growing lack of accountability in modern government. (4) They have not been missing from interpretations on British government. For example, Tony King has argued that:

> 'If Britain is becoming harder to govern, it is partly because the number of dependency relationships in which government is involved has increased substantially, and because the incidence of acts of non-compliance by the other participants in these relationships has also increased substantially'. (5)

In a similar vein, Richard Rose has suggested that:

> 'The growing complexity of government tends to make government overcomplex, reducing its efficiency and upon occasion, its effectiveness. ...Today, the chief policies of government depend for success upon the results of complex processes of interaction that can be influenced but not controlled by government'.

This 'ungovernability' or 'overload' thesis has been widely discussed and it is not without its problems. As Richard Rose has pointed out 'ungovernability' is a term 'that is ill-defined, variously defined or never defined at all'. (6) Its status as a theory is similarly elusive. Only limited attention is paid to why governments have increasingly intervened in the economy. Explanations of ungovernability stress the level of electoral expectations, complexity, competition between interest groups, scarcity of resources or some combination of all these factors for explaining policy failure. (7) A more adequate theory would explain why, for example, organised social complexity was a feature of British society in particular and advanced industrial societies in general. In fact, the 'ungovernability' thesis draws together in varying mixtures elements from the numerous theories of post-industrial society without explicitly demonstrating its links to that theory (in whatever version) or explicating the causal connections between the selected elements. Or to make the same point a different way, the ungovernability thesis explores the consequences for government of changes in its power and in the distribution of power in society without explaining the causes of those changes. For a broader ranging analysis, it is necessary to turn to theories of 'corporatism' and 'post-industrial society'.

Winkler defines corporatism in the following terms:

> 'Corporatism is an economic system in which the
> state directs and controls predominantly
> privately-owned business according to four
> principles: unity, order, nationalism and
> success'. (8)

In this definition, control refers to 'control over the
internal decision making of privately owned business'.
(9) To the extent that corporatism stresses the interdependence of government and business, therefore, there
is a marked parallel with the relationships between central and local government.

Winkler identifies four structural causes of corporatism: 'industrial concentration, declining profitability,
technological development and international competition'.
(10) Corporatism is a response to long-standing basic
trends in the British economy. The principles underlying
the administration of the corporatist economy are:
"antinomianism, inquistorial justice, strategic control,
delegated enforcement, mediated enforcement and extra-
legal power'. (11) The state avoids formal operating
procedures; uses the courts to sustain and restore
order and cooperation; regulates national economic performance through control of a few, large organisations;
uses private organisations to administer policy; con-
ducts public administration through autonomous, inter-
mediary institutions such as quasi-non-governmental and
quasi-governmental organisations (collectively termed
'quangos'); and uses private coercion in support of
public policy. (12)

This sketch of corporatist theory indicates its relevance to the study of intergovernmental relations. First,
corporatist theory emphasises the allocation of functions
not only between government and industry but also between
the various units of government. A key element in the
theory can be assessed, therefore, by exploring the
efficacy of central control over quangos as compared to
local authorities. Apart from administrative and
financial economy, Winkler argues that the state resorts
to 'mediated enforcement' 'to conceal potentially contentious state activities'. In other words, quangos are
'indirect, concealed forms of administration'. (13)
Accordingly, one would predict that quangos were less
likely to be called to account for their actions (either
by elected representatives or the electorate) than local
authorities. In more general terms, corporatist theory
suggests that differences between the different institutional forms of state actions should be analysed. What
difference does it make that a service/policy is en-

trusted to a local authority rather than a quango?

Second, the corporatist state may well view local authorities as means for legitimating its decisions and for co-opting potential dissidents; that is, as part of the machinery of delegated enforcement. For example, the creation of the Consultative Council on Local Government Finance enables local authorities to 'participate' in making public expenditure decisions. This co-option could be described as a form of social control; a way of defusing opposition to cuts in public expenditure and for turning the opponents of cuts into agents for implementing central government policy. Certainly, corporatist theory raises interesting questions about the roles of the national institutions of local government.

It is possible, of course, to identify additional, specific themes in corporatist theory which could be explored in the context of intergovernmental relations. For example, the relationships between local authorities, the Home Office and the police could be explored in the light of the (alleged) growth in the use of private coercion to support public policy. However, the most interesting feature of corporatist theory is the exploration of changing (and increasing) state power. Winkler argues that the state has some degree of autonomy (14) and then focuses on the causes of the interdependence of government and industry and the consequences of this interdependence for the form, extent and autonomy of state action. The consequences of this focus for the study of intergovernmental relations can be illustrated by a brief examination of local government finance, the study of which typically takes the form of either straightforward descriptions of the system or analyses of changing patterns of grant and expenditure. (15) There have been few analyses of the development of the system (16) and the main preoccupation has been the effects upon local authorities of increasing dependence on central grant. Corporatist theory suggests that central government's policy on local government finance will be an integral part of its economic policy: that is, just as the principles of corporatist administration are a response to the structural problems of the British economy so changes in local government finance reflect these problems. Moreover, as these problems intensify, so will central government's attempts to control local finance. Accordingly, there is need for an historical study of local government finance relating changes not only to the specific financial problems of local authorities but also to the fluctuating fortunes of the British economy. Within such a broad study a number of specific issues can be explored. Trends in local government finance could be compared with trends in the financing of other sub-national units in order to assess whether the centre's need to control both the economy and local authorities has led it to by-pass local authorities and resort to 'mediated enforcement'. The analysis could include also changes in the form of financing and explore the extent to which the centre became involved in the budgetary process of sub-national units. The changing scope of central government's involvement in the finance of local government throughout the post-war period provides a setting for the exploration of many of the themes of corporatist theory. And casting the study of local government finance in this form provides a necessary corrective to the concern with the details of the system by emphasising the evolving form of the system and its relationship to the economic context of British government.

The theory of corporatism does not just assume that there is a growing interdependence between the state and industry, it also attempts to explore the causes of this interdependence and its consequences for the state. It provides an interpretive framework within which the study of intergovernmental relations can be located.

However, there are problems with corporatist theory. As applied to Britain, analysis has been limited to the fields of economic policy and industrial relations. Nor is it clear that the state is able to maintain unity - a key corporatist notion - in these fields. Marsh and Grant argue the government, the TUC and the CBI have not been able to evolve an agreed industrial and economic policy; that there is no basic consensus underpinning the system; and that the decisions of the leadership of the CBI and the TUC are not accepted as authoritative by the membership. (17) And yet these features would seem to be essential for unity in the field of economic policy.

There are also problems with the analysis of the long-term structural changes in the British economy (18) and there are ambiguities in the concept of corporatism. For example, Winkler does not distinguish between state corporatism in which 'the state plays a directive role in the establishment of class harmony' and societal corporatism where 'the representative organisations are autonomous but cooperate with the state and each other because they recognise that they are mutually inter-dependent'. (19) And yet such a distinction would seem to be particularly appropriate to an analysis of, for example, the Labour government's 'social contract'.

Corporatist theory is, therefore, only one of a number of possible interpretative frameworks for the study of intergovernmental relations. But its major themes command attention. The interdependence of organisations, the power of the state and the broad socio-economic context of government policy are issues which cannot be ignored. Indeed, they are not the exclusive preserve of corporatist theory.

The theory of 'post-industrial society' has appeared in many variants and this very profusion no doubt accounts for the popularity and pervasiveness of a number of its central tenets. Daniel Bell defines the concept of post-industrial society as follows:

> "1. Economic sector: the change from a goods-producing to a service economy;
> 2. Occupational distribution: the pre-eminence of the professional and technical class;
> 3. Axial principle: the centrality of theoretical knowledge as the source of innovation and of policy formulation for the society;
> 4. Future orientation: the control of technology and technological assessment;
> 5. Decision-making: the creation of a new 'intellectual technology'" (20)

These 'tendencies' are reflected in, and reinforced by, three major processes in Western industrial society:

> '...the transformation of the industrial enterprise by the emergence of managers as controllers of the organisation; the changing composition of the occupational structure by the relative shrinkage of the industrial proletariat and the expansion of a new technical and professional stratum; and the transformation of the political system through the extension of the state bureaucracy and the rise of political techno-crats'. (21)

For Bell, 'the major source of structural change in society ... is the change in the character of knowledge' (22) and one of the major structural changes is the spread of bureaucracy. 'In the mid-twentieth century, bureaucracy has become the central problem for all societies' (23) and we live in an 'organisational society' where the complex web of organisations provide the 'locus of one's life'. (24) The problem is to manage this organised complexity or networks of interdependence and this task is conceptualised in terms of 'games against nature and games between persons'. (25) The conflict between the professional and populace in the locus of the organisation is seen as the distinctive form of conflict of post-industrial society. (26) Quite clearly, the theory of 'post-industrial society' treats interorganisational dependence as one of the defining characteristics of the new era.

7

Obviously, this summary neither does justice to Bell's argument - although it introduces his major themes - nor reflects the variety of approaches. (27) However, it will suffice for a discussion of the theory's relevance to the study of intergovernmental relations.

Perhaps the single most suggestive theme in Bell's analysis concerns changes in the class structure of industrial society and the consequences for the distribution of power. With the divorce of ownership and control and the growing primacy of knowledge for the process of production, the professional and technical class and the political technocrats - the 'technostructure' in Galbraith's terms (28) - have risen to pre-eminence. In the context of intergovernmental relations, this argument suggests an analysis focusing on the roles of professional local government officers and civil servants and on their power in relation to the elected representatives, interest groups and citizens. To what extent do the professionals in, for example, education constitute a group of political technocrats spanning both levels of government? Are intergovernmental relations structured around professional policy communities? To what extent is the power of the professional limited by 'the cantankerousness of politics'? Does 'the conception of a rational organisation of society' stand confounded with the professionals adhering to rationality having to re-think their premises (29) or has this rationality so permeated society that it legitimates the decisions of the technostructure? Moreover, such questions involve both trends and effects. How has the power of the professional waxed and waned over the years? (An analysis of the rise of the social work profession in the post-war period should prove of interest in charting the processes underlying 'the professionalisation of everyone'). (3) What kinds of decisions are made by the political technocrats employing what criteria? Do different professional policy communities have differing ideologies or are they linked by a common adherence to the norms of rationality? To what extent do they define the needs of clients for the clients? This list of questions is not exhaustive but illustrates the kinds of issues which the 'post-industrial society' thesis raises for the study of intergovernmental relations.

As with corporatism, there is no suggestion that the 'post-industrial society' thesis is without its weaknesses. As Burns has pointed out the very label is a nonsense because the key features of 'post-industrial society' are all present in industrial society. The description of 'super-industrial' is to be preferred if only to emphasise the continuities with industrial society rather than the discontinuities. (31) A number of the key characteristics of post-industrial society are hotly disputed. The divorce between ownership and con-

trol and the emergence of a managerial elite concerned
with 'social responsibility' as much as profit has been
asserted rather than documented. (32) In fact, the
major problems with the 'post-industrial society' thesis
are the varying emphases of its proponents and the claims
made for it. The claim that we are entering a new era
should be disregarded. The theory should be viewed as a
heuristic tool which identifies important changes in the
nature of industrial society; changes ignored or
slighted in many accounts of industrialism and which will
repay further study. And considerably more care should
be exercised in defining the content of the theory. For
example, it is not uncommon for Bell and Touraine to be
discussed together as if their versions of post-
industrial society were very similar if not identical.
In fact, Touraine's analysis of 'the programmed society'
emphasises the <u>continued</u> importance of class conflict
and he attempts to map the changing dimensions of this
conflict. (33) But the key feature of the theory for
this discussion is its ability to locate intergovernmental relations within a broader framework. The treatment
of bureaucracy as a central feature of post-industrial
society, the focus on the complex web of organisations,
and the analysis of the role of political technocrats and
of 'rational' decision-making all demonstrate that the
study of intergovernmental relations need not be pursued
in splendid isolation. It can, and indeed must, be
related to broader theoretical issues.

These brief discussions of corporatism and post-
industrial society have done no more than introduce a
number of themes which could be explored in future
research. (34) As described above and, for the most
part, as discussed by their respective authors, these
themes are extremely general. They need to be translated
into the specific context of intergovernmental relations
in Britain. The remainder of the book is devoted to this
task.

SUMMARY OF CONTENTS

In Chapter Two the existing literature on intergovernmental relations is reviewed. Employing the expository
devices of the 'conventional wisdom' and the 'conventional
critique', it is argued that the study of this topic has
been confined to a narrow range of issues. Five 'forgotten dimensions' of intergovernmental relations are
identified: namely, the need for theory, variations in
local discretion, the variety of relationships, the influence of political factors and the role of the professional. The pre-occupation with central control and
the financial aspects of the relationship between the
various levels of government has led to the relative
neglect of these dimensions.

In Chapters Three and Four, attention is focused on the need to develop a theory of intergovernmental relations. However, this search is not conducted at the macro-level. The literatures on interorganisational analysis and intergovernmental relations are explored to see what contribution they can make to repairing the defects of the existing literature on intergovernmental relations in Britain. In addition, the relationship between these 'middle-range' theories and the macro-theories discussed above are briefly explored. In the case of interorganisational analysis, it is argued that the analysis of interdependence is far more precise than that contained in either corporatism or the 'post-industrial society' thesis. However, this literature has become pre-occupied with the measurement of interactions or exchanges and it will not facilitate the analysis of intergovernmental relations unless it is located within a theory on intra and interorganisational <u>power</u>. In the case of the literature on intergovernmental relations, there is much of value in the analyses of the micro-politics of the relationships between the various tiers of government. With a few notable exceptions, however, the descriptions of intergovernmental relations have not been located within any explanatory framework. An explanation of the strategies and games of the actors presupposes a theory of the relative power of the various units of government.

In Chapter Five, a power-dependence framework for the analysis of intergovernmental relations is presented. It is argued that the discretion and the relative power of the various tiers of government is a product of their resources, the rules of the game and the values and interests supporting both the rules and the existing distribution of resources. The interactions between the units of government are analysed as if they were a 'game' in which the participants employ strategies within known rules. In the light of this analysis a number of suggestions are made for future research into intergovernmental relations in Britain.

Finally, there is an extensive, although selective, bibliography. Each section of the bibliography is prefaced with a short guide to the major books and articles on the particular topic. The bibliography is <u>not</u> limited to central-local relations narrowly defined. <u>It</u> includes items on the sociology of organisations, intergovernmental relations in the United States of America and Western Europe, and social and political theory as well as such specific topics as local government finance. Quite deliberately, the bibliography attempts to support the contention that the study of intergovernmental relations must be related to and draw upon a range of theoretical material in the social sciences.

NOTES AND REFERENCES

1.   Committee of Inquiry into Local Government Finance
(Layfield), Report Cmnd. 6453, London: H.M.S.O. 1976.
Hereafter referred to as the Layfield Report.
2.   The major research study of the last fifteen years
is Griffith, J.A.G., Central Departments and Local
Authorities London: Allen and Unwin, 1966. On the
limited amount of current research see: Barker, A.,
Central-Local Government Relationships in Britain as a
Field of Study: A commentary and research register
London: S.S.R.C., 1978.
3.   See for example: Social Science Research Council,
Central-Local Government Relationships London: SSRC,
1979 p.5.
4.   See: Smith, B.L.R., and Hague, D.C., (eds.), The
Dilemma of Accountability in Modern Government London:
Macmillan, 1971; Jones, G.W., Responsibility and
Government London School of Economics and Political
Science, 1977. Galbraith, J.K., The New Industrial
State London: Deutsch, second edn., 1972; Emery, F.E.
and Trist, E.L., 'The Causal Texture of Organisational
Environments' Human Relations Vol. 18 1965 pp. 21-32.
La Porte, T.R., Organised Social Complexity: challenge
to politics and policy Princeton: Princeton University
Press, 1974; and Toffler, Alvin, Future Shock London:
Pan Books, 1971.
5.   King, A., 'Overload: Problems of Governing in the
1970s' Political Studies Vol. 23 1975 p. 168.
6.   Rose, R., 'Ungovernability: Is there Fire Behind
the Smoke?' Glasgow: University of Strathclyde
Studies in Public Policy No. 16. 1978 p. 15, p. 16 and
p. 1.
7.   See: Brittan, S., 'The Economic Contradictions of
Democracy' British Journal of Political Science Vol. 5
1975 pp. 129-59; Douglas, J., 'The Overloaded Crown',
British Journal of Political Science Vol. 6 1976 pp.
483-505; Scharpf, F.W., 'Public Organisation and the
Waning of the Welfare State' European Journal of Political Research Vol. 5 1977 pp. 339-62; Rose, op. cit.,;
and King, op. cit.
8.   Winkler, J.T., 'Corporatism' European Journal of
Sociology Vol. 27 1976 p. 103.
9.   Winkler, op. cit., p. 104.
10.   Winkler, op. cit., p. 117.
11.   Winkler, J.T., 'The Corporatist Economy: theory and
administration' in Scase, R. (ed.), Industrial Society:
Class, Cleavage and Control London: Allen and Unwin
1977 p. 50.
12.   Winkler, 'The Corporatist Economy', op. cit.,
pp. 50-55.
13.   Winkler, 'The Corporatist Economy', op. cit.,
p. 54 and p. 55.
14.   Winkler, 'Corporatism', op. cit., pp. 134-36.
15.   See for example: Hepworth, N.P., The Finance of
Local Government London: Allen and Unwin, third edn.

1976; and Boaden, N., Urban Policy Making London:
Cambridge University Press, 1971.

16.   One of the exceptions is Rhodes, G., 'Local Government Finance 1918-1966' in Committee of Inquiry into
Local Government Finance, Appendix 6, The Relationship
Between Central and Local Government London: H.M.S.O.,
1976 pp. 102-73.

17.   Marsh, D. and Grant, W.P., 'Tripartism: reality or
myth?' Government and Opposition Vol. 12 1977 pp.194-211.

18.   See for example: Jessop, R., 'Corporatism, Parlia-
mentarism and Social Democracy' in Schmitter, P.C. and
Lehmbruch, G., (eds.), Trends Towards Corporatist
Intermediation London: Sage, 1979 pp. 185-212.

19.   Marsh and Grant, op. cit., pp. 195-96. See also:
Schmitter, P.C., 'Still the Century of Corporatism?' in
Schmitter and Lehmbruch (eds.), op. cit., pp. 7-52.

20.   Bell, D., The Coming of Post-Industrial Society
Harmondsworth: Penguin Books, 1976 p. 14.

21.   Bell, op. cit., p. 99.

22.   Bell, op. cit., p. 144.

23.   Bell, op. cit., p. 80.

24.   Bell, op. cit., p. 162.

25.   Bell, op. cit., p.28, p. 127 and p. 468.

26.   Bell, op. cit., pp. 128-29.

27.   See also: Etzioni, A., The Active Society New York:
The Free Press, 1968; Touraine, A., The Post Industrial
Society London: Wildwood House, 1974; Vickers, Sir
Geoffrey, Freedom in a Rocking Boat Harmondsworth:
Penguin Books, 1972.

28.   See: Galbraith, op. cit., pp. 59-71.

29.   Bell, op. cit., p. 366.

30.   Wilensky, H., 'The Professionalisation of Everyone'
in Grusky, O. and Miller, G.A. (eds.), The Sociology
of Organisations New York: The Free Press, 1970
pp. 483-501.

31.   Burns, T., 'On the Rationale of the Corporate
System' in Marris, R. (ed.), The Corporate Society
London: Macmillan, 1974 pp. 121-177.

32.   See for example: Nichols, T., Ownership Control and
Ideology London: Allen and Unwin, 1969; and Blackburn,
R., 'The New Capitalism' in Blackburn, R. (ed.),
Ideology in Social Science London: Fontana/Collins,
pp. 164-186.

33.   See: Touraine, op. cit., ch. 1.

34.   One theory not explored in this book is Marxism.
Various discussions of the 'local state' can be found
in Pickvance, C.G., Urban Sociology: critical essays
London: Tavistock, 1976. At the time of writing, it
is difficult to evaluate the utility of this work for
the study of intergovernmental relations, especially as
it tends to remain highly abstract not to say abstruse.
For a preliminary attempt to demonstrate the relevance
of this approach to the study of intergovernmental
relations see Dunleavy, P., 'Theories of the State and
Society and the Study of Central-Local Relations' in
Jones, G.W., Central-Local Relations in Britain

Farnborough, Hants.: Saxon House, 1980 (forthcoming).
At least three problems can be identified which would
appear to limit the applicability of the approach.
First, the theory of the state proposed by Poulantzas
and Castells would seem to be both tautological and
teleological. For a discussion of these points see:
Saunders, P., Urban Politics: a sociological interpretation Harmondsworth: Penguin Books, 1980 pp. 180-89.
Second, considerable confusion appears to surround the
concept of the 'relative autonomy of the state'. One of
the few applications of marxist theories of the state to
British local government, Cockburn, C., The Local State
London: Pluto Press, 1977 p. 47 defines the state
(including local authorities) as having 'a basic unity':
'All its parts work fundamentally as one'. The extent to
which the various institutions of the state are unified
would seem to be a matter for investigation and not for
definition. On this point see: Pickvance, op. cit.,
pp. 203-7; and Perrow, C., Complex Organisations
Glenview, Ill.: Scott, Foresman, second edn., 1979
p. 215. Finally, it is misleading in all probability,
to talk as if there were a theory of the state. There
are major differences between the various contributors
within this tradition and to subsume them all under a
single label is to conceal as much as it reveals. For
example, compare the work of Miliband, R., The State in
Capitalist Society London: Weidenfeld and Nicolson,
1969 with Poulantzas, N., Political Power and Social
Classes London: New Left Books, 1973. Such contrasts
exist also in the study of British government. Compare,
for example, Cockburn, op. cit., with Dearlove, J.,
The Reorganisation of British Local Government London:
Cambridge University Press, 1979 with Jessop, R., 'The
Transformation of the State in Postwar Britain', in
Scase, R. (ed.), The State in Western Europe London:
Croom Helm, 1980. To date, the contribution of this
tradition has been negative rather than positive - i.e.
it has highlighted the defects of conventional forms of
analysis rather than providing a redefinition of the
subject matter of research with supporting empirical
investigations.

2 Some myths in central-local relations

INTRODUCTION

> 'On a bitter winter's day, two porcupines
> moved together to keep warm, soon hurt each
> other with their quills, so they moved
> apart, only to find themselves freezing
> again. The poor porcupines moved back and
> forth freezing and hurting until they
> finally found the optimum distance at which
> they could huddle in warmth and yet not
> pain each other, too much.

> Have central and local government yet
> found the optimum distance?' (Parable)

The study of central-local relations is largely
allegorical. The literature abounds with myths embodying
popular ideas on social phenomena and parables of
imagined events. To foster an understanding of central-
local relations, therefore, it is necessary to unpick
the traditional tapestry: to separate fact from fiction.
The tools for this exercise are provided by the expository devices of the 'conventional wisdom' and the
'conventional critique'.

THE 'CONVENTIONAL WISDOM'

At the risk of some over-simplification, it can be
argued that discussions of central-local relations in the
1950s and 1960s were based on the distinction between the
agent and the partnership models. (1) In the agent
model, local authorities implement national policies
under the supervision of central departments. Local
authorities have little or no discretion. In the
partnership model, local authorities and central
departments are co-equals under Parliament. Local
authorities have considerable discretion in designing and
implementing their own policies. It is argued that local
government is moving from being a partner to being an
agent. This centralisation has come about for two reasons.
First, central government exercises increasingly tight
control over capital expenditure whilst, at the same time,
local authorities have become increasingly dependent upon
central grant. Second, central departments have acquired
more powers of detailed control. These are the myths
which accord central government a supernatural role.
Moreover, advocates of the partnership model are great
believers in local autonomy and, as a result, the trend
for local authorities to become mere agents of central

government justifies pleas for a return to the golden era of local autonomy. Myths and parable are thus entwined.

Such a brief description of the 'conventional wisdom' verges on caricature but it is nonetheless easy to illustrate the main tenets of this view of central-local relations. Thus, the Maud Report concluded:

> 'We are clear that there is a tendency for
> control and direction by the central govern-
> ment to increase, and for the financial
> independence of local authorities to decline
> still further and that both these tendencies
> weaken local government and detract from its
> effectiveness'. (2)

The Redcliffe-Maud Report was similarly of the opinion that 'there are strong centralising influences at work'. Central government was said to be 'less willing to leave local problems to local solutions'. Three reasons were advanced for this state of affairs in addition to 'the weaknesses inherent in the present structure of local government'. First, the national 'insistence on a high level of services'; second, 'national restriction of the level of capital expenditure'; and third, 'the growing proportion of (local) funds found by the central govern-ment'. (3)

The Wheatley Report was equally critical:

> 'From the practical point of view, we have
> come to the conclusion that the kinds of
> control exercised by central government
> have in total a damaging effect on the inde-
> pendence and initiative of local authorities'.
> (4)

And as with the English report, financial independence figures prominently in the recommendations for change. (5)

Official reports are not the only source of such criticisms. For example, Professor W.A. Robson was a long-standing and vehement critic of increasing central control:

> 'Can anyone seriously doubt that as the
> Treasury comes to provide more and more
> money for the local councils, the voices
> of Whitehall will speak more often and
> with greater insistence?' (6)

And in more apocalyptic vein, Edmund Dell writes:

'Local government as it exists in this
country today is far too dependent on
Whitehall to be capable of being signifi-
cantly responsive to local interests or
to local public opinion when it does
exist, if the Government rules otherwise
... Local government continues as a
matter of tradition: but it is a dying
tradition. The central government's
victory over local government is complete.
Political power in this country has never been
more centralised'. (7)

Nor is this diagnosis of recent origin. In 1956, a West
Midlands Study Group employed the metaphor of 'the local
authority ... being ground smaller and smaller between
two millstones' to describe the relationship and one of
the stones was central government 'armed with more and
more pervasive control reaching into the determination
of local policy'. (8) The second stone was professional-
ism. Twenty-one years later, the Society of Local
Authority Chief Executives similarly criticised the extent
of detailed controls, unnecessary advice and duplication
of effort. Their examples ranged from Transport Policies
and Programmes/Transport Supplementary Grant and the
Community Land Act to the length of grass after cutting
and how to measure it. (9)

It is possible to continue quoting from official
reports, books and articles throughout the post-war period
all of which mine a similar vein. (10) Developments in
central-local relations in Britain since the war have been
seen as a process of centralisation based on ever more
pervasive central control and the erosion of local
government's independent financial base. As Jeffrey
Stanyer has argued this diagnosis has achieved the status
of a 'conventional wisdom':

'For over forty years W.A. Robson has been
writing of 'the centralising tendency which
is undermining local government', 'the subordination of local autonomy to the dictates
of central power ... their (local authorities')
transformation into mere receptacles for
government policy', and his judgements have
been taken over by virtually every textbook,
Royal Commission and committee of enquiry, and
the local government world itself. The central
domination of local government and the
reduction of local authorities to will-less
agents of the Government is therefore a
common theme of the discussion of local
government and indeed part of a conventional
wisdom'. (11)

16

However, Stanyer also provides an archetypal example of the 'conventional critique'.

THE 'CONVENTIONAL CRITIQUE'

The problem with the 'conventional wisdom' is that it is difficult to substantiate its factual statements. To continue Jeffrey Stanyer's quotation:

> 'Such a view ... is misleading to a high degree and is based on a misunderstanding of local government behaviour, or rather an ignorance of what happens in local government'. (12)

The arguments of the critics on the effects of financial dependence and central controls can be briefly summarised.

Whilst it is indisputable that local authorities have received an increasing proportion of their total expenditure (13) from central government, it is difficult to identify the consequences of this trend. If 'he who pays the piper calls the tune', one would expect dependence on central grant to limit variations between local authorities in their patterns of expenditure; and to standardise the proportion of resources allocated to the various services within local authority budgets. In fact, irrespective of the size or wealth of local authorities, there is enormous variation in the patterns of expenditure. (14) Moreover, with the partial exception of the education service, increasing financial dependence did not affect the rates of change of the patterns of choice within local authority budgets. (15) This evidence has prompted the conclusion by critics of the 'conventional wisdom' that local authorities should be seen as political systems in their own right. They do not simply follow central direction: they make their own decisions about their level and pattern of expenditure.

It is also argued that although central government has an impressive list of controls at its disposal they constitute only a potential for control. Included among the available controls are general statutory provisions; circulars, departmental letters and other forms of advice; confirmatory and appellate functions; adjudicatory functions; inspection; default powers; audit; control over the appointment, dismissal, discipline, pay and conditions of work of some local authority staff; and control over local bills. (16) It is important to investigate how these controls work in practice. To what extent do central departments use their powers and to what extent do local authorities accept such attempts to control them? For example, Professor J.A.G. Griffith has argued that central departments differ markedly in their willingness to exert control. He distinguishes between laissez-faire,

regulatory and promotional departments. (17) Developing
this typology, David Regan argues that the same distinctions can be drawn between different sections or divisions
of the same department. (18) Quite clearly, therefore,
it is misleading to talk of central control. Rather there
are different types and degrees of control exerted by the
various constituent units of central government.

Similarly, it is argued that local authorities vary in
their willingness to accept control. A variety of
studies show central departments striving year after year
to cajole, bully and persuade local authorities to implement a policy. The examples include smoke control,
comprehensive education, nursery education, parking
meters, fluoridation, the introduction of insulin, building council houses and planning. (19) Very few of these
examples could be described as extreme cases of conflict
between the two levels of government, as for instance,
could Poplar and Clay Cross. And even when local
authorities have unequivocally broken the law, central
departments can have great difficulty in exercising control. John Dearlove's conclusion that the Royal Borough
of Kensington and Chelsea accepted or rejected central
interventions in the light of its own political priorities
has been seen as applicable to many other local authorities:

> '... the Royal Borough is prepared to stand out
> against the advice and direction contained in
> government White papers, circulars, private
> meetings with ministers and personal letters
> directed solely to them, if their own view as
> to what should be the proper scope of govern-
> ment is challenged. At the same time ... a
> local authority may use the supposed obstacle
> of central control for the purposes of internal
> political defence ... the impact of the central
> government upon the day-to-day decisions of
> local authorities often depends on local
> responsiveness, and the preparedness of local
> authorities to accept advice or guidance which
> in law the central government has no strict
> authority to give and no legal power to en-
> force'. (21)

THE 'CONVENTIONAL CRITIQUE' REVISITED

Ironically, this critique of the 'conventional wisdom'
has become so prevalent that it too can be labelled
'conventional'. (22) And this label is deserved
because, although it serves to correct some of the
grosser over-simplifications in the literature on central-
local relations, the 'conventional critique' has some
marked weaknesses.

First, it presents an unsympathetic reading of the

literature. The themes of the various books and reports are treated in isolation from the various qualifications made by their authors. (23) As a result, a number of suggestions or clues which could guide future research are ignored. For example, the West Midlands Study Group adds to the usual complaints about central control some comments on the role of the professional local government officer. It is argued that one of the factors eroding local autonomy is:

> ' ... a service professionalism divorced from
> the old conception of a local government
> service and finding its strongest links with
> the central government departments and, through
> it, with colleagues in other areas all over the
> country, rather than with councils and
> committees and colleagues in other departments'.
> (24)

In the haste to remove the detritus of the past, the perceptive is discarded along with the irrelevant and the wrong-headed. A number of the 'forgotten dimensions' of central-local relations (discussed below) are mentioned but not amplified in that literature characterised as the 'conventional wisdom'.

Second, the 'conventional critique' focuses on the issues raised directly in the 'conventional wisdom'. Adopting this focus begs the question of whether these issues are the ones most deserving of attention. For example, there is an almost exclusive concern with the financial aspects of the relationship. Financial considerations, although important, are not the only relevant factors affecting central-local relations. The 'conventional wisdom' has been allowed to set the parameters of debate and analysis.

Third, the 'conventional critique' presents a one-sided description of the relationship through its emphasis on local authorities as political systems in their own right. Local authorities may vary in their willingness to accept central control but not all local authorities resist central intervention or are successful in their resistance. Many local authorities comply with central instructions even when the policy is as contentious as, for example, comprehensive education. Effective non-compliance may depend on the obedience of the majority and the non-statutory basis of central government's intervention. Any satisfactory analysis of central-local relations must explain compliance as well as non-compliance with both central advice and statutory based instructions.

There is an additional problem with the argument that local authorities should be viewed as political systems

in their own right: the evidence from the analysis of
local government's patterns of expenditure is incon-
clusive. For example, the variations in the patterns of
expenditure could have been welcomed by central government, especially as it was encouraging the growth of
local expenditure for much of the period under scrutiny.
It is also possible that the 'needs element' of Rate
Support Grant (RSG) (25) itself contributed to the
variations in expenditure. In so far as central government defines local needs and provides grant on that
basis, it encourages local variation and this variation
cannot be said to provide evidence of local discretion.
And, a last example of the limitations of the evidence
used to support the 'conventional critique', the methods
of analysis employed are insensitive. It is possible
that central government's interventions are highly
specific to particular services and particular
authorities and, because such interventions either cancel
each other out or do not in total constitute a significant shift in the direction of expenditure, they are not
revealed by aggregate data analysis. Alternatively,
central government could selectively distribute resources
but because of the inevitable lag in local budgetary
responses and frequent policy changes at the centre,
these selective controls do not have an effect in a consistent direction at the aggregate level. The evidence
supporting the 'conventional critique' is not, therefore,
without its ambiguities and uncertainties.

Finally, the literature reviewed by the 'conventional
critique' is primarily the literature of the 1960s. It
presents a static picture of the state of research and,
with self-effacing modesty, ignores the extent to which
its own criticisms have changed 'the name of the game'.
The 1970s have seen a number of studies of central-local
relations which present a different picture from that contained in the 'conventional wisdom'. A review of the
literature must cover this recent work, including not
only the academic work discussed above but also government reports and other official documents (e.g. the
Layfield Report).

The 'conventional critique' has served its purpose of
insisting that conclusions on central-local relations
should be grounded in an understanding of the actual behaviour of the two levels of government rather than on a
commitment to local autonomy. But in demonstrating the
weaknesses of the 'conventional wisdom', the 'conventional
critique' has focused on a narrow set of issues. It has
demonstrated that the topic of central-local relations is
dominated by myths. Central government is not all-power-
ful. Dependence on grant does not necessarily mean a
decline in local discretion. The existence of controls
does not mean either that they are used or, when they are

used, that they are effective. But the 'conventional
critique' has remained imprisoned by these myths because
it has failed to redefine both the scope of research and
the relevant questions.

SOME RECENT DEVELOPMENTS

Any consideration of recent developments in the study of
central-local relations must begin with the Layfield
Report. Superficially, with its stress on the centralising trend of recent years and its distinction between
more central responsibility and more local responsibility, the Report seems to rehearse the agent/partner-
ship arguments all over again. However, the Report's
diagnosis of the defects of the current relationships
contains some distinctive emphases.

A three-fold distinction is offered. The term
'partnership' is seen as a synonym for the confused
sharing of responsibilities: in marked contrast to conventional usage. It is sharply distinguished from both
central responsibility and local responsibility. The
Report's list of defects in the relationship is worth
quoting in full:

'(i)   no firm guidelines have been available to
         local authorities either on the expendi-
         ture they should plan for in the medium
         term or in the grant they may expect;

(ii)   the government's efforts to control local
         authorities' expenditure in the short term
         have led to disruption;

(iii)   the true cost of expanding local government
         services has not been brought home to local
         councillors or the public;

(iv)   the arrangements for resource allocation,
         grant negotiation and loan sanction have
         not made clear where the responsibility
         rests for decisions affecting local
         authorities' expenditure;

(v)   the government puts conflicting pressures
         on local authorities;

(vi)   local authorities in England have felt out
         of touch with the government's arrangements
         for resource planning;

(vii)   the government's controls have been used
         for purposes for which they were not in-
         tended and were not suited'. (26)

21

In other words, the Report does not indulge in wild diatribes about central control but attempts to describe precisely what is wrong with the relationship. The picture which emerges is less one of central control and more one of an <u>ambiguous and confused</u> relationship in which neither level of government is clear about its responsibilities.

The consequences of ambiguity and confusion are said to be a trend towards centralisation:

> 'What has been clearly visible over recent years is a growing propensity for the government to determine, in increasing detail, the pace and direction in which local services should be developed, and the resources which should be devoted to them, and the priorities between them'. (27)

Local authorities have been caught between the pressures of demand for improved local services, an inflexible tax base and the unpopularity of rate increases. As a result, expansion has been financed out of grants. ' ... Financial pressures seem to have been critical in tipping the balance of forces to the centre', (28) and with increasing dependence on central monies there has been increasing interference by central government in the level of local taxation and increasing guidance over the pattern of local expenditure. The Report concludes that:

> 'The increasingly detailed intervention by the government is incompatible with that measured consideration of local expenditure needs and priorities, judged by local conditions and requirements and with local taxation decisions reflecting local expenditure decisions, which lies at the heart of fully responsible local government'. (29)

If confusion is to be overcome, the Report urges that a choice be made between locating responsibility firmly with central government and reversing the trend towards centralisation and reviving local accountability. The key principle for obtaining some much needed clarity is:

> ' ... whoever is responsible for deciding to spend more or less money on providing a service is also responsible for deciding whether to raise more or less taxation'. (30)

The application of this principle could lead to either more central accountability or more local accountability. Irrespective of which was adopted, the present confusions in the system would be removed and the principle of accountability would be satisfied. The consequence of the

choice is the same in both cases - the restructuring of
the pattern of central-local relations.

At first glance, this description of current trends
seems remarkably similar to the conventional wisdom outlined and criticised above. There are, however, a number
of important differences. First, the problem is not described as being one of financial dependence. The Report
is perfectly explicit in its argument that confusion and
ambiguity are the basic problems. These allied to the
financial problems have brought about the trend towards
centralisation. Second, the Report does not see the
solution of these problems wholly in financial terms:

> ' ... no financial system can do more than
> create the conditions for the development of
> the desired relationship; other measures, in-
> cluding many important non-financial ones, are
> needed to give it practical expression'. (31)

Finally, the existing relationship is not analysed
solely in legal-institutional terms. There are various
references to the political factors which sustain the
current confusion. The argument has been summarised by
George Jones:

> 'Where grant is a preponderant and growing part
> of local revenue the government will seek to
> ensure that it is spent in accordance with
> national policies and priorities. The grant
> represents money that central departments have
> fought hard to obtain against the Treasury and
> other departments with their rival programmes.
> Each department seeks to advance the particular
> service it looks after ... Civil servants and
> ministers ... are not likely to relinquish their
> concern with the money once it is handed over to
> local authorities to spend. As custodians of
> taxpayers' money and as defenders and promoters
> of particular services they wish to ensure that
> the grant is spent on their services as they
> said it would be. Civil servants also wish to
> protect their minister from criticism in
> parliament about the poor performance or
> inadequacies of services. A high grant, there-
> fore, pulls the central officials to involve
> themselves in local affairs ... local authority
> officials and councillors, recognising the high
> level of grant, feel that they have little
> justification for resisting departments. The
> political consequences of a high grant are to
> increase the pressure for central involvement in
> local government. (32)

Party politics and organisational politics rarely figure so prominently in the analysis of financial dependence.

The conclusions of the Layfield Report are reinforced by the report of the Central Policy Review Staff (CPRS). The CPRS Report rejects the criticisms that central departments issue spectacularly inconsistent advice and that local authorities are ahead of central government in the development of corporate planning. It suggests, however, that:

(i)   departments act in isolation from each other;

(ii)   the relationship is confused by un- certainties over each other's responsibilities;

(iii) there is a multiplicity of overlapping channels of communication;

       a) advice is offered in areas which are prima facie within local government's dis- cretion.

       b) the status of advice is uncertain;

       c) the same channels of communication serve different purposes;

       d) advice is either too general or too specific;

(iv)   the distribution of functions at the sub- national level is complex;

(v)   central government does not see local authorities 'in the round' as corporate entities trying to deal with inter- related problems;

(vi)   the information available on services is patchy;

       and

(vii) the controls on local authority capital expenditure are inflexible and reinforce compartmentalisation between programmes. (33)

The distinctive feature of the CPRS Report lies in its emphasis on the multiplicity of channels of communication involved in the relationship. Thus, in addition to such channels as legislation and circulars, they point to the important role of planning procedures, many of which are of recent origin, such as structure plans, transport policies and programmes, ten year social service plans, comprehensive community programmes, regional reports, local corporate plans and housing investment programmes. The CPRS Report points to the difficulties which arise from the inter-relationships of these plans. (34)

One of the curious features of the study of central-local relations is the title of the topic and the implication that intergovernmental relations in Britain are limited to links between central departments and local authorities. By default, many commentators equate local government in Britain with the English local government system. And yet there are quite different institutional arrangements for central-local relations in Scotland, Wales and Northern Ireland. Similarly, even in England, intergovernmental relations are not confined to links between central departments and local authorities. There are the links between local authorities and the regional offices of central departments and the plethora of 'fringe bodies' - the ubiquitous 'quango' under an even more opaque title. Some recognition of the complexity of intergovernmental relations can be found in the CPRS Report which notes the 'plural' nature of government and the 'multilateral' contacts of both levels of government. (35) In brief, recent official reports describe central-local relations as ambiguous, confused and complex: hardly the dominant language of the 1960s.

The problem with official reports is that of all the reasons which lead to them being written, a concern for the state of academic research is conspicuous primarily for its absence. Thus, the various features of central-local relations discussed in the Layfield and CPRS reports are not located within an explicit interpretive theoretical framework. Such reports are expected to reach conclusions not to pioneer theoretical insights or to undertake field research to test their hypotheses. Fortunately, there are other sources of evidence supporting the picture of central-local relations in the 1970s presented in official reports.

John Friend and his colleagues at the Institute for Operational Research (now the Centre for Operational and Organisational Research) have conducted, over the years, a series of studies of planning under uncertainty. (36) Although they have not been specifically concerned with central-local relations, nonetheless their analysis contains many relevant insights, primarily because the most recent work has been concerned with 'multi-organisations' and the constraints upon planning created by the need for several organisations to work together.

The central concept from which the theoretical framework for the study of the expansion of Droitwich was developed is that of the 'multi-organisation' or:

> ' ... a union of parts of separate organi-
> sations formed by the interaction of individuals
> in the pursuance of some common task'. (37)

Through a series of case studies, Friend et al demonstrate
that complex linkages are required between organisations,
if effective action is to be taken. Although they focus
on the planning problems created by such links, they
offer a number of comments on central-local relations.
Thus:

> 'Even where the opportunities for joint
> exploration are clearly limited, as in the case
> of relationships between individual local
> authorities and government departments which
> are required to operate formal systems of ex-
> ternal control over the activities of many such
> bodies, we found that a significant degree of
> informal exploration of alternatives sometimes
> took place'. (38) (emphasis added)

Moreover:

> ' ... we sometimes found it necessary to look
> on certain actors from central departments as
> themselves forming a part of the local policy
> system, rather than simply as an external
> source of recognised policy guidelines'. (39)

In other words, Friend et al provide extensive evidence
for the proposition that the relations between central
and local government are complex, involving a range of
governmental institutions, and more important, they demonstrate that ostensibly hierarchical relationships
dissolve under the exigencies of implementing a policy.
Central departments become but one of a number of actors,
all facing a common problem. Finally, they show that
these interactions have a number of consequences for
policy-making. These consequences include placing a
premium on 'reticulist' (or networking) skills and the
pre-eminence of 'partisan mutual adjustment' (or incre-
mental decision-making) over rational planning processes.

The utility of Friend et al's framework in the analysis
of central-local government relations is limited by its
specific concern with planning problems. The study does
not specifically examine central-local relations and it
does not compare and attempt to explain variations in
interactions. More important, the theoretical framework
limits any attempt at this kind of analysis. A multi-
organisation is defined in terms of the pursuit of a

common objective or task. However, this form of relationship is highly specific. Organisations could interact
with each other without pursuing a common task.
Similarly, the forms of interaction between organisations
need not be limited to partisan mutual adjustment and the
construction of networks of communication. A range of
strategies are available to organisations including, for
example, disruption, manipulation, competition and, a
particularly important strategy for central departments,
the authoritative allocation of resources. Finally, even
though only a limited number of strategies are examined,
the study does not attempt to explain why some strategies
are adopted and others rejected. Most of these limitations arise from the specific focus of the study on planning problems. Accordingly, it is more appropriate to
emphasise the simple fact that Friend et al. provide a
picture of central-local relations very different from
that prevalent in the 1960s. The starting point for
studies of central-local relations can no longer be central controls. In future, the starting point must be the
complexity of interactions and the constraints imposed
thereby on both levels of government.

The study of local government finance is not immune
to this redefinition of the field of central-local relations. The Consultative Council on Local Government
Finance was established, following the Chancellor of the
Exchequer's Budget Speech of 15 April, 1975, to promote
regular consultation and cooperation between central and
local government on major issues of common concern. To
date, there have been only two short studies of an
innovation which may be one of the most significant for
central-local relations in recent years. (40) From
these descriptions, it is clear that, although the local
authority associations have become increasingly involved
in the public expenditure survey at an early stage, this
involvement is not without problems:

'There are two practical difficulties with the
involvement of local authorities in PES: - the
timetable of PES conflicts with that of RSG ...
- the input of time and effort by the local
authority associations and their representatives
does not currently allow them to play much more
than a reactive role ...
In addition, central government departments are
most unlikely to allow local authorities into
the inner workings of the Survey and to upset
the subtle balance of the influence within
Whitehall ... A possible role for the local
authority associations within these constraints
is to work with the government departments concerned and thence to influence PES by influencing
the departments' own submissions within the
Survey machinery'. (41)

PES is a sensitive, inter-departmental political process
and the local authority associations must influence the
departmental contributions to the survey. In addition,
Harris and Shipp argue that ambiguity in the communications from central government not only serves to
reduce conflict but also 'it may preserve the freedom
of manoeuvre of local authorities to act as they see fit!
(42) The financial relationships between central and
local government can also be characterised, therefore, as
a complex set of interactions involving a range of
government institutions and placing a premium on networking skills.

The study of central-local relations has been dominated
by the myths of financial dependence and central control
and the parable of local autonomy. This allegorical
strain pervades the 'conventional wisdom' and even the
'conventional critique' is not immune in spite of the
fact that recent research suggests that a more appropriate starting point for analysis would be an exploration
of the ambiguity, confusion and complexity of the
relationship. It is now time to draw this exercise in
demythologizing to an end. A more constructive approach
is required. What additional topics need to be explored?
What are the 'forgotten dimensions' of central-local
relations?

THE 'FORGOTTEN DIMENSIONS' OF CENTRAL-LOCAL RELATIONS

Without suggesting that the following list of topics is
exhaustive, the discussion focuses on five 'forgotten
dimensions': the need for theory; variation in local
discretion; the variety of relationships; the influence
of political factors; and the role of the professional.

(i)   The Need for Theory

Both the agent and partnership models provide an inadequate basis for the analysis of central-local relations:
critics of the 'conventional wisdom' have shown both to
be descriptively inaccurate. There remains a need for a
theory which recognises that the relationship can range
from compliance to non-compliance; from a high degree of
dependence through interdependence to a high degree of
discretion. The vocabulary of central-local relations
needs to be extended to admit the possibility of bargaining between the two levels of government as well as the
fact of central control.

At least some of the existing literature does recognise
the varying degrees of dependence. Thus, Noel Hepworth
argues that:

'The "present confusion" of responsibilities
to use Layfield's expression is an extremely
convenient escape route for local politicians (and central politicians as well)'.(43)

In a similar vein, the CPRS report points to the game-
like qualities of central-local relations:

'In general, we believe that at least some
complaints by local authorities (and others)
about the non-corporateness of central
government should be discounted. Local
authorities and central government are engaged in a continual amicable struggle for
advantage: and in an age of organisation
it is no more than a conventional gambit to
decry one's opponent as disorganised'.

'It can be argued that complaints from local
authorities about ambiguity (or anything
else) are simply part of their continual
political game with central government, and
as such should not be taken too seriously'.
(44)

However, the awareness has not been translated into
explicit theories about intergovernmental relations in
Britain. The study of central-local relations will develop as much from the improvement of our tools of
analysis as it will from the description of previously
neglected features.

(ii)   Variations in Local Discretion

Any discussion of central-local relations quickly raises
prescriptive issues and, most commonly, the issue of
local autonomy. The concept of 'local autonomy' is
both an elusive and an emotive one. On the one hand,
autonomous local government can be seen as an essential
bulwark against the tyranny of the centre. On the other
hand, it can be seen as highly divisive: a way for
parochial local elites to assert their own interests over
those of the state. (45) Even without its prescriptive
connotations there remains the problem of whether the
term 'local autonomy' refers to local government or the
local community. If the latter, analysis would have to
cover the decisions of every major organisation, governmental and non-governmental to determine the extent to
which they were constrained by extra-community factors.
If the former, there is the problem of whether other
governmental units are the only source of constraints.
As Terry Clarke has argued, local autonomy is a product of
a range of factors (e.g. national factors, natural
physical resources, institutions supporting localism and
loyal local elites). (46) Intergovernmental links are

but one among these factors. Too frequently the term
'local autonomy' is used loosely with little recognition
of these problems. A study which focuses on the links
between central departments and local authorities, cannot
explain variations in local autonomy. It would be
preferable if the term 'local discretion' were reserved
for the extent to which the room for decisional manoeuvre
of local government decision-makers was constrained by
other governmental units. (47) 'Local discretion' is a
component of, rather than a synonym for, 'local autonomy'.

Even if the narrower term 'local discretion' is
employed, there remain inadequances in the literature,
notably a heavy emphasis on the impact of financial
resources. And although other resources have been
identified, including administrative, political, constitutional and professional resources they are neither precisely defined nor discussed at length. The important
questions concern the relative importance of these
resources for local discretion. For example, can political influence compensate for financial dependence?
Accordingly, there is a need to explore the range of
resources which can influence the extent of local discretion.

(iii)   The Variety of Relationships

As noted earlier, both central government and local
authorities are plural not unitary entities. Not only
can different sections of the same central department
have different attitudes and behave differently towards
local authorities but the converse may also be equally
true. In addition, there are many other public sector
organisations besides central departments and local
authorities. Future research must recognise this
variety.

First, it would be as well to confine the term central-
local relations to the links between central departments
and local authorities, employing the term intergovernmental relations to encompass the generality of relationships - i.e. the links between central government and
other sub-national public sector organisations; the links
between sub-national public sector organisations; and
the links between the Scottish, Welsh and Northern
Ireland governmental systems and both their own sub-
national public sector organisations and the British
government. It would then be possible to compare
different facets of the system of intergovernmental
relations and explore the extent to which central-local
relations were different both from other types of intergovernmental relations (e.g. 'fringe bodies') and between
different parts of the United Kingdom (e.g. Scotland).
(48)

Second, there is a distinction to be drawn between
individual local authorities and the national institutions of local government. There are numerous national
institutions including the local authority associations
(of both England and Wales, and Scotland) the various
joint bodies (e.g. LAMSAC, LACSAB, LGTB) (49) and the
professional bodies (see below). The role(s) of these
bodies is (are) shadowy. What are their links to their
members? Do they represent local government's views to
central departments or do they present the views of
central departments to local authorities? For example,
it could be argued that the co-option of the local
authority associations into the public expenditure survey
through the Consultative Council is a way of defusing
opposition to expenditure cuts and legitimating central
government's decisions. Do the various national
institutions comprise a national local government
community which provides an effective central bargaining
capability for local authorities? There has been
virtually no research on the national institutions of
local government. (50)

Third, it cannot be assumed that there is a single
pattern of links between central departments and local
authorities. Are the links functional ones - i.e.
between the equivalent departments (or sections of departments) at the two levels of government? Is there a
corporate element in the pattern of links, and if so, how
effective is this corporate element?

Finally, there is the problem of measuring the alleged
complexity of the relationships. Although a number of
studies (see above) have described the complexity of
central-local relations for specific policies or issues,
no-one has attempted to map the interactions for a major
part of the system. If the system is both a 'system' of
relationships and complex, it would be as well to document the fact and, more important, demonstrate that it is
a problem. For example, do policies fail because they
require the agreement and cooperation of too great a
number of public sector organisations? (51)

(iv)   The Influence of Political Factors

The 'conventional critique' has demonstrated that, at
least for some issues, local authorities can be viewed as
political systems in their own right, and, as argued above,
the effect of political resources on relationships needs
to be considered along with the effect of financial
resources. Little is known, however, about the political
channels of influence between central and local government with the minor exception of a few studies of the
local government background of M.P.s. Such channels do
exist and there are links between local and national
political elites. Local politicians do have 'clout' at

the national level. They are not necessarily retiring
wallflowers who shy away from the media and are over-
awed by the national eminence of the Minister. They can
impose 'political costs' on a Minister. A protracted
fight with a local authority is costly to a Minister in
time, energy and his esteem in the eyes of colleagues
and, possibly, the electorate. No Minister actively
seeks the sobriquet of 'national bully'. As Anthony
Crosland recognised, there is a degree of ambivalence in
the attitudes of Ministers to central-local relations:

> 'All governments and Ministers are a bit
> schizophrenic about their relationship with
> local authorities. On the one hand they
> genuinely believe the ringing phrases they
> use about how local government should have
> more power and freedom ... On the other hand,
> a Labour government hates it when Tory
> councils pursue education or housing policies
> of which it disapproves, and exactly the
> same is true of a Tory government with Labour
> councils. This ambivalence exists in everybody
> I know who is concerned with relations between
> central and local government'. (52)

A similar attitude can be found amongst local
authorities. Whilst they bemoan central interference
in local affairs, they are still not above requesting
specific policy guidance from central departments.

Potentially, there are many channels of influence,
including party conferences, contact with M.P.s, delegations, personal friendships, telephone calls to
Ministers at home, representation on national bodies and
even parties aboard yachts on the Thames. (53) But we
do not know how extensive political contacts are or how
important they are for particular decisions. Are formal
links (e.g. delegations) more numerous and important than
informal links? To what extent and under what
conditions can local politicians embarrass national
politicians and affect changes in policy? What is the
influence of variations in party composition at the
local level upon the relationship between the two levels
of government? How significant are national party
decisions on policies for the local party? Have local
authorities been 'nationalised' in more than name? What
are the roles of the Labour Party's Local Government
Section and the NEC's Regional-Local Government Committee
and how much influence do they have on local parties?
The same questions can be asked of the Conservative
Party's Local Government Department and National Local
Government Advisory Committee. What are the links of
individual local authorities/local authority associations
with M.P.s/Parliament and how effective is this lobbying?
These and similar questions can be raised but, given the

existing evidence, they cannot be satisfactorily answered.

(v)   The Role of the Professional

The professional officers have many opportunities to exert influence on behalf of their employing authority, the local authority associations, and their professional associations although they are conspicuous for their absence in the literature on central-local relations. For the local authority they have one-to-one contacts with counterparts at the centre and, if necessary, they can lobby anyone who will listen on behalf of the local authority.   In the capacity of advisers to the committees of local authority associations they are part of the delegations to, and meetings with, central departments.   Through the professional associations they can lobby or advise central departments about preserving or improving professional standards. (54)   But again the extent and consequences of this involvement remain obscure.   Do they form part of a national professional community - a community including civil servants - which pursues its own professional interests?   Does some legislation, although seen by some as yet another imposition on local government, have its origins in the aspirations of, and lobbying by, a profession?   What is the relationship between the professional associations and other national institutions of local government?   If the professionals are prominent in central-local relations, is it possible to identify, in Galbraith's terms, a 'technostructure'. (55)   Certainly, it is surprising that the concern about the power of the official in local government has not spread to an analysis of their role in central-local relations.

CONCLUSIONS: the rationality of ambiguous confusion?

The normal description of central-local relations is domi-nated by the myths of financial dependence and detailed control and the parable of local autonomy.   Even the 'conventional critique' falls victim to mythology by re-stricting its analysis to the subject matter of the 'conventional wisdom'.   However, more recent official reports and research studies suggest that there are a number of 'forgotten dimensions' in the study of central-local relations including the game-like nature of relations;   the variety of resources underpinning local discretion;   the variety of relationships;   and the in-fluence of political and professional factors.   The 'problem' of central-local relations is not, therefore, one of central control but of ambiguity, confusion and complexity.   This state of affairs means that attempts at control by central departments are irritating and frustrating for local authorities not because they are effective but because they are ad hoc, even random measures. And there are advantages for both parties in this situation. Ambiguity bestows room for manoeuvre. Freedom of action can be negotiated and renegotiated. Even the most stringent controls can be circumvented. It is possible that both parties have a vested interest in at least some degree of ambiguity, even confusion. The clarification of responsibilities could be a painful process. It is convenient to be able to blame central government for cuts in, for example, education. There is a rationality underlying the complex and ambiguous confusion: the rationality of the 'game'. The relations between central and local government are too often seen in an over-simplified light. The intricate pattern of linkages is both a constraint and a source of opportunities. Both the 'conventional wisdom' and the 'conventional critique' serve to obscure this fact.

However, the discussion of the 'forgotten dimensions' of central-local relations bears rather too close a resemblance to a shopping list of future research studies for comfort. It is important to indicate the range of questions which need to be answered. But it is equally important to develop the tools of analysis: to expand the vocabulary of central-local relations. A plethora of detailed, descriptive case studies, even if they are on the topics discussed above, will not necessarily advance the study of central-local relations. Barefooted empiricism needs the guidance and insight of a framework of analysis.

Allied to this point is the historical parochialism of the study of central-local relations. Too often the sole preserve of Public Administration, the subject needs to break out of these confines. It can illuminate facets of modern government of general concern to social scientists. It can provide a fruitful locus for the analysis of the power of the professional: for exploring the problems of accountability created by the interdependence of a multitude of complex governmental bureaucracies; and for the incidence and causes of policy failure. Building bridges between the study of central-local relations and theoretical issues in the study of Western industrial society is an essential step in the development of an adequate framework of analysis. It cannot be achieved by the traditional methods of legal-institutional case studies.

NOTES AND REFERENCES

1.   See: Hartley, O.A., 'The Relationship Between Central and Local Authorities'. Public Administration Vol. 49 1971 pp. 439-56.
2.   Committee on the Management of Local Government (Maud) Vol. 1 Report London: H.M.S.O., 1967 p. 76.

3.   Royal Commission on Local Government in England
1966-69 (Redcliffe-Maud), Vol. 1 Report Cmnd. 4040,
London: H.M.S.O., 1969 p. 11, p. 12 and p. 133.
4.   Royal Commission on Local Government in Scotland
1966-69 (Wheatley) Report Cmnd. 4150, Edinburgh:
H.M.S.O., 1969 p. 243.
5.   Royal Commission on Local Government in Scotland,
op. cit., p. 246; and Royal Commission on Local
Government in England, op. cit., pp. 133-4.
6.   Robson, W.A., Local Government in Crisis London:
Allen and Unwin, 1966 p. 53.
7.   Dell, E., 'Labour and Local Government' Political
Quarterly Vol. 31 No. 3 1960 p. 335.
8.   West Midlands Study Group, Local Government and
Central Control London: Macmillan, 1956 p. 244.
9.   'Supplementary Memorandum by the Society of Local
Authority Chief Executives on Unnecessarily Detailed
Control by Government Departments' in Eleventh Report
from the Expenditure Committee, The Civil Service,
Vol. II, Minutes of Evidence, HC 535, London: H.M.S.O.,
1977 p. 1085. See also: Association of County Councils
et al., Review of Central Government Controls Over
Local Authorities London, 1979.
10.   See amongst others: Chester, D.N., Central and
Local Government London: Macmillan, 1951 p. 337;
Birley, D., The Education Officer and His World London:
Routledge and Kegan Paul, 1970 p. 30; Green, L.P.,
Provincial Metropolis London: Allen and Unwin, 1959
p. 156; Hill, F., 'The Partnership in Theory and
Practice' Political Quarterly Vol. 37 1966 pp. 169-79;
Lord Redcliffe-Maud and Wood, B., English Local
Government Reformed London: Oxford University Press,
1974 p. 24, p. 135 and p. 160; Richards, P.G., The
Reformed Local Government System London: Allen and
Unwin, first edn., 1973 pp. 165-70; Sharp, Dame E.,
'The Future of Local Government' Public Administration
Vol. 40 1962 pp. 375-86; and Swaffield, J.C., 'Local
Government in the National Setting' Public Administration Vol. 48 1970 p. 310-11.
11.   Stanyer, J., Understanding Local Government London:
Fontana/Collins, 1976 p. 211.
12.   Stanyer, J., op. cit., p. 211.
13.   The statistics supporting the argument that local
authorities are financially dependent on central grant
usually cite grant as a proportion of current relevant
expenditure. These figures accentuate the degree of
dependence. If grant is treated as a proportion of
total local income, - i.e. if 'other income' (rents,
trading income) is included - the increase in grant
between 1949 and 1970 - i.e. the period covered by the
quotes in the text - was six per cent. This increase
is not a dramatic one when spread over twenty-one years.
Between 1970 and 1974 the increase was five per cent and
this increase is obviously more in line with the
financial dependence thesis. Unfortunately, diagnosis

preceeded the symptons.

Figures from: Committee of Inquiry into Local Government Finance (Layfield) Report Cmnd. 6453, London: H.M.S.O. 1976, p. 384. Hereafter referred to as the Layfield Report. For a detailed discussion of the financial statistics see: Crispin, A., 'Local Government Finance: assessing the central government's contribution' Public Administration Vol. 54 1976 pp.45-61.

14. See: Boaden, N., Urban Policy Making London: Cambridge University Press, 1971 chs. 1 and 2.

15. See: Ashford, D., 'The Effects of Central Finance on the British Local Government System' British Journal of Political Science Vol. 4 1974 pp. 305-22.

16. Griffith, J.A.G., Central Departments and Local Authorities London: Allen and Unwin, 1966 pp. 54-62.

17. Griffith, J.A.G., op. cit., pp. 515-28.

18. Regan, D.E., Local Government and Education London: Allen and Unwin, 1977 pp. 33-4.

19. See: Blackstone, T., A Fair Start: the provision of pre-school education London: Allen Lane, The Penguin Press, 1971; Brier, A.P., 'The Decision Process in Local Government: a case study of fluoridation in Hull' Public Administration Vol. 48 1970 pp. 153-68; Dearlove, J., The Politics of Policy in Local Government London: Cambridge University Press, 1973 Ch. 1; Hartley, O.A., op. cit., pp. 448-50; Scarrow, H., 'Policy Pressures by British Local Government: the case of regulation in the public interest' Comparative Politics Vol. 4 1971 pp. 1-28; Swann, B., 'Local Initiative and Central Control' Policy and Politics Vol. 1 1972 pp. 55-63; Friend, J.K., Power, J.M, and Yewlett, C.J.L., Public Planning: the intercorporate dimension London: Tavistock, 1974; Isaac-Henry, K., The Politics of Comprehensive Education in Birmingham 1957-1967 Birmingham: Unpublished M.Soc. Sc. Thesis, University of Birmingham 1970; and the various case studies of the reorganisation of secondary education listed in: Ribbins, P.M. and Brown, R.J., 'Policy Making in English Local Government: the case of secondary school reorganisation' Public Administration Vol. 57 1979 pp. 188-9.

20. See: Keith-Lucas, B., 'Poplarism' Public Law Spring 1962 pp. 52-80; Mitchell, A., 'Clay Cross' Political Quarterly Vol. 45 1974 pp. 165-78; and Skinner, B. and Langdon, J., The Story of Clay Cross Nottingham: Spokesman Books, 1974.

21. Dearlove, J., op. cit., p. 20.

22. See the criticisms of the literature on central-local relations in: Boaden, N., op. cit., Chs. 1 and 2; Dearlove, J., op. cit., Ch. 1.; Stanyer, J., op. cit., Ch. 10; Smith, B.C., Policy Making in British Government London: Martin Robertson, 1976 Ch. 7; and

36

Smith, B.C., and Stanyer, J., <u>Administering Britain</u>
London: Fontana/Collins, 1976 pp. 122-9.
23. For example, a number of writers with a clear
legal-institutional focus recognise the 'informal
pressures' in the relationship. See: Cross, J.A.,
<u>The Principles of Local Government Law</u> London: Sweet
and Maxwell, 1974 p. 178. Also compare Chester, D.N.,
<u>op</u>. <u>cit</u>., p. 121 with Hartley, O.A., <u>op</u>. <u>cit</u>., p. 450.
Both authors point to the problems created for central
government by local authority inactivity.
24. West Midlands Study Group, <u>op</u>. <u>cit</u>., p. 244.
25. At the time of writing, RSG contains three elements:
the domestic element which provides rate relief for
domestic ratepayers; the resources element which
ensures that all local authorities have a minimum
rateable value per head of population; and the needs
element which 'compensates for differences between
local authorities in the amount they need to spend per
head of population'. For further details see:
Layfield Report, <u>op</u>. <u>cit</u>., pp. 454-9 (the quote is
from p. 456); and Hepworth, N.P., <u>The Finance of
Local Government</u> London: Allen and Unwin, third edn.
1976 Chs. 3 and 12 and Appendix 3. However, the Local
Government Planning and Land (No.2) Bill contains
proposals to replace the needs and resources elements
with a block grant.
26. Layfield Report, pp. 45-6.
27. Layfield Report, p. 65.
28. Layfield Report, p. 72.
29. Layfield Report, p. 72.
30. Layfield Report, p. 50.
31. Layfield Report, p. 64.
32. Jones, G.W., <u>Responsibility and Government</u> London:
London School of Economics and Political Science, 1977
p. 11. The relevant sections of the Layfield Report
are pp. 65-8, p. 78 and p. 265. This discussion of the
Layfield Report is concerned with their description of
central-local relations and <u>not</u> their proposed reforms.
For a discussion of the Report's recommendations compare Jones, <u>op</u>. <u>cit</u>., pp. 8-20 with Cripps, F., and
Godley, W., <u>Local Government Finance and its Reform</u>
Cambridge: Department of Applied Economics, 1976.
33. Central Policy Review Staff, <u>Relations Between
Central Government and Local Authorities</u> London:
H.M.S.O. 1977 pp. 1-3. Hereafter cited as the CPRS
Report.
34. CPRS Report, pp. 12-15.
35. CPRS Report, pp. 15-18, pp.21-22, pp.24-25, pp.35-37
and pp. 40-41. For a discussion of the 'plural'
nature of British government, see ch. 4.
36. See: Friend, J.K., and Jessop, W.N., <u>Local Government and Strategic Choice</u> London: Tavistock, 1969;
Friend, J.K., et al., <u>op</u>. <u>cit</u>., (1974); Friend, J.K.,
'Planners, Policies and Operational Boundaries: some
recent developments in Britain' <u>Policy and Politics</u>
Vol. 5 No. 1 1976 pp. 25-44; Friend, J.K., 'The

Dynamics of Policy Change' <u>Long Range Planning</u> Vol. 10
February 1977 pp. 40-7.

37. Friend, J.K., et al., (1974), op. cit., p. 42.
38. Friend, J.K., et al., (1974), op. cit., p. 350.
39. Friend, J.K., et al., (1974), op. cit., p. 351.
40. Brief background information on the Consultative
     Council is given in Layfield Report, pp. 408-9. The
     two studies referred to are: Harris, R., and Shipp,
     P.J., <u>Communications Between Central and Local Govern-</u>
     <u>ment in the Management of Local Authority Expenditure</u>
     Coventry: Institute for Operational Research, 1977;
     and Taylor, J.A. 'The Consultative Council on Local
     Government Finance: a critical analysis of its
     origins and development' <u>Local Government Studies</u> Vol.
     No. 3 1979 pp.7-36.
41. See: Harris and Shipp, op. cit., p. 85; and Taylor,
     op. cit., pp. 25-9 and pp. 30-1.
42. See: Harris and Shipp, op. cit., p. 88.
43. Hepworth, N.P., 'Local Government and Central
     Control' <u>Public Administration</u> Vol. 55 1977 p. 16.
44. CPRS Report, p. 43 and p. 47.
45. For a more detailed discussion see: Sharpe, L.J.,
     'Theories and Values of Local Government' <u>Political</u>
     <u>Studies</u> Vol. 18 1970 pp. 153-74.
46. Clark, T.N., 'Community Autonomy in the National
     System' in Clark, T.N. (ed.), <u>Comparative Community</u>
     <u>Politics</u> New York: Halsted Press, 1974 pp. 21-45.
47. This definition of local discretion is modified
     from that contained in: Jowell, J., 'The Legal Con-
     trol of Administrative Discretion' <u>Public Law</u> Autumn
     1973 p. 179.
48. For a study which is beginning to explore these
     differences see: Hogwood, B.W., 'The Tartan Fringe'
     Glasgow, University of Strathclyde: <u>Studies in Public</u>
     <u>Policy No. 34,</u> 1979, especially pp. 30-5.
49. For those unfamiliar with the 'alphabet soup' of
     local government, the acronyms refer to the Local
     Authorities Management Services and Computer Committee
     (LAMSAC) the Local Authorities Conditions of Service
     Advisory Board (LACSAB) and the Local Government
     Training Board (LGTB).
50. The major exception is Griffith, J.A.G., op. cit.,
     pp. 33-49 but this book is now out of date. A brief
     history of the associations can be found in Keith-Lucas,
     B. and Richards, P.G., <u>A History of Local Government in</u>
     <u>the Twentieth Century.</u> London: Allen and Unwin, 1978,
     Ch. 9. The role of the associations in the reorgani-
     sation of local government is discussed in: Wood, B.,
     <u>The Process of Local Government Reform</u> 1966-74 London:
     Allen and Unwin, 1976; and Isaac-Henry, K., 'Local
     Authority Associations and Local Government Reform',
     <u>Local Government Studies</u> Vol. 1. No. 3 1974, pp. 1-12
     The role of the associations in the negotiations over
     RSG is outlined in: Harris and Shipp, Taylor, op.
     cit. It is important to note that the above studies
     refer to the local authority associations and not the

national institutions of local government. There has
been a marked increase in the number of joint bodies
and future research can no longer ignore their role(s)
in central-local relations.

51. On the effects of the need to secure the agreement and
cooperation of a number of organisations on the implementation of a policy see: Pressman, J. and
Wildavsky, A., Implementation Berkeley and Los Angeles:
University of California Press, 1973; and Hood, C.C.
The Limits of Administration London: Wiley, 1977
pp. 17-20.

52. Boyle, E., Crosland, A., and Kogan, M., The Politics
of Education Harmondsworth: Penguin Books, 1971 p.171.

53. An interesting, anecdotal source of information is:
Crossman, R.H.S., The Diaries of a Cabinet Minister
Volume 1, Minister of Housing London: Jonathon Cape/
Hamish Hamilton, 1975 p. 39, pp. 60-1, pp. 352-3,
p. 391, p. 410, p. 429, p. 525, p. 563, p. 598 and
p. 612. On the political influence of local
authorities, Ashford concludes:

> 'The complex interactions of mayors, local and
> central officials and national politicians so
> common in France, is unknown in Britain'.

Ashford, D., 'Are Britain and France Unitary?'
Comparative Politics Vol. 9 1977 p. 489. Ashford
overstates his case. Comparatively, such interactions
may be less common but they are not unknown in Britain.
However, it is too early for this kind of generalisation. The real distinction between Britain and
France may reside in the greater importance of
organisational (or small 'p') politics in British
central-local relations whereas the local politician
plays the more important role in French central-local
relations. Whichever generalisation is most
appropriate, it would be as well to collect some
evidence.

54. For examples see: Lee, J.M. Wood, B., et al., The
Scope for Local Initiative London: Martin Robertson,
1974, pp. 39-52 and pp. 75-84; and Harris and
Shipp, op. cit., pp. 19-21.

55. Galbraith, J.K., The New Industrial State London:
Deutsche, 2nd., edn., 1972. See also the distinction
between 'technocrats' and 'topocrats' discussed below
in Ch.4.

3 Interorganisational analysis

INTRODUCTION

If the study of central-local relations in Britain has been preoccupied with the detailed description of a narrow range of topics and has demonstrated a marked aversion for theory; if recent theories of advanced industrial society are at a level of generality which does not admit of easy application to the study of facets of British government, the problem to be confronted in the following chapters can be succinctly stated. How can these two levels of analysis be reconciled? In the next two chapters, the literatures on interorganisational analysis and intergovernmental relations will be examined to see if they are capable of affecting such a reconciliation and what light they can shed on the 'forgotten dimensions' of intergovernmental relations. Before turning to these particular tasks, however, one preliminary issue must be dealt with. What is the justification for applying theories developed by different disciplines and in different governmental contexts to the study of British government?

The relevance of the literature on intergovernmental relations seems obvious. It is exploring the equivalent of central-local relations in different governmental systems. Its importance does not reside solely in the fact of shared subject matter. Not only has there been a growing awareness of the 'plural' nature of British government (1) but a number of commentators have pointed to the parallels between allegedly 'unitary' systems and federal systems. Thus Jesse Burkhead reflects that:

> 'It may be some comfort for students of federalism that unitary governments have problems of inter-governmental relations not unlike those that emerge in a formal system of national-state-local relationships'. (2)

In a similar vein, William Riker comments:

> ' ... it is clear that county councils in Britain can do about as much as local governments in the United States. Certainly dissident national groups in the peripheral provinces (e.g. Welsh and Scottish nationalists) probably feel no more put upon by central authority than do the states' rights partisans of the American South'. (3)

Unfortunately, the literature on central-local relations in Britain has had a marked parochial streak. At times, it seems as if any books or articles which lack the phrase 'central-local relations' in their titles are automatically deemed irrelevant. As a result, the parallels between intergovernmental relations in unitary and federal systems have not been explored in any detail. The next chapter takes at least a first step in repairing the omission.

The dangers of applying inappropriate theories to the study of British government seem most acute in the case of organisation theory and its off-spring interorganisational analysis. Although there is a shared concern with the interdependence of organisations, nonetheless organisation theory has been frequently criticised for its management orientation. The alleged concern with questions of efficiency, with techniques and with the interests of managers do not seem particularly promising starting points for the study of government. However, these criticisms reflect an unduly narrow conception of organisation theory and a palpably inaccurate characterisation of a great deal of research on organisations. Martin Albrow's distinction between organisation theory and the sociology of organisations is useful in this context:

> 'The organisation theorist is concerned to help managers and administrators. By contrast, the perspective of the sociologist is 'impractical'. His search is for understanding, untrammelled by the needs of men of affairs. Therefore he cannot accept the conceptual framework of the organisation theorist as setting the limits to his research interests in organisations'. (4)

Instead the sociology of organisations is 'devoted to discovering the causes and consequences of various types and features of organisations'. (5) Accordingly, the term 'sociology of organisations' is to be preferred in order to emphasise that the literature discussed in this chapter is not exclusively management-oriented.

In short, both literatures are concerned to explore the relationships between various types of organisations and, therefore, offer the prospect of insights into the relationship between central departments and local authorities. It is the task of the next two chapters to determine precisely what contribution they can make and the remainder of this chapter evaluates the literature on interorganisational analysis.

The study of organisations has burgeoned in the post-war period and during the past decade there has been a growing interest in the relationship between organisations and their environments and, in particular, in the links between organisations. Interorganisational analysis has aroused considerable interest: Perrow describes it as 'exciting work' which is leading to the 'revitalisation of organisation theory'; Scharpf argues that the perspective is central to an understanding of policy failures and policy implementation; and Elkin suggests that the perspective 'provides a language to handle some of the fundamental problems of comparative urban political inquiry'. (6) Any attempt to assess the validity of such claims is hampered, however, by the lack of agreement on either the key concepts or their definition. At its simplest, interorganisational analysis suggests that within the environment of an organisation are other organisations upon which it is dependent and with which it interacts. This environment has manifold consequences for the structure of, behaviour in, and performance of an organisation. A typical summary of this complex of interactions is provided by Elkin.

> 'At the same time as the focal organisation attempts to manage its dependencies by employing one or more ... strategies, other organisations in the network are similarly engaged. The consequence is that behaviour within the network is complex and dynamic: there are multiple, over-lapping relationships, each one of which is to a greater or lesser degree dependent on the state of others'. (7)

But once analysis proceeds beyond this general picture, there is considerable diversity in approaches to the topic, a diversity which can be best understood by examining those issues which divide the various contributors - i.e. the nature of the environment, the appropriate unit of analysis, organisational goals, power and exchange and the consequences of the interactions. The following assessment suggests the conclusion that the literature on interorganisational analysis has become preoccupied with classification and with methodological questions and does not facilitate the analysis of intergovernmental relations. However, it is not the sole, or even the main, objective of this chapter to itemise the inadequacies of interorganisational analysis. Rather, the intention is to argue that, if the emphasis is placed on intra- and interorganisational power, interorganisational analysis can provide a series of concepts of considerable value. (8)

THE NATURE OF THE ENVIRONMENT

A basic assumption in the literature on interorganisational analysis is that the organisation is an open system. Emery and Trist have pointed out that:

' ... there has been something of a tendency
to continue thinking in terms of a 'closed'
system, that is, to regard the enterprise as
sufficiently independent to allow most of
its problems to be analysed with reference to
its internal structure and without reference
to its external environment'.

Instead they argue for recognition of the 'mutual per-
meation of an organisation and its environment' (9) and
suggest that environmental changes are a major source of
uncertainty for organisations. They identify four types
of 'causal texture of organisational environments' -
placid, randomised environment; placid, clustered
environment; disturbed-reactive environment; and
turbulent fields. (10) The first three types correspond to, respectively, the economist's classical market,
imperfect competition, and the oligarchic market.
Finally, the turbulent field involves an increase in the
area of 'relevant uncertainty': that is, it is both complex and rapidly changing. This formulation has been influential and the study of organisations has been dominated by open system models. (11) However, it is
important to know which aspects of the environment are
'relevant' since an organisation will probably be confronted by several environments.

Aldrich and Pfeffer have suggested that there are two
views of the link between the organisation and its
environment. The first view sees the link as an exchange
of resources. Thus, a particular organisation needs
resources - e.g. money, raw materials. The environment
is a stock of these needed resources. Consequently, an
organisation bargains for its share of these resources.
The second view sees the link in terms of information
rather than resources; uncertainty is the most important
feature of the environment; complexity and instability
generate uncertainty which the organisation acts to
reduce or remove. (12) Unfortunately, the problems
associated with the concept of environment cannot be reduced to a choice between competing definitions. As
Karpik has argued the words 'system' and 'environment'
are ambiguous: both terms having a 'semi-descriptive,
semi-theoretic status'. He phrases the problem as
follows:

'the systemic approach ... is only capable of
setting up a standard of judgement in the
sociological community provided it is founded
upon a parallel theory that constructs the
object of study, states its particularities,
and shows how it fits into society as a whole'.
(13)

In other words, some rationale has to be found for focusing on the environment. A study interested in the process of managing structural change and the development of interorganisational learning processes would ask very different questions from a study interested in the legitimation of the power of administrative and managerial personnel in society. (14) The inadequacies of systems theory are too well known to warrant detailed repetition (15) but the consequences of these weaknesses for interorganisational analysis are severe because they mean there are no internally generated criteria for defining the relevant aspects of the environment.

THE UNIT OF ANALYSIS

The introduction of the concept of 'organisation set' was central to the development of interorganisational analysis. This phrase was used to describe the environment of organisations by Blau and Scott. (16) Credit for its development is usually accorded to Evan who defined the organisation set as 'an organisation or a class of organisations' and its 'interactions with the network of organisations in its environment'. Evan refers to the organisation that is the point of reference as the 'focal organisation'. (17) The external environment is treated as a series of discrete units to be mapped and analysed from the standpoint of one particular unit. Some of these other organisations provide inputs of resources to the focal organisation - the input set. Others consume the output of the focal organisation - the output set.

However, the focal organisation and its organisation set has limitations as the unit of analysis. The links with other organisations are seen as an extension of intraorganisational characteristics and processes. But the links between a variety of organisations may have characteristics completely different from the characteristics of any one, or even every single, organisation involved in those interactions. The network of linkages may have characteristics in its own right. The concept of the organisation set arbitrarily limits the analysis. It would be preferable to focus on the network or the patterns of direct and indirect linkages between organisations. In this way, the extent to which the links are an extension of intraorganisational processes can be explored rather than asserted. The problem is to limit the number of links to be studied. Ultimately, a very large number if not all organisations could be linked directly and indirectly. The network has to be bounded. But if the analysis is grounded in systems theory, there are no clear criteria for specifying these boundaries. The concept of network warns of the dangers of arbitrarily limiting the number of links to be studied but it raises again the problem of selecting and defining the object of study.

To complicate the picture further, there is the thorny
issue of organisational goals, because the goals of the
organisation will influence the resources it needs to
acquire and the uncertainties to which it responds. It
is common practice to talk of the goals or the mission of
the organisation; in fact, the pursuit of goals continues
to be seen as a defining characteristic of organisations.
However, a number of objections have been raised to the
use of the concept. First, it is argued that organisations do not have goals. To explain organisational
activities in terms of the organisation's goals is to
reify the organisation, i.e. to imply that it has the
power of thought and action. Second, when the formal
goals of an organisation are studied, either they are
found to be inoperative or the organisation seems
ineffective because it does not achieve the stated goals.
Finally, it is difficult to distinguish between goals and
means. One person's goal can be another's means en route
to another 'higher' goal (18).

These difficulties led Etzioni to reject the 'goal
model' and suggest that a 'systems model' should be
adopted. Rather than judging an organisation by its
success or failure in achieving stated goals, it should
be evaluated by its capacity to find an optimal allocation of resources to ensure its survival. (19)
Alternatively, Yuchtman an Seashore suggest that an
organisation's effectiveness should be evaluated by its
capacity to acquire resources. (20)

However, neither of these formulations offers a
satisfactory solution to the problem. In order to find
an optimal balance of resources the criteria for determining the optimal balance have to be specified. Similarly,
criteria for determining the resources to be acquired
have to be stated. These criteria can be specified by
appealing either to the stated goals of the organisation
or to system needs - i.e. the optimal balance or resources
required are determined by the need for system self-
regulation and survival. But, as Silverman has pointed
out, the concept of self-regulating activities also
implies that the power of thought and action lies in
social constructs. (21) An air of philosophic
resignation pervades much of the discussion of goals.

Such resignation seems premature. Thompson's work on
organisational goals suggests a way of resolving at least
some of the difficulties. He uses the term 'domain' to
define 'needed' or 'relevant' resources. Domain refers
to the claims which an organisation makes for itself in
terms of the services provided and the population served.
The goals an organisation pursues will determine which
other organisations it will interact with. However, these

goals are themselves a product of the relationship of an
organisation to other organisations. Unless domain
consensus is established, that is, unless there is some
agreement that the goals an organisation pursues are
legitimate, that organisation will be in a state of conflict with other organisations. To avoid this conflict,
an organisation will negotiate with other organisations
about its goals. Thus the needed resources and the relevant uncertainty are defined by the goals of the organisation and the domain consensus. (22)

Just as domain consensus is negotiated, so the goals of
a particular organisation are the product of a political
process. Thompson suggests that goals be seen as the
product of an internal process of negotiation and bargaining between groups. Out of this process, there will
emerge a dominant coalition with an agreed set of
temporary goals. (23) Over time, however, an organisation has multiple and conflicting goals. Formal
statements of the mission of an organisation are replaced
by a focus on the identification of the goals of specific
groups and on descriptions of the process of goal
setting.

This approach avoids the twin problems of reification
and formalism. The merit of Thompson's approach resides
in the emphasis on negotiation. Not only are the goals
of a particular organisation the outcome of politics
within the organisation but also of bargaining between
organisations. Moreover, the stress on the negotiation
of goals implies that the perceptions of the dominant
coalition are important to an understanding of an
organisation's response to changes in its environment.
In other words, the environment is both constitutive and
constituted. (24)

This approach differs markedly from the dominant view
of the environment, which emphasises its importance as a
source of constraints upon the organisation. For example,
Pugh and Hickson emphasise the effects of size, dependence
and technology on the organisation's structure. (25)
Similarly, Lawrence and Lorsch argue that the structure
of the organisation is shaped by environmental constraints.
(26) These writers invoke a form of environmental
determinism to explain changes in organisation structure.
The organisation does not shape its environment but is
shaped by it.

Thompson's analysis of the relationship between the
organisation and the environment suggests that it is by
no means clear that the environment exercises such a
determinant influence. A number of studies have
developed his suggestions. Child suggests that decision
makers can choose which aspects of the environment they
will respond to:

'The critical link lies in the decision-
makers evaluation of the organisation's
position in the environmental areas they
regard as important ... ' (27)

The power of the dominant coalition is seen as crucial to
an understanding of the relationship between an organisation and its environment. Chandler has shown in a
study of some seventy American corporations, that
structure follows strategy:

'Strategic growth resulted from an awareness of the opportunities and needs ... to
employ existing or expanding resources
more profitably. A new strategy required
a new or at least refashioned structure if
the enlarged enterprise was to be operated
efficiently'. (28)

Perrow has reversed the determinist argument. He
suggests that the most significant failure of organisation theory is ' ... the failure to see <u>society</u> as
adaptive to <u>organisations</u>'. The position is trenchantly
stated:

'To see ... organisations as adaptive to a
'turbulent', dynamic ever-changing environment is to indulge in fantasy. The environment of most powerful organisations is well
controlled by them, quite stable, and made
up of other organisations with similar
interests, or ones they control'. (29)

In a later edition of the same book, he distinguishes
between ground and figure, suggesting that organisations
and the links between organisations are the figure and
that values and power distribution are the ground which
give the figure definition. He sketches a theory of the
role of organisations in society in which the state is
not primarily a 'tool' of the capitalist class but:

' ... an independent entity with organisational
needs of its own, thus serving as a broker
between the capitalist class and other classes,
and meeting its own needs for growth and
power in the process'. (30)

The theme common to these studies is that the relationship between the organisation and its environment can
only be understood by exploring the intra- and interorganisational distribution of power. Systems theory
cannot specify the 'relevant' aspects of the environment,
provide the criteria for bounding the network, or define
goals without reifying the organisation. Karpik has
argued that systems theory has to appeal to a 'parallel

theory' in order to overcome these problems. (31)
Thompson and others have identified one form of such a
parallel theory. In the next section, the concept of
organisational power will be explored in some detail.

POWER AND EXCHANGE

Dependence is the key concept in the analysis of power
and exchange. Its origins lie in exchange theory and the
analysis of the processes which govern the relationships
between individuals. Thus, Blau defines dependence in
the following terms:

> 'By supplying services in demand to others, a
> person establishes power over them. If he
> regularly renders needed services they cannot
> readily obtain elsewhere, others become depen-
> dent on andobligated to him for these services,
> and unless they can furnish other benefits to
> him that produce interdependence by making him
> equally dependent on them, their unilateral
> dependence obligates them to comply with his
> requests lest he cease to continue to meet
> their needs'. (32)

The most important single statement of the concept of
dependence in the context of interorganisational analysis
is that by Thompson. He suggests that any given organisation is dependent upon other organisations:

> ' ... (1) in proportion to the organisation's
> need for resources or performance which that
> element can provide, and (2) in inverse prop-
> ortion to the ability of other elements to
> provide the same resource or performance'.

And dependence is the obverse of power:

> ' ... an organisation has power, relative to
> an element of its task environment, to the
> extent that the organisation has the capacity
> to satisfy needs of that element and to the
> extent that the organisation monopolises that
> capacity'. (33)

The importance of the concept of dependence, and the
reason that it is stressed more than the concept of
power, lies in the fact that it admits of reciprocity.
Thus, dependence is a source of constraints upon an
organisation but, at the same time, an organisation can
act to loosen those constraints. An organisation can be
both dependent upon another organisation and have power
over that organisation. As Crozier and Thoenig point
out:

'Even if one partner appears to completely dominate the other, the dependence remains reciprocal'. (34)

Many problems surround the concept of dependence. In the first instance, and to set the context for the rest of the discussion, the ways in which the concept is deployed in the literature on interorganisational analysis will be criticised. Subsequently, three approaches to the complexities of the concepts of power and dependence are explored: power as resources; power as rule-governed interaction and power as the mobilisation of bias. It is argued that the analysis of organisational power cannot be restricted to any one of these approaches but must encompass all three.

The Classification and Measurement of Interactions

For the most part, writers on interorganisational analysis have not been pre-occupied with the concepts of power and dependence. There is a marked tendency simply to cite Thompson's definition and then get on with the business of classifying and measuring interactions. There are disagreements, of course, about the best way of pursuing this activity. For example, should the analysis focus on the exchange of resources or adapting to uncertainty? And the resource/uncertainty dichotomy does not exhaust the possible contents of exchanges. Litwak and Hylton measure dependence using the indicators of awareness of other organisations, acquaintances and interactions between organisations and written agreements. (35) Thompson and McEwen stress resource exchanges, overlapping board membership and joint programmes. (36) Benson has criticised the measurement of dependence by the examination of interactions as putting the cart before the horse: ' ... interactions at the service delivery are ultimately dependent on resource acquisition'; (37) and two resources are said to be basic - money and authority. And one final example of this particular pre-occupation with measuring interactions is Klonglan's 'cumulative index of cooperative inter-organisational relations'. Moving from low intensity to high intensity, it contains the following items - director awareness of the existence of other organisations, director acquaintance between organisations, director interaction between organisations, information exchange, resource exchange, overlapping board membership, joint programmes and written agreements. (38) The proliferation of measures of interorganisational relations is symptomatic of a literature too often dominated by methodological refinement at the expense of research into substantive problems. (39)

Thus, Crozier and Thoenig comment:

' ... organisational students tend either to
try to build an abstract theory from which
they deduce from (sic) a set of cybernetic
axioms and derive normative prescriptions or
to measure those empirical relationships about
which one can get reliable data even if they
are meaningless for understanding how the
system really functions ... Even when such
empirical analyses are set forth, they are
comparatively weak and quite inadequate in
view of the scientific objectives stated'.
(40)

Thus, Levine and White investigated twenty-two health
organisations in New England and reported their initial
impressions on unanalysed data from some fifty-five other
health organisations. Links were measured by examining
referrals between agencies; the transfer of labour
services; the transfer of resources; written communications and joint activities. (41) And yet it is quite
common for essentially limited studies to begin with
grandiose assertions that networks are a fundamental
feature of modern industrial society. (42)

The attempt to develop measures of dependence is not
in itself a foolish or irrelevant expenditure of effort.
The problem is the extent of this pre-occupation. It has
led to a focus on the structure of interactions and
consequently important issues have been ignored. What is
the relationship between resources and power? To what
extent are interactions constrained by pre-existing
rules of the game? To what extent is the distribution of
power between organisations sustained by shared values?
It is as important to examine these questions as it is to
measure the amount and classify the types of interaction.

'Structuralist' vs. 'Game' Approaches

Although Thomson's formulation of the concept of interorganisational dependence has been influential, it is not
without problems. Because its origins lie in exchange
theory, there is the problem of explaining why a given
distribution of power exists. Only if it is assumed that
there is a given distribution of power can exchange
theory explain the relationships between the various
parties.

Birnbaum has criticised Blau in these terms:

' ... the structural distribution of resources
can often give rise to opposition directed
against the beneficiaries of social organisation when their power does not result from
the previous exchange relationship. But he
does not investigate the origin of this unequal
distribution of resources'. (43)

There has been some recognition of this problem in the literature on interorganisational analysis. For example, Benson has argued that:

' ... interorganisational power relations cannot be fully understood without attention to the larger patterns of societal dominance'. (44)

Similarly, there are ambiguities in Thompson's discussion of goal-setting as a political process. He draws heavily on the work of Cyert and March but their account does not discuss the origins of the goals of the contending parties within the organisation; does not explore explicitly the effects of inequalities in the distribution of power for goal-setting; and tends to focus only on those goals relevant to the formal structure and to ignore the range of individual commitments to the organisation. (45) It is necessary, therefore, to treat Thompson's formulation as a starting point and to pursue in more detail some of the objections which have been raised. (46)

Recently, the discussion of the concepts of power and dependence has polarised between 'structuralist' and 'game' approaches. A detailed exploration of this debate will serve, incidentally, to demonstrate the inadequacy of the distinction and, more important, to identify the ways in which the study of organisational power needs to be developed if it is to become an adequate alternative to systemic approaches.

The difference between structuralist and game approaches is summarised as follows by Crozier:

In the structuralist approach:

' ... some environmental variables or problems determine the structure of an organisation, and the structure of an organisation or the fit between the structure and the problem determine its effectiveness'.

On the other hand, the game approach analyses the behaviour of individuals in organisations as:

' ... the result of the strategy each one of them has adopted in the one or several games in which he participates ... These games are played according to some informal rules which cannot easily be predicted from the prescribed roles of the formal structure. One can discover, however, these rules, as well as the pay-offs and the possible rational strategies of the participants, by analysing the players' recurrent behaviour'. (47)

Crozier is one of the major contributors to the study of intra and interorganisational power 'games'. He argues that:

> 'The literature has rightly underscored the fact that the relation of the organisation to its environment is a relationship of dependence. Yet studies usually describe and classify the resources of power employed in this relation more than show the mechanisms of the game between the partners'. (48)

The starting point for Crozier's analysis of the game rather than the structure of interactions is the power relations within the organisation. (49) Every organisation has areas of uncertainty within it and power lies in the ability to control this uncertainty:

> 'Each participant in an organisation, in an organised system ... wields power over the system he belongs to and over the members of this system insofar as he occupies a strategically favourable position as regards the problems on which the success of the system depends'. (50)

Control over such uncertainty places a participant in a favourable position with other members of the organisation: he can blackmail them.

> 'It is anyway impossible to eliminate blackmail ('chantage'), since it is related to the perennial need for adjustment and innovation. No human enterprise can adapt to its environment if it is reduced to its formal power, to the theoretical pact which defines it'. (51)

However, anyone who has control over uncertainty is at one and the same time dependent upon others within the organisation. His ability to use 'chantage' is, therefore, limited. He is forced to bargain and negotiate with other members of the organisation. Crozier stresses the ways in which participants experience their participation. The contrasting perceptions of the participants enable the researcher to identify their strategies and the rules under which they are deployed. (52) In this scheme resources are not 'objective', but are defined by the participants, and control of a resource does not necessarily confer power on the controller. They only become important when so perceived by the participants and deployed in support of strategies. (53) The constraints under which 'chantage' takes place and the strategies used are described as a game:

'The terms of the exchange result neither from
chance nor from some abstract and theoretical
balance of power. They are the result of a
game whose constraints create compulsory
hurdles and opportunities for manipulation for
the players, and therefore determine their
strategy'. (54)

Crozier does not, therefore, classify the resources
available to the various participants or measure the
amount and type of interactions between them. Rather,
he focuses on the relationships between the various
participants and, in particular, on the strategies they
employ:

'The nature of the relationship does not depend
upon the resource of each player, but on the
powers which they use in the game...
Power in the relationship cannot be deduced by
an objective analysis of opposing forces'. (55)

Nor is the game confined to relationships within the
organisation. It can be applied to relations between
organisations:

'Regulation is the basic mechanism of organisations. From that point of view, there is no
difference in kind, but only a difference in
degree between an organisation and an interorganisational network. Both are social and
human systems, more or less stable and structured,
integrating various units, regulating their
behaviours, and imposing a collective game on
their members'. (56)

The 'games' in French local government involving the prefect and and local notables (especially mayors) provides
a striking illustration of Crozier's thesis. Convention-
ally, the prefect has always been regarded as representing the interests of the 'state' and the 'notable' as the
defender of local interests. Yet both are interdependent:
the success of one depends upon the other. The prefect
will be concerned that no strong local interests oppose
central policies and thus reduce his efficacy as a prefect. The mayor derives his power in his relationship
with the prefect from his claim to represent 'the whole
community'. Both have an interest in 'bending the
rules'. The prefect does not want to appear as merely
the executor of decisions taken at the centre, but he will
have to secure the complicity of the notables, since such
rule-bending is potentially open to criticism. Conversely, the notables have an interest in the bending of
rules since they derive status within the local
community from getting 'something special' for the
community. (57)

Thoenig has extended the concept of the game to the whole structure of 'territorial administration' in France. (58) At each level there exist relations of dependence around which games evolve. He identifies two separate channels of territorial administration, the elected and the administrative. There are areas of common interest between members of each of the channels and within each channel. But communication is not structured vertically or horizontally. Rather the system is one of 'cross-regulation'. Each member of a channel tries to have his interests favoured by members of the other channels upon whom they are dependent. The complexity of these interactions places a premium on playing several roles. It is an enormous advantage to be involved in more than one game. Thus, mayors become general councilmen and deputies. In spite of the complexity of this 'honeycomb' pattern of relations, however, the game is remarkably stable because it provides benefits to each participant. All have a vested interest in preserving the <u>status quo</u>. (59)

Crozier's 'game' model of interorganisational relations leads to a re-interpretation of central-local relations in France - one which lays considerably less emphasis than usual on central direction and hierarchical control. Moreover, its emphasis on the strategies of participants in a game appears to be very different from those studies which focus on measuring the resources of organisations and the structure of interactions. This 'structuralist' approach is illustrated by the work of Scharpf and his colleagues.

In their analysis of policy-making in the Federal Republic of Germany, they focus on the ways in which the structure of interactions contributes to policy failure. They argue that the welfare state has failed in three ways:

> ' - the failure of <u>effectiveness</u> in the management of the economy,
> - the failure of <u>efficiency</u> in the management of the social service sector, and
> - the failure of <u>responsiveness</u> to differenti-ated, qualitative demands in the performance of all government functions'. (60)

This 'crisis of ungovernability' requires that policy analysis relate public sector structures and processes to substantive policy outcomes. (61) How does the frag-mented decision-making structure of the Federal Republic affect policy outcomes? Central to their answer is the analysis of empirical networks of interorganisational dependence. The various studies emphasise the 'goodness of fit' between prescriptive policy networks - i.e. the 'objective' policy problem and the feasible alternatives within given constraints - and empirical networks - i.e. actual policy performance. (62) Any 'mismatch' is seen as an important predictor of policy failure.

The analysis of the networks focuses on the structure of inter-actions; an approach explicitly defended by Scharpf:

> 'At this time, it is still an open question whether the attempts by Michel Crozier and his group ... to develop a theory of intra- and interorganisational 'games' will eventually succeed in identifying a limited number of relatively stable, recurring game patterns which would help to reduce (and thus explain) the bewildering variety of observable inter-actions.
> As long as the empirical-theoretical break-through of a 'transactional' sociology of organisations is still uncertain, however, interorganisational policy studies might do well to follow a 'structuralist' approach that focuses upon the more stable ('structural') factors facilitating or impeding the employ-ment of specific influence strategies'. (63)

The 'semi-permanent relationships of unilateral and mutual dependence' are discussed in terms of resource acquisition (64) and they are explored in a series of case studies in such policy areas as modernising the dairy industry, pollution, urban renewal, federal highway construction and regional industrial policy.

Scharpf's theory of interorganisational relations is based on the 'classic' resource dependence model with the definition of resources 'extended to cover the range of all Laswellian values, including such intangibles as 'respect', 'affection' and 'rectitude' ". (65) The dis-cussion focuses on the exchange and substitutability of resources. In brief, the concept of power is defined in terms of the resources of participants.

At first glance, these summaries of the work of Crozier and Scharpf would seem to reveal a marked difference in approach. Important differences certainly exist but the distinction between structuralist and game approaches serves only to obscure them.

The problem with virtually all dichotomies is the implication that the alternatives are mutually exclusive. It is as misleading for Scharpf to label Crozier's work 'transactional' as it is for Crozier to assert that studies focusing on resource acquisition have ignored the strategies of participants. Crozier identifies a range

of constraints on the 'game' and specifically recognises
the importance of structural constraints. (66) Conversely, Scharpf et al. describe explicitly the
strategies deployed by decision-makers in the government
of the Federal Republic of Germany. (67) Similarly,
various authors have essayed lists of strategies that
decision-makers can employ. (68) Many of these authors
may list hypothetical strategies rather than documenting
the strategies employed in particular circumstances but
this is not Crozier's complaint. The distinction between
game and structuralist approaches polarises the field
when the differences are only ones of relative emphasis.
And in so doing, some important differences are obscured.

First, it is inaccurate to suggest that the structuralist approach is necessarily concerned to measure the
resources available to the interacting organisation. A
distinction needs to be drawn between those studies which
classify and measure the interactions between organisations and those which focus on the prior question of
resource acquisition. (69)

Second, those studies which do concentrate on resource
acquisition tend to define power in terms of the resources
commanded by decision-makers. Such a conception of power
is unduly limited. For example, there is no guarantee
that the researcher's list of resources would correspond
to that of the participants; that the same resource would
be of equal use in a variety of situations; or that the
various resources can be compared. Such limitations
underlie Crozier's critique of structuralist approaches,
his stress on perceptions of power, and his denial that
resources are 'objective'. And at this point, the major
difference between proponents in the field of interorganisational analysis can be specified. The structura-
list/game dichotomy obscures the fact that the difference
concerns the concept of power, and whether it derives from
and consists of command over resources or whether it
derives from perceptions of power and consists of rule-
governed interactions.

Replacing one dichotomy with another, however, does
little to advance the analysis. By emphasising that the
differences lie in the concept of power, the objective is
not to argue in favour of one or other conception but to
suggest that both facets of power are relevant to an
understanding of interorganisational linkages. Although
a focus on power as resources is limited, it is not thereby rendered irrelevant. Similarly, perceptions of power
can be an unreliable guide. An actor's (perceived)
power may stem from his command of resources and the
conditions under which the various resources can be
effectively deployed may influence the choice of
strategies. The precise nature of the relationship be-

tween resources and strategies cannot be explored by a focus on perceptions alone. In Britain, central departments control far greater financial resources than local authorities. It is important to find out when and how the control of financial resources provides support for, and affects the choice of, strategies by central departments. As Benson has argued, the choice of strategies is a function of the amount and distribution of resources. For example, authoritative strategies are said to require a dominant position in the flow of resources whereas cooperative strategies require some minimal degree of equality in the distribution of resources. (70) It would be misleading to suggest that Crozier is unaware of the intricacies of the relationship between resources and strategies. He points to the constraints of technology, law, formal organisational structure and other elements of the environment on the participants in the game. The emphasis on perceptions reflects, therefore, his desire to avoid the determinism associated with many conceptions of the organisation-environment link and to show that the rules of the game are only partially governed by technical, historical and environmental constraints.

This ability of participants to make and remake the rules of the game introduces a third aspect of the concept of power. Clegg, reviewing Crozier's earlier work, has argued that the power of many of the lower participants in the organisational game is power at the margin, i.e. it is restricted in scope. (71) In a similar vein, Fox remarks that union or worker representatives:

' ... have already been socialised, indoctrinated and trained by a multiplicity of influences to accept and legitimise most aspects of their work situation: a situation designed in the light of the values and purposes of the major power holders'. (72)

As a result, the power of the worker is limited not only by inequality in the distribution of resources within the organisation but also by a consensus which limits the area of negotiation to issues which do not threaten the values and purposes of major power holders - i.e. management.

In other words, it is possible to distinguish between power as resources, power as rule-governed interactions and power as the 'mobilisation of bias'. Although each group may control some resources; although there may be scope for 'chantage' within and between organisations, this bargaining does not necessarily mean there is equality in the distribution of power. The existence of shared values may limit the bargaining to a narrow range of issues and stipulate rules of the game which favour one of the contending parties.

The major problem with this third aspect of power lies in the assumption by some writers that such inequalities in the distribution of power can be identified with the domination of the organisation by one group - i.e. management. Both Clegg and Fox are criticising the assumption in some versions of pluralism that there is an equal distribution of power in organisations. It does not follow, however, that an assumption of strict equality is an essential component of a pluralist approach, or that the consensus is designed by and for one specific group of participants. In arguing for a recognition of the plurality of social systems within the organisation, the intention is to explore the relative power of the participants; the bases of their power; the ways, if any, in which the rules of the game are 'negotiated'; (73) and the pervasiveness of unobtrusive controls or control of decision premises. (74) As Crozier argues, although social and economic inequalities are important in the game and managers have greater room for manoeuvre, nonetheless management cannot ignore the rules of the game. <u>All</u> participants are constrained by the rules. They <u>are</u> not unilaterally determined by any one group nor are they determined equally by all groups. (75) Nonetheless, the critique suggests that the ways in which the rules of the game are negotiated and have evolved over time is a key area of investigation. Much of the so-called 'pluralist' literature on organisational power has focused on issues and power resources (or bases) to the exclusion of other facets of power. (76)

The concept of the 'mobilisation of bias' is a product of the community power debate in political science and, to date, it has not figured prominently in the analysis of organisational power. (77) Bachrach and Baratz discuss the 'mobilisation of bias' (and the allied concept of 'non-decisions') as follows:

> 'When the dominant values, the accepted rules of the game, the existing power relations among groups, and the instruments of force, singly or in combination, effectively prevent certain grievances from developing into full-fledged issues which call for decisions, it can be said that a non-decision-making situation exists'. (78)

As interpreted by Parry and Morriss this critique requires that we distinguish between the many kinds of decisions whether they be 'key issues' or routine, administrative decisions and, for each kind of decision, between the types of power involved. Three types of power are discussed - the power to initiate a routine; the power by which a routine is maintained; and the distribution of power following from the performance of a routine. (79) Of particular relevance in this formulation is the focus on

routines, and the values and power distribution sustaining them. It is precisely this focus which is required
in the study of organisational and interorganisational
power and so prominent in Crozier's work. However, it is
not simply a matter of describing the rules of the game
operative at a given point in time. Clegg distinguishes
between power, rules and domination, arguing that pluralist theory has focused on the surface manifestations of
power - i.e. participation in key issues. He argues for
an analysis of the rules supporting and constraining such
participation and for an analysis of the structure of
domination which supports the rules. (80) The analysis
of power must explore the origins of the rules, the values
and distribution of power supporting them and the
pressures changing them. At this juncture, the limits of
Crozier's analysis can be specified more precisely. He
focuses on power and, more important, the rules underlying
the exercise of power but he does not analyse the gener-
ation of rules. He explains why actors continue to
support pre-existing rules of the game but he does not
explore variations in the degree of commitment to these
rules. Shared values can not only limit the scope of
'chantage' but also the form of the rules. The bases of
support for the rules thus becomes of central importance.

There have been few studies of this aspect of organisational power. (81) In the context of interorganisational analysis, the value of exploring power as the
mobilisation of bias has been demonstrated by Warren et
al.'s study of 'institutionalised thought structure', and
its effect on the pattern of relationships between organisations involved in the Model Cities programme. The
existence of shared values is said to explain the lack of
competition and even contact between the organisations
involved. And yet the lack of coordination between
agencies was assumed to be a major contributory factor to
the failure to solve urban problems. Moreover, the new
agencies of the Model Cities programme were quickly
assimilated to the shared values. Not surprisingly, they
record little evidence of innovative attacks on problems.
(82) The 'institutionalised thought structure' was, to
employ Perrow's term, the 'ground' against which the
'figure' of organisational interactions had to be viewed.
(83) And Warren et al. document the ways in which the
rules of the game and the distribution of power between
organisations are sustained by the shared values of the
organisational network.

The analysis of the concepts of power and exchange in
the literature on interorganisational analysis cannot be
adequately summarised by distinguishing between
structures and games. The major distinctions reside in
the differing approaches to the concept of power. However,
these approaches are not mutually exclusive. It needs to

be more readily appreciated that power can no more be reduced to the sum of each participant's resources than it can be viewed solely in terms of each actor's perceptions; that the rules governing interactions cannot be treated as given nor can they be viewed in a deterministic manner as the product of the values and interests of any one group. Power is a multi-faceted concept and its utility in the analysis of the relationships between organisations will not be improved if it is arbitrarily limited to but one of the facets.

CONSEQUENCES

Given that organisations are interdependent and employ strategies to manage their dependence, what are the consequences of this activity? This question has not figured prominently in the interorganisational analysis literature. Some attention has been given to the structural consequences of dependence. For example, networks have been compared by size, compactness, density and diversity. (84) Some attention has also been paid to the interoganisational decision-making process, and these studies are often concerned to prescribe for improved decision-making. (85) In its preoccupation with measuring interactions, the literature has omitted to, ask why such networks matter. Indeed, Perrow argues that far too much time has been devoted to the study of 'trivial organisations'. (86) There would be little point in studying organisational networks if, as much of the literature implies by default, little of consequence follows from their existence. The roots of this litera- ture often lie in some version of the post-industrial society thesis but only rarely are the links between the macro-theory and the specific studies of networks clearly articulated. The location of empirical work within a broader, interpretative framework is not a feature of interorganisational analysis - a point discussed in more detail below. Fortunately, clues about the importance of networks can be culled from other sources.

For example, a number of studies have pointed to the problems created for the implementation of a policy by the need to work with and through a large number of separate organisations. Each organisation has its own interests and commands resources of its own. Compliance or cooperation is not automatically forthcoming and in negotiating agreement the original policy can be changed. (87) Similarly, Sampson has documented the activities of ITT, demonstrating that the actions of large multi- national companies are not necessarily benevolent; that they are by no means the passive victims of a turbulent environment; and that governments experience major problems in controlling them. (88) These and other sources suggest that the relative power of organisations in a network has crucial effects on both the process of policy-making and political accountability. (89)

Although the interactions between organisations are not
the only influence upon policy-making, it is clear that
they are sufficiently important on a range of issues to
warrant far more attention than they have received to
date. The failure of the literature on interorganisational analysis to explore such consequences can be
numbered amongst its greatest failings.

CONCLUSIONS

Models in the social sciences are never wholly satisfactory; they are more or less useful. This chapter has
reviewed the literature on interorganisational analysis
and in so doing it has criticised the bulk of the contributions. The objective has not been to demonstrate the
truism that all models are incomplete but to identify the
ways in which the existing models can be developed. As
Karl Weick has argued much criticism in the sociology of
organisations is not balanced by a concern with affirm-
ation: with the need to enlarge our understanding of the
phenomenon of organising in the act of criticising. (90)
This chapter has at least attempted to approach its
subject matter in a constructive manner.

To recap, it has been suggested that the systems
approach to the study of the link between organisations
and their environment is inadequate because the theory
cannot specify the 'relevant' aspects of the environment;
or provide the criteria for bounding the network; or
define goals without reifying the organisation. Moreover,
there is no one theory of interorganisational analysis.
The field has been described as a set of issues. Building
upon the work of Thompson, it has been argued that a focus
on intra- and interorganisational power can provide both
the analytical cutting edge lacking in systems theory and
a coherent perspective. Thus the goals of the organisation are described as the outcome of an intra- and
interorganisational political process: they are negotiated. The environment does not determine the goals and
decisions of an 'organisation'. The environment is constitutive but it is also constituted by the dominant
coalition. However, much of the literature on interorganisational analysis has adopted a deterministic or
constitutive position on the effects of the environment on
organisational decision-makers. There has been a pre-
occupation with classifying and measuring interactions.
Even those authors who have built upon Thompson's work
have tended to adopt a narrow conception of the exchanges
with the environment. A review of structuralist and game
approaches to the study of organisational links suggests
that it is necessary to distinguish three facets of
organisational power: power as resources: power as rule-
governed interactions: and power as the mobilisation of
bias. None of these aspects of power is adequate if
examined in isolation from the others. To comprehend the

links between organisations, analysis has to encompass all three facets of power. And the concern with intra- and interorganisational power is also a concern with the consequences which arise from the activities of organisations, whether these consequences take the form of either frustrating the implementation of policy or obscuring the accountability of organisations for their actions.

The discussion of interorganisational analysis in this chapter forms part of the search for a more adequate theoretical framework for analysing intergovernmental relations and to assess the contribution which recent theoretical developments in the field of interorgani- sational analysis might make to an understanding of such relations. Criticism of the interorganisational litera- ture has not sought, therefore, to expose inherent weak- nesses but to high-light key common concerns and potential areas of development. It has been argued that the literature contains a number of useful concepts and it is appropriate to ask what contribution they can make to the study of the 'forgotten dimensions' of British central-local relations?

First, the concept of organisational <u>networks</u> draws attention to the variety of relationships in which a central department or a local authority could be engaged. It is no longer adequate to limit analysis to the central department/local authority link. At the very least, the concept of networks enjoins the analysis of links between public sector organisations in all their various guises and there is no necessary reason why analysis could not be extended to private sector organisations also. The view that Britain is a unitary state has worked against recognition of the fact that its intergovernmental relations are complex. And equally important, the literature on interorganisational analysis provides tools for measuring and comparing networks. (91) If intergovernmental relations in Britain are complex, it would be as well to document this ostensibly simple point as precisely as possible.

Second, the concept of <u>goals</u> as the outcome of a politi- cal process within and between organisations acts as a corrective to the 'top-down' view of intergovernmental relations - for example, the view that goals are determined by central departments and implemented by local authorities. There are many prescriptions in the literature on central-local relations for central depart- ments to make their policy explicit. (92) The view of goals as temporary and the product of bargaining suggests that it would be more profitable to explore the process of goal-setting in public sector organisations; to identify the constraints on making explicit policy settlements. Indeed, it is relevant to ask if goals are

determined at the centre: to what extent is there a
'bottom-up' dimension to goal setting? Moreover, this
perspective suggests that there will be a variety of
competing goals. Accordingly, it is important to compare
different policy areas and ask if they have distinct
organisational networks.

Third, the concepts of power and exchange emphasise
that the relationship between centre and periphery is not
a 'control' relationship. Rather central departments and
sub-national public sector organisations are interdependent. And recognition of this point opens up a
series of questions about intergovernmental relations
which until recently have been conspicuous only for their
absence. To what extent do the participants control
different amounts and types of resources? To what extent
do they recognise and work within agreed rules of the
game? Do they employ strategies to manage their relationships? Do they compete for discretion in designing and
implementing policies? To what extent do the participants
share values which limit the scope of negotiations? In
addition, within these general areas, a number of more
specific questions can be raised. For example, attention
is focused on the identification of the rules of the
game: describing how they are applied in specific
situations; analysing how they are adjusted to meet
changed situations; and most important, exploring their
origins.

Finally, the interorganisational model suggests that
institutional complexity can have marked consequences
for governmental effectiveness and accountability.
Crozier and Thoenig describe French central-local
relations as a 'game' that is 'closed and secret' in
which the participants 'fear public opinion and hide from
the sanctions of electoral suffrage'. (93) It is
certainly relevant to ask if the ambiguity and confusion
of British central-local relations has similar consequences. (94) But the discussion in this chapter has
directly confronted the relationship between interorganisational analysis and theories of advanced
industrial society only in brief. The relationship
between these two levels of analysis must now be explored
in a little more detail.

As already noted, interorganisational analysis tends to
adopt some version of the post-industrial society thesis,
albeit implicitly. The focus on the complex web of
organisations, the analysis of interdependence, the
separation of ownership and control and the stress on the
power of large-scale organisations in modern society are
shared themes. (95) Similarly, corporatist theory
stresses interdependence between organisations and, in
Winkler's case, specifically appeals to Thompson's
analysis of organisational interdependence. (96)

On the face of it, therefore, there would appear to be
marked affinities between the two levels of analysis.
But in this case appearances are deceptive. The argument
that interorganisational analysis needs to be located
within a theory of inter- and intra-organisational power
is but one way of saying that it has become divorced from
any broader interpretative framework. Whatever the roots
of interorganisational analysis, those roots do not inform
the interpretation of empirical results. In other words,
interorganisational analysis is capable of informing the
analysis of the 'figure' or the surface level of interactions between the various units of government but it is
not able to explore the 'ground' or the deep structures
of power, values and interests which support and sustain
those interactions. Appearances to the contrary, interorganisational analysis does not affect a reconciliation
between levels of analysis. (97) Not that this problem
is peculiar to interorganisational analysis in particular
or even the sociology of organisations in general. It
will be considered again in the discussion of the
literature on intergovernmental relations.

NOTES AND REFERENCES

1. See for example: Rose, R., 'The United Kingdom as a
    Multi-National State' in Rose, R. (ed.), Studies in
    British Politics London: Macmillan, third edn., 1976
    pp. 115-50.
2. Burkhead, J., 'Federalism in a Unitary State:
    regional economic planning in England' Publius Vol. 4
    1974 p. 61.
3. Riker, W.H., 'Six Books in Search of a Subject or
    Does Federalism Exist and Does it Matter?' Comparative
    Politics Vol. 2 1969 p. 142.
4. Albrow, M., 'The Study of Organisations: objectivity
    or Bias?' in Salaman, G., and Thompson, K., (eds.),
    People and Organisations London: Longmans, 1973 p.412.
5. Albrow, op. cit., p. 412.
6. Perrow, C., Complex Organisations Glenview, Ill.,:
    Scott, Foresman, second edn., 1979, preface and p. 237:
    Scharpf, F.W., 'Interorganisational Policy Studies:
    issues, concepts and perspectives' in Hanf, K., and
    Scharpf, F.W., (eds.), Interorganisational Policy
    Making London: Sage, 1978; and Elkin, S.L.,
    'Comparative Urban Politics and Interorganisational
    Behaviour' in Young, K., (ed.), Essays on the Study of
    Urban Politics London: Macmillan, 1975 p. 183.
7. Elkin, op. cit., pp. 175-6.
8. A subsidiary objective of this chapter is to draw the
    attention of political scientists to the literature on
    the sociology of organisations. Compared to, for
    example, the literature on intergovernmental relations,
    this literature is relatively unknown to British
    political scientists. Hopefully, this chapter will
    pursuade them that it will repay exploration.

9.   Emery, F.E. and Trist, E.L., 'Socio-Technical Systems' in Emery, F.E., (ed.), Systems Thinking Harmondsworth: Penguin Books, 1969 p. 281 and p. 282.

10.   Emery, F.E. and Trist, E.L., 'The Causal Texture of Organisational Environments' in Emery, op. cit., pp.245-49.

11.   See for example: Katz, D., and Kahn, R.L., The Social Psychology of Organisations New York: Wiley, 1966; and Terreberry, S., 'The Evolution of Organisational Environments' Administrative Science Quarterly Vol. 12 1968 pp. 590-613.

12.   Aldrich, H.E., and Pfeffer, J., 'Environments of Organisations' in Inkeles, A., (ed.), Annual Review of Sociology Vol. II Palo Alto, California: Annual Review Inc., 1976 pp. 79-105.

13.   Karpik, L., 'Preface' in Karpik, L., (ed.), Organisation and Environment: theory, issues and reality London: Sage, 1978 p. 9.

14.   Compare, for example: Metcalfe, L., 'Policy Making in Turbulent Environments' in Hanf and Scharpf, op. cit., pp. 37-55 with Habermas, J., Toward a Rational Society London: Heinemann, 1971 pp. 81-122.

15.   For a summary of the weaknesses of systems theory and appropriate citations see: Silverman, D., The Theory of Organisations London: Heinemann, 1970 chs. 2 and 3.

16.   Blau, P.M., and Scott, W.R., Formal Organisations London: Routledge and Kegan Paul, 1963 p. 195.

17.   Evan, W.M., 'The Organisation-Set: toward a theory of interorganisational relations' in Thompson, J.D., (ed.), Approaches to Organisational Design Pittsburgh: University of Pittsburgh Press, pp. 175-91.

18.   For a discussion of the concept of organisational goals see: Gross, E., 'The Definition of Organisational Goals' British Journal of Sociology Vol. 20 1969 pp. 277-94: Mohr, L., 'The Concept of Organisational Goal' American Political Science Review Vol. 67 1973 pp. 470-81: and Perrow, C., Organisational Analysis London: Tavistock, 1970.

19.   Etzioni, A., 'Two Approaches to Organisational Analysis: a critique and a suggestion' Administrative Science Quarterly Vol. 5 1960 pp. 257-78.

20.   Yuchtman, E., and Seashore, S.E., 'A System Resource Approach to Organisational Effectiveness' American Sociological Review Vol. 32 1967 pp. 891-903.

21.   Silverman, op. cit., p. 4.

22.   See: Thompson, J.D., Organisations in Action New York: McGraw-Hill, 1967 pp. 27-9. See also: Levine, S., and White P.E., 'Exchange as a Conceptual Framework for the Study of Interorganisational Relationships' Administrative Science Quarterly Vol. 5 1961 pp. 583-601; and Thompson, J.D. and McEwen, I., 'Organisational Goals and Environment: goal-setting as an interaction process' American Sociological Review Vol. 23 1958 pp. 23-31.

23.   Thompson, Organisations in Action, op. cit., pp.
       127-30. See also Cyert, R.M. and March, J.G.,
       A Behavioural Theory of the Firm Englewood Cliffs, N.J.:
       Prentice Hall, 1963.
24.   Ranson, S., Hinings, C.R. and Greenwood, R. 'The
       Structuring of Organisational Structures' Administrat-
       ive Science Quarterly Vol. 25 1980 pp. 1-17.
25.   Pugh, D.S. and Hickson, D.J., Organisational
       Structure In its Context Farnborough, Hants.: Saxon
       House, 1976.
26.   Lawrence, P.R., and Lorsch, J.W., Organisations and
       Environment Boston: Graduate School of Business
       Administration, Harvard University, 1967.
27.   Child, J., 'Organisation Structure, Environment and
       Performance: the role of strategic choice' in
       Salaman and Thompson, op. cit., p. 98.
28.   Chandler, A., Strategy and Structure Cambridge,
       Mass.: MIT Press, 1962 p. 15.
29.   Perrow, C., Complex Organisations Glenview, Ill.:
       Scott, Foresman, first edn., 1972 p. 199.
30.   Perrow, Complex Organisations, second edn., op. cit.,
       p. 215.
31.   Karpik, op. cit., p. 9.
32.   Blau, P.M., Exchange and Power in Social Life New
       York: Wiley, 1964, p. 118.
33.   Thompson, Organisations in Action, op. cit., pp.
       30-31. See also: Emerson, R.M., 'Power-Dependence
       Relations' American Sociological Review Vol. 27
       1962 pp. 31-41.
34.   Crozier, M., and Thoenig, J.C., 'The Regulation of
       Complex Organised Systems' Administrative Science
       Quarterly Vol. 21 1976 p. 562.
35.   Litwak, E., and Hylton, L.F., 'Interorganisational
       Analysis: a hypothesis on co-ordinating agencies'
       Administrative Science Quarterly Vol. 6. 1962 pp.395-
       415.
36.   Thompson and McEwan, op. cit., pp. 25-8.
37.   Benson, J.K., 'The Interorganisational Network as a
       Political Economy' Administrative Science Quarterly
       Vol. 20 1975 p. 231.
38.   Klonglan, G.E., Warren, R.D., Winkelpleck, J.M. and
       Paulson, S.K., 'Interorganisational Measurement in the
       Social Services Sector: differences by hierarchical
       level' Administrative Science Quarterly Vol. 21. 1976
       pp. 675-87.
39.   See for example the debate over the Aston measure of
       dependence. The measure includes items on both other
       organisations and on relations to the owning group.
       See: Pugh, D.S., and Hinings, C.R., Organisational
       Structure: extensions and replications Farnborough,
       Hants.: Saxon House, 1976 pp. 23-4. Mindlin, S.E.
       and Aldrich, H., 'Interorganisational Dependence: a
       review of the concept and a re-examination of the
       findings of the Aston Group' Administrative Science

Quarterly Vol. 13 1976 pp.382-92 point out thatthe items on relations to the owning group skew the dependency measure. To conclude a typical exchange, Pugh and Hinings reply: 'We consider this criticism to be very well taken conceptually and that the distinction between inter- and intraorganisational dependence needs to be retained and developed in future work' p. 174.

40. Crozier and Thoenig, op. cit., p. 562 and p. 548.
41. Levine and White, op. cit., p. 585 and p. 589. See also: Evan, W.M., Interorganisational Relations Harmondsworth: Penguin Books, 1976; and Turk, H., 'Interorganisational Networks in Urban Society' American Sociological Review Vol. 35 1970 pp. 1-19.
42. See for example: Turk, H., Organisations in Modern Life San Francisco: Jossey-Bass, 1977 ch. 1.
43. Birnbaum, P., 'Power Divorced from its Sources: a critique of the exchange theory of power' in Barry, B.M. (ed.), Power and Political Theory New York: Wiley, 1976 p. 29.
44. Benson, op. cit., p. 233.
45. For a more detailed critique see: Burns, T., 'On the Plurality of Social Systems' in Burns, T., (ed.), Industrial Man Harmondsworth: Penguin Books, 1969 pp. 232-49; and Pettigrew, A.M., The Politics of Organisational Decision-making London: Tavistock, 1973 chs. 1 and 2.
46. For a more detailed discussion of organisational politics see: Rhodes, R.A.W., 'Organisational Politics' in Brown, M, and Muir, L. (eds.), Social Work: a theory and practice text London: Macdonald and Evans 1980 (forthcoming).
47. Crozier, M., 'Comparing Structures and Comparing Games' in Hofstede, G., and Kassem, M.S. (eds.), European Contributions to Organisation Theory Assen/Amsterdam: Van Gorcum, 1976 p. 195 and p. 196.
48. Crozier and Thoenig, op. cit., p. 563.
49. I would like to thank Ed Page (University of Strathclyde) for his assistance with, and translations of, various passages in books and articles by Michel Crozier not available in English. Where possible, I have referred to translated work only.
50. Crozier, M., 'The Problem of Power' Social Research Vol. 40 1973 pp. 220-21. This article is a translated chapter from: Crozier, M., La Société Bloquee Paris Ed. du Seuil, 1971.
51. Crozier, 'The Problem of Power' op. cit., p. 223.
52. For a detailed description of his methodology see: Crozier, M., 'The Relationship between Micro and Macro Sociology' Human Relations Vol. 25 1972 pp. 239-51.
53. Crozier, M., and Friedberg, E., L'acteur et le système Paris: Ed du Seuil, 1977 p. 71.
54. Crozier, 'The Problem of Power' op. cit., p. 219.

55. Crozier and Thoenig, op. cit., p. 563.
56. Crozier and Thoenig, op. cit., p. 562.
57. See also: Becquart-Leclerq, J., 'Relational Power
     and Systemic Articulation in French Local Polity' in
     Karpik, L., (ed.), op. cit., pp. 253-92; Kesselman,
     M., The Ambiguous Consensus New York: Alfred A. Knopf,
     1967; and Worms, J.P., 'Le Prefet et ses notables'
     Sociologie du Travail Vol. 8 1966 pp. 249-75.
58. Thoenig, J-C., 'State Bureaucracies and Local
     Government in France' in Hanf and Scharpf, op. cit.,
     pp. 167-97.
59. Crozier and Thoenig, op. cit., p. 559. See also:
     Thoenig, J-C., 'Pouvoir d'etat et pouvoirs locaux'
     Pouvoirs Vol. 4 1978 pp. 25-37.
60. Scharpf, F.W., 'Public Organisation and the Waning
     of the Welfare State' European Journal of Political
     Research Vol. 5 1977 p. 343.
61. A broader ranging analysis of policy-making in the
     Federal Republic of Germany can be found in Mayntz, R.
     and Scharpf, F.W., Policy-Making in the German Federal
     Bureaucracy Amsterdam: Elsevier, 1975.
62. See: Scharpf, F.W., Reissert, B., and Schnabel, F.,
     Politikverflechtung Kronberg; Scriptor, 1976; and
     Scharpf, F.W., Reissert, B., and Schnabel, F., 'Policy
     Effectiveness and Conflict Avoidance in the Inter-
     governmental Policy Formation' in Hanf and Scharpf,
     op. cit., pp. 57-112.
63. Scharpf, 'Interorganisational Policy Studies' op.
     cit., p. 353.
64. Scharpf, 'Interorganisational Policy Studies,
     op. cit., p. 366.
65. Scharpf, 'Interorganisational Policy Studies,
     op. cit., p. 354.
66. Crozier, 'The Problem of Power', op. cit., p. 214.
67. Scharpf, et al., 'Policy Effectiveness and Conflict
     Avoidance in Intergovernmental Policy Formation'
     op. cit., pp. 100-106.
68. See inter alia: Elkin, op. cit., p. 175; Selznick,
     P., TVA and the Grass Roots Berkeley and Los Angeles:
     University of California Press, 1949 p. 13; Thompson
     and McEwan, op. cit., pp. 159-63; Thompson Organisat-
     ions in Action, op. cit., pp. 134-37.
69. Benson, op. cit., p. 231.
70. Benson, op. cit., pp. 241-46.
71. Clegg, S., Power, Rule and Domination London:
     Routledge and Kegan Paul, 1975 p. 49.
72. Fox, A., 'Industrial Relations: a social critique
     of pluralist ideology' in Child, J., (ed.), Man and
     Organisation London: Allen and Unwin, 1973 p. 217.
73. See: Strauss, A., Schatzman, L., Ehrlich, D.,
     Bucher, R., and Sabshin, M., 'The Hospital and its
     Negotiated Order' in Friedson, E., (ed.), The Hospital
     in Modern Society New York: Macmillan, 1963 pp. 147-69.
74. Perrow, Complex Organisations. second edn., op. cit.,
     pp. 149-53.

75. See: Crozier and Friedberg, op. cit., p. 70; and Burns, T., The BBC: Public Institution and Private World London: Macmillan, 1977 p. 86.
76. See for example: Hickson, D.J., and Hinings, C.R., Lee, C.A., Schneck, R.E., and Pennings, J.M., 'A Strategic Contingencies' Theory of Intraorganisational Power' Administrative Science Quarterly Vol. 16 1971 pp. 216-29. For critiques see: Clegg, op. cit., pp. 43-53; Bachrach, P., and Baratz, M.S., 'Two Faces of Power' American Political Science Review Vol. 56 1962 pp. 947-52; and Lukes, S., Power: A Radical View London: Macmillan, 1974.
77. One of the major charges levelled against critics of the pluralist literature is their inability to specify satisfactory methods for the study of the 'mobilisation of bias'. Ignoring the easy retort that methods should not dictate the subject matter of research, a number of studies have begun to develop an appropriate methodology. Some of the relevant issues can be seen by comparing Crenson, M.A., The Un-politics of Air Pollution Baltimore: John Hopkins Press, 1971 with Polsby, N., 'Empirical Investigations of Mobilisation of Bias in Community Power Research' Political Studies Vol. 37 1979 pp. 527-41. For further discussion see Ch. 5 below.
78. Bachrach, P., and Baratz, M.S., 'Decisions and Nondecisions: an analytical framework' American Political Science Review Vol. 57 1963 p. 641.
79. Parry, G., and Morriss, P., 'When is a Decision not a Decision?' in Crewe, I., (ed.), The British Political Sociology Yearbook, Vol. 1 Elites in Western Democracy Croom Helm, 1974 pp. 317-36.
80. Clegg, op. cit., Chs. 4 and 5.
81. But see: Perrow, Complex Organisations, second edn. op. cit., pp. 59-68; and Bendix, R., Work and Authority in Industry New York: Wiley, 1956.
82. Warren, R., Rose, S., and Bergunder, A., The Structure of Urban Reform Lexington, Mass.: Heath, 1974 pp. 19-25.
83. Perrow, Complex Organisations, second edn., op.cit., p. 236.
84. See: Evan, Interorganisational Relations op. cit., Part 4; and Mitchell, J.C., 'The Concept and Use of Social Networks' in Mitchell, J.C., (ed.), Social Networks in Urban Situations Manchester: Manchester University Press, 1969 pp. 1-29.
85. See for example: Friend, J., Power, J.M., and Yewlett, C.J.L., Public Planning: the inter-corporate dimension London: Tavistock, 1974; the various publications of F.W. Scharpf (above notes 60-62); and Tuite, M., Chisholm, R., and Radnor, M., Interorganisational Decision Making Chicago: Aldine, 1972.
86. Perrow, Complex Organisations, second edn., op. cit. p. 193.

87.   See for example: Bardach, E., The Implementation
Game Boston: MIT Press, 1977; Hood, C.C. The Limits
of Administration London: Wiley, 1976; Hanf and
Scharpf, op. cit., especially chs. 8 and 12; and
Pressman, J., and Wildavsky, A., Implementation
Berkeley: University of California Press, 1973.

88.   Sampson, A., The Sovereign State London: Coronet
Books, 1974.

89.   See inter alia: Bailey, M., Oilgate London:
Coronet Books, 1979; Galbraith, J.K., Economics and
the Public Purpose Boston: Houghton Mifflin, 1973;
Perrow, C., The Radical Attack on Business New York:
Harcourt Brace Jovanovich, 1972; and Sampson, A.,
The Seven Sisters London: Coronet Books, 1976.

90.   Weick, K.E., The Social Psychology of Organising
Reading, Mass.: Addison-Wesley, second edn., 1979
p. 12.

91.   See note 84 above; and Laumann, E.O., and Pappi,
F.U., Networks of Collective Action New York: Academic
Press, 1976.

92.   Griffith, J.A.G., Central Departments and Local
Authorities London: Allen and Unwin, 1966 pp. 537-39.

93.   Crozier and Thoenig, op. cit., p. 556. And compare
these remarks with the quotations on p.29   above.

94.   The description 'game' is potentially misleading.
Although it is a striking metaphor which serves
admirably to highlight the differences between interorganisational and traditional approaches to the study
of intergovernmental relations, it is only a shorthand
expression covering situations in which decision-
makers employ strategies within known rules of the game
to pursue their goals. However, it can all too easily
be taken to refer to certain theories of transactional
psychology (See for example: Berne, E., Games People
Play Harmondsworth: Penguin Books, 1968) or it can
obscure the differences between games proper and
social interaction (Silverman, op. cit., pp. 210-12).
Finally, continual reference to 'the game' can serve to
obscure the point that there is an 'ecology of games'
See for example: Long, N., 'The Local Community as an
Ecology of Games' American Journal of Sociology Vol.
64, 1958 pp. 251-61. In an effort to avoid some of
these misleading connotations, I have occasionally substituted the more prosaic term 'rule-governed interactions for the 'game' metaphor.

95.   See for example: Clegg, op. cit., pp.46-48 and his
analysis of the use of the concept of power in the study
of organisations.

96.   See: Winkler, J.T., 'Corporatism' European Journal
of Sociology Vol. 17, 1976 pp. 130-31.

97.   On 'deep structures' see Clegg, op. cit., pp. 70-79
and the discussion below in Ch. 5.

4 Intergovernmental relations

The literature on intergovernmental relations (IGR) is
extensive and, since no short review could possibly draw
together all the disparate threads, this chapter does not
attempt to provide a detailed survey or to describe IGR
in particular countries. Rather, it emphasises the
various theoretical models which have been used to
analyse variations in the relationships between tiers of
government and, in particular, those research studies
which suggest potentially fruitful approaches to the study
of British central-local relations. As with the literature on interorganisational analysis, however, it will be
argued that there is no ready-made theory which can simply
be transposed to the British context.

A number of additional themes will also be explored.
First, it will be argued that the IGR literature can shed
light on the 'forgotten dimensions' of British central-
local relations because it has focused increasingly on the
complex interdependencies of levels of government and
because discussions of the politics of IGR have stressed
the prevalence of bargaining, the strategies of participants and the importance of the rules of the game.
Second, and in sharp contrast to the interorganisational
analysis literature, there have been a few systematic
attempts to explain the origins of, and changes in, the
rules of the game. In other words, the relationship
between the 'ground' or the underlying distribution of
power and the 'figure' or the interactions of participants
has been explored. However, in spite of this concern with
the distribution of power between levels of government, it
will be argued that the analysis is limited partly because
it is country-specific. Finally, the contrasts and
parallels between the IGR and the interorganisational
analysis literatures will be explored to determine whether
or not the IGR literature can make a distinctive contribution to our understanding of British intergovernmental
relations.

The two major objectives of this chapter are, therefore,
to determine the extent to which the IGR literature provides a basis for future research into British intergovernmental relations; and to assess the extent to
which specific explanations of the relationships between
units of government are located within a broader interpretative framework.

A number of commentators have noted the similarities between allegedly 'unitary' systems of government and 'federal' systems. (1) In fact, the comparison of these two types of governmental system can be viewed as one of the classic topics of political science. Given the growing awareness of the plural nature of British government, it is appropriate to begin the discussion of the IGR literature by exploring in at least some detail the distinctive features of federal systems. However, the discussion will not focus on either normative or definitional questions, although there is an extensive literature on both topics. (2) The emphasis is placed on the models or theories of the relationship between the various units of government. More specifically, the development of the study of federalism into the more general study of intergovernmental relations will be explored. (3)

A useful starting point for examining the wealth of material on federalism is Birch's distinction between the institutional, sociological, process and bargaining approaches. (4) The institutional approach is well illustrated by Wheare. His approach is to construct an 'ideal type' model of the features of federalism in a manner somewhat reminiscent of Weber on bureaucracy. The definition of federalism in terms of general and regional governments having co-ordinate and independent powers (5) may not apply to all countries describing themselves as federal, but it does provide a benchmark against which to evaluate them. This approach has been oft-criticised. It is claimed that the definition is too restrictive and that the approach is legalistic although, as Birch points out, it is not immediately apparent why this last point should be viewed as a criticism. Perhaps the major weakness of the approach has been that many new federations simply do not conform to the model. (6) One is reduced to concluding that most so-called federal systems are not really federal.

The sociological approach to federalism argues that it cannot be understood in legal or constitutional terms. As Livingston has pointed out 'the essence of federalism lies not in the constitutional or institutional structure but in society itself'.(7) Federalism is a reflection of social diversity. Thus:

' ... Federalism is ... not an absolute but
a relative term; there is no identifiable
point at which a society ceases to be unified
and becomes diversified ... All communities
fall somewhere in a spectrum which runs from
what we may call a theoretically wholly inte-
grated society at one extreme to a theoretically
wholly diversified society at the other'. (8)

The process approach views federalism as the process of federalising. Birch quotes Friedrich to the effect that a federation is 'a union of groups, united by one or more common objectives, but retaining their distinctive group character for other purposes'. (9) Thus the emergence of the European Community is an example of the federalising process.

Finally, the bargaining approach to federalism emphasises that it is ' ... a bargain between prospective national leaders and officials of constituent governments for the purpose of aggregating territory, the better to lay taxes and raise armies'. According to Riker, such a bargain is a federal bargain when:

> ' ... (1) two levels of government rule the same land and people, (2) each level has at least one area of action in which it is autonomous, and (3) there is some guarantee (even though merely a statement in the constitution) of the autonomy of each government in its own sphere'. (10)

Birch's classification is useful for drawing attention to the sheer variety of approaches to the study of federalism. However, it is also important to place these four approaches in perspective and view them not as separate models but as representing a brief history of the development of federalism. Thus, Livingston's spectrum of federalism is probably the first major attempt to move away from a static to a more flexible approach which recognises the interdependence of the two levels of government. This shift reflects the growing recognition that 'dual federalism' had given way to 'cooperative federalism' - that the concurrent powers were in all probability a more significant feature of federalism than the separate powers. (11)

The need to incorporate this development into the definition of federalism is recognised even by those writers who do not belong to the behaviourist school of thought in these matters. Vile modifies Wheare's approach and emphasises that interdependence is as important to understanding federalism as independence. (12) Similarly, in an earlier book, Birch pointed to the massive growth in concurrent powers and his definition of federalism emphasised the coordinate division of powers rather than their separation. (13) But neither Vile nor Birch go far enough for a number of other writers. Thus, Friedrich's definition noted above could apply to any situation in which there is some kind of sub-division of powers. Sawyer talks of the 'federal situation'. He uses this phrase to refer to:

' ... a situation where geographical distribution of the power to govern is desired or
has been achieved in a way giving the several
governmental units of the system some degree
of security ... '. (14)

In other words, federalism can merge imperceptibly into
decentralisation of any form. And Riker has gone so far
as to ask 'does federalism exist and does it matter? His
answer to both parts of the question is a resounding 'No'.
Federalism is only significant when states are being
founded. It has little practical significance afterwards.
(15)

The four approaches identified by Birch are not, therefore, simply separate models of federalism. They represent a brief history of the development of the concept.
With the growing recognition of the importance of concurrent powers, approaches to federalism have laid
increasing emphasis on the interdependence of the two
levels of government. This theme directly corresponds to
the concerns of the interorganisational analysis
literature. However, it does not take us very far for-
ward. What models have been developed in the literature
to describe and analyse this interdependence? In order
to explore this question, it is necessary to go beyond
Birch's four-fold classification for three reasons.
First, the differences between the process and bargaining
approaches have become increasingly difficult to sustain.
Second, his discussion of bargaining is limited almost
exclusively to the work of Riker. Finally, the analysis
is limited to state-centre relationships and does not give
sufficient attention to the multiplicity of institutions
and relationships within a federal system.

The process approach has been very prominent in the
study of the European Community, but it has not been the
only one. Briefly, three broad approaches to the study of
European integration have been identified. (16) The
federalist approach stresses the constitutional division
of powers and the role of political institutions in
creating a United States of Europe. (17) It corresponds
to the institutional approach discussed above. The
transactionalist approach stresses the importance of the
underlying socio-economic conditions and a 'sense of
community' for integrating a particular region. (18) Such
a sense of community cannot emerge without some degree of
interdependence, and such interdependence can only be
established by transactions between the various parties.
It corresponds to the sociological approach. Finally, the
neofunctionalist approach stresses that integration is a
process.(19) As a reaction against earlier approaches, the
neofunctionalists are careful not to suggest either that
there is an ideal typical system of government (federalism) or that integration is an 'assembly line process'
which will necessarily occur if the underlying conditions

74

are met. Rather they emphasise the pluralist nature of modern society. It is argued that political elites will see supra-national institutions as a means of meeting their pragmatic interests. They will negotiate and bargain across national boundaries and, as a result, there will be changes in their loyalties, expectations and political activity. The locus of decision-making will shift from national to supra-national institutions. The process of integration involves the gradual politicisation of the issues considered. There is a 'spill-over' effect as actors discover that to satisfy their pragmatic, technical interests they have to broaden the agenda. More controversial issues come within the ambit of the supra-national institutions. If the bargaining and negotiation on these issues is successful, national actors will entrust yet more issues to supra-national institutions. Such a brief account scarcely does justice to the various strands of neofunctionalist thought. Nor does it raise the very real difficulties of this theory. But such problems are not of direct concern here. (20) Of greater importance is the fact that the neofunctionalist theory is a combination of both the process and bargaining approaches. And a great deal of the recent literature similarly draws no such distinction. Rather, the emphasis falls on the continuously evolving nature of the bargaining relationship between states and the centre. The literature on European integration is just one of the more conspicuous examples of this combination of approaches.

The discussion of bargaining in the federal context also needs to be broadened. Riker's contribution may be of value but his discussion of bargaining focuses on the historically unique federal bargain and, more specifically, on the structure of the party system which he views as crucial to the survival of a federation. But bargaining continues after the original federal compact has been struck. It is an ever present, day-to-day feature of the relationships between the states and federal government. Thus, May emphasises that:

> ' ... despite the formal division of decision-making, decisions taken by the central government and decisions taken by the unit governments affect the same people, and therefore affect each other. Because of this interdependence the two levels of government, although they cannot dictate one another's decisions, can and do seek to persuade, influence and bargain with one another'. (21)

It is necessary, therefore, to stress that the interdependence of states and centre generates extensive bargaining and negotiation.

Finally, it must be recognised that a major feature of

federal systems is the sheer number and complexity of interactions between a variety of governmental institutions. A great many discussions of federalism, including that by Birch, focus on the state-centre relationship. But interactions between centre and locality, between states and between localities - in fact, between all the various units of government - are important. They are not only of interest in their own right but the complex of relationships affects the links between states and centre - a point clearly illustrated by the experience of the American federal government in its attempts to intervene in urban areas. (22)

The effect of incorporating the above three features into the discussion of federalism is to broaden the scope of the analysis considerably. In recognition of the fact that the subject has been extended beyond its traditional confines, the term intergovernmental relations (IGR) has been coined. Although IGR has been described as a new field, this claim should be treated with a degree of caution. As with many such claims, there are great similarities with what went before. Nonetheless, the IGR literature does have some distinctive emphases. According to Anderson, IGR designates:

> ' ... an important body of activities or
> interactions occurring between governmental
> units of all types and levels within ...
> the federal system'. (23)

This general definition has been elaborated by Wright who identifies five elements within the field. (24) First, IGR recognises the multiplicity of relationships between all types of government. Second, it emphasises the interactions between individuals, especially public officials. Third, these relationships are continuous, day-to-day and informal. They are not fixed by agreements or rules and they are not spasmodic, although both the formal and informal basis of the links must be examined. Fourth, although the role of the politician has been recognised in federal relations, too little attention has been paid to the role of the administrator. IGR insists on the important role played by all public officials, be they politicians or administrators. The final distinctive feature of IGR is its policy component. Wright suggests that federalism translated questions of policy into questions of law. IGR emphasises the political nature of the relationship and focuses on substantive policies, especially financial issues such as who raises what amounts and who shall spend it for whose benefit with what results. In summary, Wright claims that:

' ... The term IGR alerts one to the multiple,
behavioural, continuous and dynamic exchanges
occurring between various officials in the
political system. It may be compared to a
different, novel and visual filter or concept
that can be laid on the American political
landscape. It permits one to observe,
classify and cumulate knowledge without
obscuring other relevant data which prior
political concepts have provided'. (25)

And the usefulness of this 'visual filter' is not
limited to the American political system. Recent work on
the Federal Republic of Germany has emphasised the
'fragmented and complex' inter-relationships between the
Länder and the Bund. Coordinate and independent powers
are of limited importance in German federalism. The
horizontal division of powers between legislation and
implementation are of greater significance. And yet:

' ... there are no grounds for concluding that
this horizontal division is less ' federal' than
the American-style vertical division'. (26)

Complexity and interdependence have become the key
concepts in the analysis of federalism. However, there
are problems with this development. Vile suggests that a
state of 'complete indeterminacy' has been reached and
that:

' ... the slippery slope upon which W.S.
Livingston embarked in the nineteen-fifties
has reached its reductio ad absurdum. The
time has come to reassess federal systems in
terms of a definition which actually does help
us to distinguish between different kinds of
political system'. (27)

Federalism has become virtually synonymous with
decentralisation. Discussion is no longer limited even to
the more prominent federal institutions. The stage has
probably been reached where the term 'federalism' has no
distinct meaning. It can now be taken to refer to any
division of powers between national and sub-national and
supra-national institutions. (28) This process of definition and redefinition has created the field of intergovernmental relations but it too faces the problem of
indeterminacy. Walker points to the 'conflicting concepts'
and the plethora of 'divergent interpretations'. (29)
Further, he suggests that the main concerns are defining
the federal role, interpreting the partnership ideal and
methods. The current pre-occupations are fiscal arrangements (30) and muddled intergovernmental management. (31)
In other words, the emphasis has fallen on the operational
aspects of IGR rather than on developing theory. (32). As

in the case of interorganisational analysis, it would appear that the literature on IGR provides a set of themes to be explored rather than a theory to be applied in a variety of contexts.

The suggestion that the literature on federalism and IGR has emphasised the themes of interdependence and complexity is scarcely novel. Fortunately, the IGR literature also contains models of the bargaining process in federal systems. It is necessary, therefore, to supplement the above general characterisation of the literature with a discussion of some of these specific models.

BARGAINING, DIPLOMACY AND TOPOCRATS

Although May's study of federalism is primarily concerned with the effects of differences in size and wealth between units and with the financial relations between governments, these specific issues are analysed with a bargaining model of federal decision-making.

May contends that a federation is not two independent political systems but a single system containing within it a number of overlapping sub-systems. He suggests that the earlier literature did not pay sufficient attention to the diversity of units and the bargaining between them because interest was concentrated on questions of legal form. But to understand decision-making in a federal system attention has to be focused on the bargaining process and the interdependence of units of government. The characteristics of decision-making in federal systems are summarised as follows:

> ' a) public policy decisions are taken at the
> two levels of government; neither level can
> dictate the decisions of the other;
> b) the decisions taken by the central govern-
> ment will be determined by three main factors:
> (1) the demands of the central government's
> electorate, which will largely determine the
> goals set; (2) the decisions taken by the unit
> governments, which, because they affect the same
> people on whom the impact of the central
> government's decisions fall, will act as a con-
> straint on the central government's scope for
> effective action; and (3) the central govern-
> ment's power potential vis-a-vis the units as
> determined by (i) the provisions of the con-
> sitution and other rules of the game which at
> any time provide the framework within which
> bargaining takes place, and (ii) the central
> government's bargaining capabilities, which
> depend on such factors as the number of units in
> the federation, the structure of the federal system,
> and the role of particular personalities or

78

groups:
c) the decisions taken by each unit government,
in a similar way, will depend on four main
factors: (1) the demands of its electorate;
(2) the decisions taken by the central government; (3) the decisions taken by other unit
governments; and (4) the unit government's
power potential vis a vis other units and the
central government'. (33)

This summary statement is elaborated in later chapters
and May introduces a number of additional factors which
influence bargaining capabilities. First, the civil
service in a federation can exert influence in a variety
of ways. Civil servants may take attitudes favourable
to unit governments with them when they move to the
central administration. The interchange of staff and the
cooperation of staff in equivalent functions may foster
the growth of national attitudes and standards. (34)
Second, although 'the rules of the game and other
environmental factors go a long way towards determining
the pattern and outcome of bargaining', the way the
government operates in a specific situation - strategic
factors - is nonetheless important. A number of general
strategies can be identified. A common strategy is to
establish the legitimacy of ones demands by appeal to the
constitution or, if this strategy is inadequate, to 'the
intentions of the founding fathers', 'the national
interest', or 'state's rights'. To give added weight to
demands, there are a variety of methods for building up
agreement including formal and informal negotiations with
parliamentary leaders, petitions and intergovernmental
conferences. Alternatively, it is possible to resort to
commissions or committees of inquiry. This method can
either take the issue out of the bargaining process or delay
any decision. Other strategies include the mobilisation
of electoral support, the use of sanctions/threat of
secession, log-rolling and coalitions between unit
governments. And in such bargaining the timing of one's
intervention, the ability to release and withhold
information and to make apparent concessions can have a
decisive influence on the outcome. (35)

This bargaining model is used to analyse fiscal adjustment in a variety of federal systems. May argues that
grants do not 'necessarily imply a loss of "sovereignty"
to units', and he suggests that:

' ... the impact of grants on a unit depends
not so much on the method of payment as on
the strength of the bargaining powers of that
unit in relation to the central government and
the other units and the importance of unit
governments as separate entities in the overall national political system'. (36)

Such a brief summary scarcely does justice to May's work but enough has been said to show that this view of IGR has a marked affinity with the power-dependence model of interorganisational analysis. (37) Moreover, it has an obvious relevance to the study of central-local relations in Britain. Although a number of writers have recognised the bargaining relationship between the various units of British government, May's approach has the singular advantage that it presents an explicit model of this process.

Some of the disadvantages of May's model are obvious ones. His characterisation of the bargaining process refers to a federal system. Accordingly, detailed adjustments have to be made for its application to Britain. The constitution as a source of rules of the game has to be modified to recognise the uncodified nature of the British constitution and the importance of ultra vires for local government. Secession, the SNP notwithstanding, is not yet a viable strategy in the UK. Such details need not detain us. However, there are three other reservations about the model which require a more extended treatment. First, May's discussion of the basis of interdependence is limited. His emphasis falls on the fact that the two levels of government serve a common electorate and the demands of this electorate act as a constraint on both. But there are many bases to interdependence - a point emphasised in the interorganis-ational analysis literature. Second, his analysis concentrates on fiscal adjustment. He does not explore the consequences of this bargaining process for sub-stantive policy. Finally, there is no analysis of either the causes of interdependence or of changes in the rules of the game. Fortunately, other studies enable us to fill some of these gaps.

In his analysis of federal-provincial relations in Canada, Simeon argues that 'neither sociological nor institutional factors can account for the actual per-formance of political systems or for their policy-making processes'. (38) He specifies three sets of factors: broad social and cultural characteristics; institutional and constitutional factors; and the particular norms, attitudes, goals and perspectives of decision-makers. The analytical framework is summarised as follows:

> ' ... there is a set of interdependent actors, or partisans; they operate within a certain social and institutional environment; they share some goals but differ on others ... ; they have an issue or set of issues on which they must negotiate; none has hierarchical control over the others; they have varying political resources; they use these resources in certain strategies and tactics; they arrive at certain outcomes; and these out-

comes have <u>consequences</u> for themselves,
for other <u>groups in the</u> society, and for
the system itself'. (39)

Simeon stresses that this framework is dynamic, by which
he means that the background factors (e.g. socio-
cultural characteristics), immediate factors (e.g.
issues, goals and resources) and the consequences of
actions interact with each other. Thus, the consequences
of a particular decision can affect the process and the
background factors. The overwhelming proportion of the
book is concerned with tracing the interactions between
the several components of the framework. Three features
of the argument warrant more detailed discussion - the
context of interactions, political resources, and outcomes and consequences.

Simeon is primarily concerned with the goals, perceptions and attitudes of individual decision-makers but
he sees the social and institutional environments as the
'essential determinants' of these factors. (40) This
context is broken down into a number of constituent
factors including geography, regional economic disparities
and different historical traditions, all of which are
seen as contributing to the greater salience of regional
and ethnic cleavages relative to class and economic
cleavages. The institutional environment is also said to
influence federal-provincial relations. Traditional
institutions are said to be ineffective in resolving
federal-provincial disputes and, as a result, direct
intergovernmental negotiations have developed as the
mechanisms for managing relations between governments.
Similarly, the party system does not serve as a mechanism
for intergovernmental adjustment. Another feature of the
institutional environment is the centralised internal
organisation of government departments which focuses
issues at the political level rather than diffusing them
through the bureaucracy. Finally, the constitution sets
parameters to the decision-making process. The important
feature of Simeon's discussion is that the interactions
between governments are <u>not</u> seen as the prime determinant
of policy outcomes. There is an essential prior stage of
analysis, namely the socio-cultural context. The discussion of the interorganisational analysis literature
concluded that, for the most part, it did not specify
the context of interactions. Although Simeon's discussion
is specific to Canada, nonetheless, he clearly makes the
point that a focus on interactions is, of itself,
inadequate. Any similar framework for the analysis of
intergovernmental relations in Britain will obviously
have to include some discussion of the broader context
within which interactions take place.

Simeon's discussion of political resources similarly
serves as a useful corrective to some of the major pre-

occupations of the interorganisational analysis literature. That literature tended to measure exchanges of
resources such as manpower, information and money. For a
political scientist, political resources are conspicuous
only for their absence. Simeon not only recognises the
importance of such resources but also emphasises that
' ... their distribution is highly variable and relative
to both the issues and the time'. In a similar vein to
Crozier, he points out that such resources are 'predominantly subjective', depending upon the beliefs and
perceptions of the individual decision-maker. (41) A
number of types of political resource are discussed:
legal authority, political support, skills and expertise,
'objective' information, size and wealth, procedures and
rules of the game and factors specific to the negotiations. However, it is stressed that no fixed a priori
classification of political resources will be adequate.
Such resources are 'rooted in the social context, the
issues, and the time, and, even more important, in the
minds of the participants'. Resources are subtle, complex, continually shifting and double-edged. (42) This
emphasis is a valuable pointer to the distinctive
nature of intergovernmental relations as distinct from
interorganisational relations.

Finally, in this brief synopsis, Simeon argues that
the process of intergovernmental diplomacy has important
effects on outcomes and important consequences for other
actors in the political system. Thus, on the outcomes of
particular issues, he comments:

> 'Because of the way federal-provincial negot-
> iations brings in to the decision-making pro-
> cess certain interests and concerns which would
> not otherwise be involved, and because it gives
> provincial governments, as institutions, a
> major voice in national policy-making, the kinds
> of decisions made in the system and the
> interests brought to bear in policy-making are
> distinctive ... differences in some central
> characteristics of this adjustment process help
> to explain why the results in one case differ
> from that in others'. (43)

Furthermore, the 'most important determinant of the outcome, and of the relative influence of different actors,
is the distribution of political resources. (44) Similarly, federal-provincial diplomacy has consequences for
other actors in the political system, including parliament, interest groups, the status of governments and
ethnic conflict. Simeon summarises the position as
follows:

'It is clear, then, that the process of
federal-provincial negotiations has some
important consequences for Canadian federalism - for the policies generated, for the
participants themselves, for the way the
process operates in other cases, for the
constitutional and institutional arrangements of Canadian government, for
different groups within the system, for
responsiveness of the system to democratic
values, for individual interest groups, and
for political change itself. On the one
hand the process is dependent on the wider
environment; on the other hand it is an
instrument through which the participants alter
that environment'. (45)

To select particular elements from a framework is
invariably misleading but in this case the very act of
selection serves to highlight its real contribution to
understanding intergovernmental relations. The analysis
of the context of interactions, the stress on political
resources and the concern with outcomes and consequences
were all identified as important omissions from the
interorganisational analysis literature. Moreover,
Simeon's analysis not only acts as a valuable corrective
to that literature but also complements it with its
analysis of perceptions, tactics and strategies. The
description 'diplomacy' serves to highlight the
parallels with, for example, Crozier's 'game'.

It would be misleading, however, to suggest that an
appreciation of the 'game-like' quality of intergovernmental relations was restricted to only a few
commentators. There are now a variety of case studies
which draw attention to this feature of the relationships.
Most important in recent studies has been the emphasis on
bargaining not only between elected representatives but
also between non-elected officials. Simeon's analysis
reflects the distinctive features of Canadian federalism
with its emphasis on bargaining between political actors.
It is necessary to turn to other sources for an analysis
and description of bargaining between officials. A useful summary statement is provided in Wright's review of
IGR in the United States of America. (46)

Wright distinguishes between three models of intergovernmental relations: the separated, the overlapping
and the inclusive. In the separated model, the states
and the national government are independent and the
authority pattern is one of autonomy. In the inclusive
model, the states are dependent on the national government and the authority pattern is hierarchical. In the
overlapping model, the various units of government are
interdependent and the authority pattern is one of
bargaining. This latter model is seen as the 'most

representative' of IGR practice and its chief characteristics are described as limited dispersed power; interdependence; limited areas of autonomy; bargaining-exchange relationships; and cooperation and competition. Bargaining is defined as 'negotiating the terms of sale, exchange or agreement'. (47) Much of the remainder of Wright's book is devoted to a description and analysis of this bargaining. The nature of this analysis will be illustrated by examining briefly his discussion of the actions and attitudes of local officials.

Without claiming that all officials follow all of the rules all the time, Wright provides illustrations of two categories of rules: pervasive and particularistic. Pervasive rules guide the behaviour of nearly all local officials. Particularistic rules are specific to one particular arena of local action, namely obtaining grants. Included amongst the pervasive rules are:

'1. Maximize federal and state dollar revenues and minimize local taxes...
2. Maximise local flexibility and discretion while minimizing federal/state controls, regulations, guidelines etc...
3. Accept the IGR Law of Gravity: 'The buck drops <u>down</u> to local officials'...
4. Maximize public participation and satisfaction while implementing an effective and efficient grant program...
5. Maximize respect and gain the confidence of other IGR participants by using the following sub-rules:
    a) demonstrate honorable and decent intentions;
    b) develop evidence of capable personnel and program performance; and
    c) package and 'sell' agency (or unit) accomplishments.
6. Mobilize marginal resources...
7. Retain and enhance political/organisational 'clout' by:
    a) using favourable constituencies and contacts;
    b) neutralising hostile interests;
    c) trying not to appear greedy;
    d) husbanding power as if it were a finite currency...'

The particularistic rules are sub-divided into grant-seeking and grant-approval activities. Included amongst the grant-seeking rules are:

'1. Know the regulations...
 2. Know the application deadlines...
 3. Know what the grantors want to hear...
 4. Know where the dollars are...
 5. An alternative rule to number 4 is: Know
     who knows where the dollars are.
 6. Know the best matching ratios or formulas'.

Finally, Wright identifies a number of intergovernmental
games. These include: 'Liberty' or don't tell us how
to spend your money; 'Equality' or distribute the
dollars evenly; 'Fraternity' or programme professionals
stick together; 'We are all in the same mess' or appeals
for intergovernmental cooperation and coordination;
'Turf protection' or defending the programme against all
attacks and challenges; 'Project perfectionism' or defining grant requirements so strictly that only angels
can qualify; and 'End Run' or by-pass the states. (48)
Wright concludes by describing IGR in the United States
as 'a huge, complex building that is under continuous
construction and reconstruction. (49)

Simply describing the current rules of the game, however, is insufficient. It is equally important to
explore the question of, and changes in, such rules.
One important change in IGR in the United States in
recent years, it is claimed, is the centralisation of
government and 'the transformation of the American polity
into virtually a unitary system'. (50) Wright's analysis
clearly suggests that any such argument is an over-
simplification. He points to the intensification of
competition between governments in the 1960s and 1970s
and especially the conflict between programme specialists
and public interest groups (PIGS). (51) This development
has been analysed in some detail by Beer who argues that:

' ... more important than any shifts of power
or functions between levels of government has
been the emergence of new arenas of mutual
influence among levels of government. Within
the field of intergovernmental relations a
new and powerful system of representation has
arisen...' (52)

The new centres of influence have arisen within government and two have been particularly important over the
past decade: technocrats and topocrats. The former are
the professional programme specialists whose growing
influence, Beer suggests, has 'promoted the rise of a
counter-veiling power in the form of the intergovernmental lobby'. (53) This lobby encompasses the PIGS or
the 'Big Seven': i.e. the Council of State Governments,
the National Governors Conference, the National Conference
of State Legislatures, the National Association of County
Officials, the National League of Cities, the U.S.

85

Conference of Mayors and the International City
Managers Association. Beer describes these bodies as
topocrats, meaning that their authority is derived from
place and thus they promote or defend the interests of a
particular geographical area. (54) The interests of
technocrats are narrowly defined by their professional
expertise. The interests of topocrats are not so constrained. They speak for a range of interests which are
limited only by the geographic area of the governmental
unit from which they are drawn. In other words, technocrats are sectional groups whereas topocrats speak for
the public interest of their area. This development has
added a new system of representation to American federalism.

The analysis of intergovernmental relations has moved
away from a focus on legal forms to a concern with the
processes of interaction between various units of
government. The studies discussed in this section have
described these interactions as bargaining, as diplomacy
and as a game. However, each of the models discussed
has emphasised different features of the relationships.
Some have focused on financial resources whereas others
have stressed the decisive influence of political
resources. Some concentrate on the analysis of the
process whereas others stress the effects of this process on policy outcomes. Some describe and analyse the
role of the politician whereas others stress the role of
the official. Finally, some examine the existing rules
of the game whereas others have explored changes in the
rules and, in particular, the conflict between technocrats and topocrats and the ways in which this conflict
has changed the system of representation in federal
structures of government. But to what extent are these
models and themes relevant to the analysis of British
IGR? What are the strengths and weaknesses of the
models?

CONCLUSIONS

Perhaps the clearest way to assess the contribution that
the IGR literature could make to the analysis of British
IGR is to demonstrate the similarities and the differences with the literature on interorganisational analysis.

The ways in which the two literatures correspond are
relatively obvious. The complexity of the environment
of organisations is a theme common to both. In the
interorganisational analysis literature, other organisations are a key component of the environment of any
organisation and the environment and the organisation
permeate each other. The discussion of federalism
demonstrated that the environment of any unit of government was similarly complex. Analysis could no longer be
limited to the more prominent, traditional federal
institutions. This shift of emphasis is consistent with

the argument that the study of central-local relations in Britain cannot be limited to the links between central departments and local authorities. The complexity of the institutional environment must be recognised and analysis extended to include all public sector organisations.

An organisation does not simply face a complex environment. It is also dependent upon elements in that environment. This essential interdependence of organisation is a major theme of the interorganisational analysis literature. To modify an old proverb, 'no organisation is an island'. The IGR literature similarly lays considerable emphasis on interdependence. The growing recognition of the interdependence of levels of government in federal systems led to the slippery slope of the 'spectrum of federalism'. However, the IGR literature seldom defines and explores the bases of interdependence. There have been few attempts to measure variations in the degree of dependence. Rather, there has been a preoccupation with describing and analysing the bargaining between levels of government. Nonetheless, the theme of interdependence is also relevant to the analysis of British central-local relations. Local authorities are not 'mere agents' of central government. They are political systems in their own right with the capacity to resist central demands. Moreover, central government is dependent upon local authorities for information, for expertise and for the implementation of policy. Thus, any discussion of the relationship must recognise that it can range from dependence to independence and that there are many bases to the relationship.

Given that any organisation faces a complex environment composed of organisations upon which it is dependent, it has to find ways of managing that dependence. Both literatures emphasise the bargaining which takes place between organisations. This process can be described in terms of strategies for managing uncertainty, or as a 'game', or simply as a bargaining model: whichever way it is clear that the relationship is rarely one of control. There are 'rules of the game' known to the participants and within these rules 'strategies' are employed. And the success of participants in employing strategies depends upon their relative power. This power is not purely a function of the resources they possess, but also of the ability to translate the potential of these resources into desired results through the use of strategies. Moreover, no actor is ever powerless. The terms dependence and interdependence are employed to emphasise the reciprocal nature of relationships. Similarly, the emphasis on bargaining is a recognition of the fact that no actor is ever wholly controlled. And although the current literature on

British central-local relations does not systematically describe the rules of the game and the strategies, it is clear that bargaining does take place.

The IGR and the interorganisational analysis literatures share a number of common themes, therefore, and are capable of illuminating the 'forgotten dimensions' of British intergovernmental relations. Both stress the complex linkages between organisations, their interdependence and the importance of bargaining; all elements conspicuous mainly for their absence in both the conventional wisdom on, and the conventional critique of, British central-local relations. However, the existence of common themes does not mean that there are no significant differences between the two literatures. For example, although both stress the rules of the game, strategies and bargaining, the interorganisational analysis literature rarely explores the consequences of this behaviour for policy and policy-making. It tends to be concerned with variations in the patterns of interaction for their own sake. Important though this difference may be, it is not the most significant. Three aspects of the IGR literature are especially noteworthy.

First, there has been far more attention paid to the context of interactions. The interorganisational analysis literature emphasised the 'figure' or the interactions of organisations but it did not explore the 'ground' or the values and distribution of power supporting these interactions. As Simeon's analysis of Canadian federalism makes perfectly clear, contextual factors are the prime determinants of such interactions.

Second, various analyses of federal systems have emphasised the importance of political factors. This emphasis can take the form of an analysis of the effects of the party system on federalism; or the effects of a shared electorate on central government and unit government decisions; or an analysis of the distribution of political resources between the unit governments. In each case, analysis is not limited to exchanges of personnel, equipment, clients, information or money.

Finally, a small number of studies have explored changes in the rules of the federal game. Much of the interorganisational analysis literature tends to take the rules of the game as 'given', thereby failing to recognise the ways in which the bargaining process can be skewed in favour of one set of participants. But the IGR literature, as in the case of Beer's analysis, has moved beyond bemoaning the trend towards centralisation and explored the emergence of new arenas of influence.

Although it would appear that the IGR literature offers a valuable corrective to many of the weaknesses in the interorganisational analysis literature, it too has limitations especially when applied to Britain.

First, many of the models which have been developed are country-specific. Thus, Simeon's analysis of the context of interactions is specific to the Canadian system. It is not related to, for example, a theoretical characterisation of advanced industrial society. Similarly, many of the discussions of the rules of the game treat the constitution of the particular federal system as a major source of such rules, often drawing no clear distinction between the formal rules and the behaviour of actors. Such limitations make it difficult to translate the details of the analysis in to the British context.

Second, although there is an explicit awareness of the interdependence of the various units of government, the bases of that interdependence are rarely explored in any detail. Rather strikingly, there is a tendency to emphasise financial transactions between governments as the measure of interdependence. However, as the interorganisational analysis literature demonstrates, it is possible to identify a number of bases, not just the oft-cited financial basis. The consequence of this omission is that the IGR literature does not analyse the relative power of the various units of government by comparing their resources or by assessing the extent to which one resource can be substituted for another. Just as the interorganisational analysis literature tends to provide formal models of patterns of interaction without locating them in an analysis of the distribution of power, so the IGR literature tends to discuss broad trends in relative influence of units of government without specifying the bases of variations in their relationship.

Finally, and to return to the second major objective of this chapter, although the context of the relationships and changes in the rules of the game have been discussed in the IGR literature, the relationship between this level of analysis and the micro-level of the games and strategies of actors has not been clearly articulated. Two criticisms should be noted. First, at the specific level, the effects of changes in the distribution of power on the 'game' are not fully explored. For example, topocrats may have emerged as a counterveiling power to the technocrats but to what extent do they still need to legitimise their own interests and actions by appeal to scientific-professional standards? Conversely, to what extent does the power of the technocrats depend upon their ability to find support for their programmes amongst a broader constituency than their professional community and bureaucratic actors? Second, at the general level, only a cursory attempt is made to explain the change in the distribution of power. The emergence of topocrats may be a reaction to the power of the technocrats but why have the latter come to exercise such influence? As argued in Chapter 1, there have been a number of attempts to explain change in advanced industrial societies but these macro theories, whether of post-industrial society or of corporatism, do not inform the analysis of changes in intergovernmental relations. However, although the literature on IGR may not have succeeded in reconciling the analysis of the context with the analysis of interactions, nonetheless it has demonstrated that the link between ground and figure is an essential component of any attempted explanation of interactions and their consequences for policy-making. The problem of the relationship between levels of analysis is by no means peculiar to the study of IGR and it will be discussed in more detail in the final chapter.

At the very outset, it was suggested that the IGR literature would not provide any ready-made model for the study of British IGR. However, it does suggest a number of themes which could be pursued in the British context. Recent work on the United Kingdom as a 'multi-national state' emphasises that the 'visual filter' of IGR can add to our understanding of British government. (55) The emphasis on bargaining, strategies and rules of the game appears potentially fruitful. Recognition of the variety of institutions involved in British IGR seems long over-due. (56). An exploration of the relative importance of professional groups as against the national institutions of local government is particularly apposite given recent attempts to change the relationship between central departments and the national institutions. But these comments and suggestions for future avenues of exploration are in themselves inadequate. Future research needs to be guided by a framework of analysis and it is precisely such a framework that the IGR literature does not provide. It can suggest items any framework will have to encompass. It provides warnings about potential pitfalls for the un-wary. However, the task of constructing a framework remains to be done.

NOTES AND REFERENCES

1) See the references in notes 1 - 3 of Chapter 3.

2) For references see: Wright, D.S., and Peddicord,
    T.E., Intergovernmental Relations in the United
    States: selected books and documents on Federalism
    and National-State-Local Relations Philadelphia,
    Pa.: Centre for the Study of Federalism. Temple
    University, 1975.

3) An alternative starting point for the discussion of
    IGR is the concept of decentralisation. However,
    the term is fraught with difficulty. Not only is it
    treated as a value in its own right which, it is
    claimed, promotes democracy but it is also seen as
    a variable for comparing administrative structures.
    Even if the realms of normative political theory are
    foresworn, the problems do not cease because there
    are few indices capable of distinguishing between
    the various degrees of centralisation/decentralis-
    ation. There is a marked tendency to concentrate
    on either definitional questions or on describing
    particular forms of decentralisation rather than
    comparing and explaining variations. This chapter
    concentrates on specific forms of decentralisation
    in advanced industrial societies of which federal-
    ism is one of the most conspicuous examples. In so
    far as the concept of decentralisation is employed
    it is treated as a variable. Units of government
    range along a continuum from centralised to
    decentralised: there is no one state of affairs
    which can be labelled 'decentralised'. The seminal
    review of the literature on decentralisation is:
    Fesler, J.W., 'Approaches to the Understanding of
    Decentralisation' Journal of Politics Vol. 27 1965
    pp. 536-66. For an excellent discussion of the
    values served by decentralisation see: Maass, A.,
    Area and Power Glencoe, Ill.: The Free Press, 1959.
    For attempts to construct indices of decentralis-
    ation see: Sherwood, F.P., 'Devolution as an
    Organisational Strategy' in Daland, R.T., (ed.),
    Comparative Urban Research Beverley Hills,
    California: Sage, 1967 pp. 60-87; Clark, T.N.,
    'Community Autonomy in the National System: federal-
    ism, localism and decentralisation' in Clark, T.N.,
    (ed.), Comparative Community Politics New York:
    Halsted Press, 1974; and Smith, B.C., 'The Measure-
    ment of Decentralisation' in Jones, G.W., (ed.),
    Central-Local Relations in Britain Farnborough,
    Hants.: Saxon House, 1980 (forthcoming).

4) Birch, A.H., 'Approaches to the Study of Federalism'
    Political Studies Vol. 14 1966 pp. 15-23.

91

5) Wheare, K.C., Federal Government London: Oxford University Press, 1946 p. 11.

6) For examples see: Carnell, F.G., 'Political Implications of Federalism in New States' in Hicks, U.K., and others, Federalism and Economic Growth in Underdeveloped countries London: Allen and Unwin, 1961. pp. 16-69.

7) Livingston, W.S., Federalism and Constitutional Change Oxford: The Clarendon Press, 1956 p. 2.

8) Livingston, op. cit., p. 4.

9) Birch, op. cit., p. 18.

10) Riker, W.H., Federalism: Origin, Operation, Significance Boston: Little, Brown, 1964 p. 11.

11) The concept of 'cooperative federalism' has been oft-elaborated, especially in the American context. Thus, we have Creative Federalism and the New Federalism. Both should be viewed as species of cooperative federalism, the major differences lying in their respective methods and views on how the partnership ought to work. As noted at the outset, this section will not discuss in any detail the workings of particular federal systems. The various species of American federalism are not discussed, therefore, because they are viewed as operational variants of the one theory - cooperative federalism. For a detailed discussion see: Reagan, M.D., The New Federalism New York: Oxford University Press, 1972; and Elazar, D., et al., Cooperation and Conflict in American Federalism Itasca, Illinois: Peacock, 1969.

12) Vile, M.J.C., The Structure of American Federalism Oxford: The Clarendon Press, 1961 pp. 198-9.

13) Birch, A.H., Federalism, Finance and Social Legislation Oxford: The Clarendon Press, 1955 p. 306.

14) Sawyer, G.F., Modern Federalism London: Watts, 1969, pp. 2-3.

15) Riker, W.H., 'Six Books in Search of a Subject or Does Federalism Exist and Does it Matter?' Comparative Politics Vol. 2 1965 pp. 135-46.

16) This account follows Hodges, M., 'Introduction' in Hodges, M., (ed.), European Integration Harmondsworth: Penguin Books, 1972 pp. 12-28.

17) See, for example: Hallstein, W., Europe in the Making London: Allen and Unwin, 1972.

18) See, for example: Deutsch, K.W., et. al., Political Community and the North Atlantic Area Princeton: Princeton University Press, 1957.

19) See, inter alia: Haas, E.B., Beyond the Nation State Stanford: Stanford University Press, 1964; Lindberg, L.N., The Political Dynamics of European Economic Integration Stanford: Stanford University Press, 1963; and Lindberg, L.N., and Scheingold, S.N., Europe's Would be Polity Englewood Cliffs, N.J.: Prentice Hall, 1970.

20) For critical discussion see: Hodges, op. cit., pp. 24-8; Pentland, C., International Theory and European Integration London: Faber and Faber, 1973; and Wallace, W., Wallace, H., and Webb, C., Policy-Making in the European Communities London: Wiley, 1977.

21) May, R.J., Federalism and Fiscal Adjustment Oxford: The Clarendon Press, 1969 p. 3.

22) See, for example: Martin, R.C., The Cities and the Federal System London: Athlone Press, 1965.

23) Anderson, W., Intergovernmental Relations in Review Minneapolis: University of Minnesota Press, 1960 p. 3.

24) Wright, D.S., 'Intergovernmental Relations: an analytical overview' The Annals No. 416 November 1974 pp. 1-16.

25) Wright, op. cit., p. 4.

26) Johnson, N., Government in the Federal Republic of Germany Oxford: Pergamon, 1973 p. 101 and p.132. See also: Merkl, P.H., 'Executive-Legislative Federalism in West Germany', American Political Science Review Vol. 53 1959 pp. 732-41; and Mayntz, R., and Scharpf, F.W., Policymaking in the German Federal Bureaucracy Amsterdam: Elsevier, 1975.

27) Vile, M.J.C., Federalism in the United States, Canada and Australia Research Paper 2 to the Commission on the Constitution, London: H.M.S.O. 1973 p. 35.

28) The relationship between the concepts of federalism, decentralisation and devolution is discussed in more detail in Rhodes, R.A.W., 'Regional Policy and a "Europe of Regions"' in Gillingwater, D., and Hart, D.A., (eds.), The Regional Planning Process Farnborough: Saxon House, 1978 pp.50-51 and pp.54-55.

93

29)   Walker, D.B., 'How Fares Federalism in the Mid-
      Seventies?' The Annals No. 416 November 1974 pp.
      17-31.

30)   A useful general survey of recent fiscal issues can
      be found in: 'General Revenue Sharing and Federal-
      ism' The Annals No. 419 May 1975; and Wright,
      D.S., Understanding Intergovernmental Relations
      North Scituate, Mass.: Duxbury Press, 1978
      chs. 4-7.

31)   The seminal work on this topic is Sundquist, J.D.,
      Making Federalism Work Washington, D.C.: The
      Brookings Institution, 1969. He argues that 'the
      federal system is too important to be left to
      chance' (p.31). The maze of relationships and the
      increase in the number of levels of government are
      said to require a coordinated approach in the form
      of a new regional coordinator or supra-department-
      al official (p.273). Management is the key to
      transforming a jumble into a system of relation-
      ships. This view has been sharply challenged in
      Wildavsky, A., A Bias Towards Federalism
      University of California, Berkeley: Graduate
      School of Public Policy, November, 1975. He
      defends the conflict and bargaining of the present
      system and points to the difficulties of planning
      and coordination in a pluralistic political
      system. See also: Landau, M., 'Redundancy,
      Rationality and the Problem of Duplication and
      Overlap' Public Administration Review Vol. 39
      1969 pp. 346-58; and Ostrom, V., The Intellectual
      Crisis in American Public Administration Alabama:
      University of Alabama Press, 1974.

32)   Walker, op. cit., p. 18.

33)   May, op. cit., pp. 3-4.

34)   May, op. cit., pp. 29-30.

35)   May, op. cit., pp. 31-35.

36)   May, op. cit., p. 164 and p. 166.

37)   For further discussion see: May, R.J., 'Decision-
      Making and Stability in Federal Systems',
      Canadian Journal of Political Science Vol. 3 1970
      pp. 73-87.

38)   Simeon, R., Federal-Provincial Diplomacy: the
      making of recent policy in Canada Toronto and
      Buffalo: University of Toronto Press, 1972 p. 8.

39)   Simeon, op. cit., pp. 11-12.

40) Simeon, op. cit., p. 20.

41) Simeon, op. cit., p. 201.

42) Simeon, op. cit., p. 223 and p. 226.

43) Simeon, op. cit., p. 277.

44) Simeon, op. cit., p. 266.

45) Simeon, op. cit., p. 297.

46) Wright, D.S., Understanding Intergovernmental Relations North Scituate, Mass.: Duxbury Press, 1978.

47) Wright, op. cit., pp. 16-29.

48) Wright, op. cit., pp. 188-93. See also: Simeon, op. cit., pp. 229-31.

49) Wright, op. cit., p. 329.

50) Beer, S.H., 'Federalism, Nationalism and Democracy in America' American Political Science Review Vol. 72 1978 p. 9. On the centralisation of American government see: Reagan, op. cit., p. 163; Elazar, op. cit., and Lowi, T.J., 'Europeanization of America: from United States to United State' in Lowi, T.J., and Stone, A., (eds.), Nationalizing Public Policies in America London: Sage, 1978.

51) Wright, op. cit., pp. 61-3.

52) Beer, op. cit., p. 9.

53) Beer, op. cit., p. 18.

54) Beer, op. cit., p. 18. See also: Beer, S.H., 'The Modernisation of American Federalism' Publius Vol.3 No. 2 1973 pp. 49-95; and Beer, S.H., 'The Adoption of General Revenue Sharing: a case study in public sector politics', Public Policy Vol. 27 1976 pp. 127-95.

55) An invaluable bibliography on this theme is: Pollock, L., and McAllister, I., A Bibliography of United Kingdom Politics: Scotland, Wales and Northern Ireland University of Strathclyde, Glasgow: Studies in Public Policy Vol. III 1980. Useful discussions of Britain as a multi-national state can be found in: Birch, A.H., Political Integration and Disintegration in the British Isles London: Allen and Unwin, 1977; and Rose, R., 'The United Kingdom as a Multi-National State' in

95

Rose, R., (ed.), <u>Studies in British Politics</u>
London: Macmillan, third edn. 1976 pp. 115-50.

56)   Some of the differences between the constituent
      units of the U.K. are discussed in: Page, E.,
      'Why Should Central-Local Relations in Scotland Be
      Different to Those in England?' <u>Public Admini-
      stration Bulletin</u> No. 28 December 1978 pp. 51-72:
      Madgwick, P., and James, M., 'The Network of Con-
      sultative Government in Wales' in Jones, G.W.,
      (ed.), <u>Central-Local Relations in Britain</u>
      Farnborough, Hants.: Saxon House, 1980; and
      Birrell, D., 'The Centralisation of Local Govern-
      ment Functions in Northern Ireland - an appraisal'
      <u>Local Government Studies</u> Vol. 4 No. 4 1978 pp. 23-
      37.

5 A framework for analysis

INTRODUCTION

At the outset, it was argued that the subject of central-local relations seemed to be divorced from more general issues in the study of government. In addition, the existing theories or models of the relationship were seen to be inadequate, ignoring a number of important dimensions. However, it is possible to provide both a framework of analysis and to relate the study of central-local relations to broader issues by drawing upon a wider range of literature than is normally associated with the subject. Both the sociologists who have explored inter-organisational linkages and the political scientists who have explored intergovernmental relations have produced models or theories capable of illuminating the inter-actions between British governmental units. These litera-tures are limited, however, in a variety of ways. In this chapter, the attempt is made to construct a framework of analysis which draws upon the interorganisational analysis and IGR literatures but avoids some of their more obvious weaknesses. Most important, the framework does not focus solely upon the interactions between central and local government - the figure. Drawing upon corporatist theory, the analysis of the interactions is located within a broader context - the ground. More specifically, the changing role of government and its effects on the rules of the game will be explored.

Before turning to these particular tasks, however, a number of preliminary issues must be touched upon. The first issue concerns the distinctions between frameworks, analogies, models and theories. This area is a contentious one in the social sciences and there is limited agreement on the definition of the various terms. (1) The framework presented here is a systematic inventory or classification of elements to be explored in the study of central-local relations. From this definition, it does not follow that the framework contains no explanatory statements. At various stages, explanations for variations in both the patterns of links and in the behaviour of various actors in central-local relations will be suggested. This lack of specificity is unavoid-able for two reasons. First, there is a paucity of research upon which to base detailed explanations and, second, 'Generating a theory involves a process of research'. (2) Accordingly, the reader will not find a series of hypotheses for testing or refutation. 'Grand

theory' (such as systems theory) with its hypotheses
deduced from general axioms can become a futile exercise.
Either attention becomes distorted onto trivial issues
because they can be measured or the theory becomes the
(mandatory) padding which prefaces the case studies but
otherwise bears tangentially upon the substance of the
research. The framework offered here is of a far more
modest nature. Its rationale lies in its ability to
focus attention on key features of central-local
relations; to suggest, in as precise and systematic a way
as current research permits, how the interactions between
the two levels of government vary; and to provide an
interpretation of the existing form(s) of such interactions.

Finally, it must be emphasised that the scope of the
framework has been deliberately restricted. First, it
does not purport to explain policy-making at either the
central or the local level. Intergovernmental relations
are but one of many influences on policy. This chapter
focuses on the intergovernmental aspects of policy-making.
In so doing, it is not claimed that such links are the
most important influence on policy, only that they are
important for some policies. Second, the exposition is
cast in terms of central-local relations narrowly con-
strued. As argued earlier, the networks of intergovernmental relations is far broader than central-local
relations. However, for ease of presentation, the
narrower focus has been adopted. The framework could be
extended to cover the range of public sector organisations and to compare the component parts of the system
of intergovernmental relations.

FIGURE: the analysis of interactions

That aspect of the framework concerned with the analysis
of interactions and the effects of interactions on local
discretion contains five propositions:

a) Any organisation is dependent upon other organisations for resources.

b) In order to achieve their goals, the organisations
   have to exchange resources.

c) Although decision-making within the organisation
   is constrained by other organisations, the dominant
   coalition retains some discretion. The appreciative
   system of the dominant coalition influences which
   relationships are seen as a problem and which
   resources will be sought.

d) The dominant coalition employs strategies within
   known rules of the game to regulate the process of
   exchange.

e) Variations in the degree of _discretion_ are a product of the goals and the relative power potential of interacting organisations. This relative power potential is a product of the resources of each organisation, of the rules of the game and of the process of exchange between organisations.

The remainder of this section discusses these propositions and their application to the study of central-local relations in more detail.

(a) Dependence and Resources

Central to the analysis of the relationship between the organisation and its environment is the concept of power-dependence. To repeat Thompson's definition, an organisation is dependent upon another organisation:

'(1) in proportion to the organisation's needs for resources ... which that element can provide and (2) in inverse proportion to the ability of other elements to provide the same resource'. (3)

And dependence is the obverse of power. Thus a local authority is dependent upon a central department to the extent that it needs the resources controlled by the department and cannot obtain them elsewhere.

The power-dependence concept is employed in preference to the concept of power for a simple but nonetheless important reason. Many discussions of power treat it as a zero-sum phenomenon. In other words, a central department can only increase its power at the expense of a local authority. But it is possible that two interdependent organisations could both increase their power. As Talcott Parsons concludes:

' ... though under certain specific assumptions the zero-sum condition holds, these are not constitutive of power systems in general, but under different conditions systematic 'extensions' of power spheres without sacrifice of the power of other units is just as important a case'. (4)

By employing the power-dependence concept, the intention is to focus attention on the reciprocal nature of power relationships. No matter how great the power of a central department over a local authority, it is still dependent to some degree on that local authority.

The advantages of this formulation of the relationship between an organisation and its environment are three-fold. First, the term 'environment' is no longer treated as a residual category covering everything 'outside' the

organisation. It refers solely to those other organisations with which a focal organisation interacts.
Second, complexity is given an explicit meaning. It
refers to the number of other organisations and the scale
of interaction. Finally, it identifies the bases of the
power-dependence relationship between organisations - i.e.
resources.

The availability, distribution and substitutability of
resources underpin the power-dependence relationships
between organisations; these aspects are central to
understanding the relative power of interacting organisations. The term 'resources' is defined broadly to
encompass all those means for supplying the needs of
public sector organisations. In the context of central-
local relations there has been a considerable emphasis on
the effect of financial resources on the relationship.
This view of the resources available to both central
departments and local authorities is too narrow. At a
minimum it is possible to identify four other resources:
constitutional and legal, hierarchical, political and
informational. Even this listing is incomplete. Given
the existing research and the subjective nature of
resources, it is only possible to note some of the more
obvious examples. Future research into central-local
relations may well identify additional resources - e.g.
task and technological resources, physical resources. (5)
Moreover, the five resources discussed below may be
capable of further sub-division - e.g. constitutional-
legal resources could be sub-divided into generic and
specific responsibilities. (6) Whatever the defects of
the current list, it does have the advantage of drawing
attention to the range of resources which can underpin
the interactions of central departments and local
authorities.

(1) Constitutional-legal resources - the mandatory and
discretionary powers allocated between local authorities
and central departments by statute and constitutional
convention.

(2) Hierarchical resources - the authority to issue
commands and to require compliance conferred by the
position of an actor in an organisational hierarchy.
Although the authority to obtain compliance will have a
legal basis, hierarchical resources are treated as
analytically distinct from constitutional-legal resources
in order to emphasise the supervisory element in the
relationship between centre and locality. This element
can become routinised and elaborated to such an extent
that the legal basis becomes a poor guide to the actual
position. For example, the circulars issued by central
departments may have no specific statutory basis but they
may also be seen as legitimate interventions and as a

means of central supervision.

(3) Financial resources - the money raised by a public sector organisation from services provided, from taxes levied (or precepted) and from borrowing.

(4) Political resources - the access to decision-making in other government units bestowed on elected representatives by political office, the legitimacy deriving from the fact of election and the right to build public support.

(5) Informational resources - the information and expertise possessed by actors. This resource can be organised in many ways but, in the context of central-local relations, the most notable examples are the professional groups in local government and the civil servants of central departments.

It should not be thought that the above resources will be employed in isolation from each other. In any particular interaction, a local authority or central department may well deploy a number of resources. Thus, a professional group ostensibly providing technical information may also act to further its own values and interests. Such complexities do not invalidate the distinctions. Unless a range of resources is identified in the first instance, there is no way of exploring the bases of any interaction.

Finally, it is worth noting that the concept of power-dependence has the advantage of admitting that local authorities and central departments may be dependent upon each other to different degrees in different circumstances. Without denying that financial resources may be crucial in central-local relations, the framework recognises the sheer variety of possible relationships. The resources required by central departments and local authorities are multifarious and this leads to complex patterns of power-dependence within the network of relationships. Local discretion (see below) can be viewed as a multi-dimensional concept and a local authority dependent along one dimension can have a high degree of discretion along another. Thus a financially dependent authority is not necessarily lacking in political or informational resources.

To this point, the discussion has focused on defining resources. It is also necessary to analyse resources in terms of the amount (or their availability and distribution), in terms of scope (or their substitutability), and in terms of means (or the strategies for managing relationships). A few examples will suffice by way of elaboration.

In the first instance it is clear that there are differences between local authorities, and between central departments, in the availability and distribution of resources. For example, the Layfield Report demonstrates that local authorities differ markedly in their constitutional-legal and financial resources. Moreover, for individual services, the Report identifies the varying mixture of discretionary and mandatory powers and the differing degrees of precision with which powers are allocated between central and local government. In other words, central departments differ in the extent and precision of their controls over local authorities. (7) Similarly, there are inequalities in the distribution of political resources. For example, not all local authorities are politically controlled and, in these circumstances, party channels of communication will be unavailable to councillors.

There may be inequalities in the distribution of resources but it does not necessarily follow that these inequalities are cumulative. The fact that a local authority or a central department lacks one resource does not mean it lacks others. One resource could be substituted for another. For example, a central department lacking the constitutional-legal resources to prevent (or encourage) a specific local initiative can attempt to get its way by withholding (or supplying) financial resources. Conversely, a local authority which has been refused financial resources can attempt to reverse this state of affairs by embarrassing the central department. Press and television reports on the adverse consequences of the centre's decision may lead to the decision being reconsidered.

At this juncture, the various resources have been defined and it has been argued that they are distributed unequally and that one resource can be substituted for another. The availability, distribution and substitutability of resources will affect the choice of means by a central department or a local authority for regulating its relationships. Before examining the various strategies in central-local relations, however, it is necessary to explore why a local authority or a central department 'needs' some resources and not others.

(b) Goals

The second proposition states that the goals of a central department and of a local authority will determine which resources are needed. A local authority which wants to build council houses will have to raise the capital for such a development. This 'goal-model' of organisations has been much criticised. It is argued that only individuals, not organisations, have goals - i.e. the problem of reification - and that formal statements of goals are

102

useless guides to actual behaviour - i.e. the problem of formalism. However, these problems are not insurmountable. Organisational goals can be seen as the product of an internal political process of negotiation and bargaining between groups. Out of this process there will emerge a dominant coalition with an agreed set of temporary goals. Over time, however, goals are multiple, conflicting and changing. In this way, formal statements of the organisation's goals are replaced by an emphasis on identifying the actual goals of specific groups within the organisation as they change over time. (8)

Goal setting is a constrained political process. The dominant coalition's discretion is limited not only by past decisions and its relations with other groups within the organisation but also by the need to establish domain consensus, and by the goals and decisions of other organisations. Thus, a central department may view a local authority's goals as 'illegitimate' and deny it needed resources. As a result, the local authority will have to negotiate its goals, or the claims it makes for itself in terms of the services it intends to provide and the population it intends to serve, with the central department and establish agreement or consensus about the scope of its activities and access to needed resources - domain consensus. (9) There are some obvious examples of domain consensus, or lack of it, in central-local relations, including subsidised bus fares and rents for council houses.

Goals as defined above, therefore, are general stances or frameworks to guide decisions. Decisions are choices between specific, alternative courses of action. The concepts of goal and decision differ also in that only the former are statements about future or preferred domains. As John Friend has noted, decisions are acts which pass into history once carried out. (10) Accordingly, decisions made within the context of broad, even vague, goals translate these goals into specific actions. In this process, decisions can elaborate and reformulate the original goal. Past decisions can certainly limit a local authority's or a central department's freedom to set new goals or even to elaborate existing ones. Thus, a local authority and a central department must take account of each other's current goals and of both their own past decisions and those of the other organisation. The dominant coalition is not writing on a clean slate. Options will have been foreclosed or slanted in certain directions. Past commitments and deployment of resources will limit today's ability to commit and deploy resources.

(c) Dominant Coalitions and Appreciative Systems

Although goal setting is a constrained process, the response of the dominant coalition to these constraints is not that of a parking meter to a ten pence piece. The dominant coalition will only perceive some relationships as problematic and negotiate with some departments over its goals. Such perceptions can differ markedly between decision-makers even when they face what is ostensibly the same problem. They may disagree about the definition of the problem, its importance, the ways of solving it and the likely consequences of the various alternatives. The 'appreciative system' (11) of the decision-maker influences the goals pursued, perceptions of what is a problematic relationship and the definition of the resources required.

The concept of appreciative systems refers to that combination of factual and value judgements which describe the 'state of the world' or 'reality'. It is a record of past goals and decisions - the accumulated wisdom of a central or local department or its 'departmental philosophy' (12) - and a general map for understanding and steering a course through the environment. Three components or dimensions of appreciative systems can be identified - interests, expectations and values or ideology. 'Interests' refers to the stakes of individuals in the organisation; a stake commonly expressed in terms of demands for retaining or increasing control over the resources of the organisation. 'Expectations' refers to the behaviour expected of an individual in a particular position within the organisation by himself and by others. 'Values' refers to the most general evaluative standards used by the decision-maker to interpret the environment and his relationship to it. In practice, of course, these components of the appreciative system are interwoven. (13)

Although there are many difficulties in exploring the various facets of the appreciative systems of government actors, (14) the concept is important for understanding central-local relations. For example, it may be possible to explain why so many local authorities accept central intervention in terms of the expectations of local decision-makers - i.e. they do not expect action on their part to have any effect on a central department and, as a result, they simply implement the central department's policy.

The relationship between central departments and local authorities is not solely determined, therefore, by the resources of the various participants. It is also affected by the goals and perceptions or appreciative systems of the participants. Nor are these the only influences. The control of needed resources by a central department will only make it relatively more powerful than

104

a local authority if those resources are deployed
effectively. In other words, the discussion of resources
has been a discussion of the relative power <u>potential</u> of
central departments and local authorities. It is
necessary to explore the process of exchange between
centre and locality in order to extend the analysis
beyond a discussion of potential power.

(d)   The Process of Exchange, Rules of the Game and
      Strategies

The preceding pages have drawn upon the (admittedly
diffuse) literature on the sociology of organisations. In
examining the process of exchange between central departments and local authorities, this particular literature is
less helpful than that on intergovernmental relations.
Whereas the former tends to emphasise the bases of interactions, the latter more commonly focuses on describing
and analysing the process of interaction. Thus, a number
of studies have emphasised the bargaining or diplomatic
relationship between levels of government. (15) To avoid
the specific or narrow connotations of the terms 'bargaining' and 'diplomacy', the term 'process of exchange' is
used to cover the variety of forms which interactions
between central and local government can take. Accordingly, bargaining can be viewed as that specific form of
exchange involving concessions by one participant for
resources controlled by the other.

It has been argued that the degree of discretion of
participants in central-local relations is a product of
the goals and decisions of each level of government and
of their relative power in terms of resources. However,
this relative power remains only potential power unless
the resources are effectively deployed. Such effective
deployment is affected by both the rules of the game and
the process of exchange between the two levels of
government.

Rules of the game are the less formal but no less
important rules which 'largely define the institutions of
society ... they set the approximate limits within which
discretionary behaviour may take place'. (16) Thus,
'There emerges complicity among ... groups based on the
sharing of mutual experience and complementary interests
and on adherence to the same collective norms'. (17)

There is one obvious reason for emphasising that rules
of the game exist in British central-local relations - the
fact that they have never been studied. And the lack of
research means that it is difficult to identify examples
of such rules and their effect on discretionary behaviour.
However, two examples can be tentatively offered. First,
it can be argued that there is a rule asserting the value
of local democracy or local self government. In fact,
Mackenzie has argued that 'local self government' is now

part of the English constitution'. (18) The rule is considerably vaguer than such explicit legal rules as <u>ultra</u>
<u>vires</u> but it is not without importance. It requires that
the rights and duties of local authorities be respected
and any derogation of these rights and duties will be met
with an outcry. Thus, Crosland has suggested that
Ministers believe the ringing phrases about local democracy and, at one and the same time, hate it when local
authorities pursue policies diametrically opposed to
those of the government of the day. (19) Such an
ambivalent or schizophrenic response is one way of
recognising the existence of the rule.

The second possible example can be labelled the rule of
consultation. Thus, for a given policy initiative, local
authorities have a right to be consulted by central
government before the policy becomes law. Quite clearly,
local authorities are not always consulted but it is not
uncommon in these circumstances for protests to be made
to the responsible Minister. Breaches of a rule are
often the clearest indicator of its existence.

A number of other possible rules could be identified but
the exercise becomes increasingly speculative. It is perhaps more important to stress both that such rules do
exist and that there is considerable scope for research
designed to identify them and to describe their application, adjustment and decline.

The key characteristic of the process of exchange
between central and local government is the strategies of
the participants. The term strategies refers to the means
employed by either a central department or a local
authority for imposing upon the other level of government
its preferences concerning the time of, the conditions
for, and the extent of the exchange of resources.
Unfortunately, there is no existing classification of
strategies which can be applied to the relationships
between central and local government. There are, of
course, a number of studies which identify strategies
employed either in other governmental systems or between
private sector organisations. (20) These include such
obvious strategies as forming a coalition, co-optation,
and confrontation as well as the less obvious such as the
use of a supra-organisation and appeals to legitimacy. It
is also possible to identify examples of strategies being
used in central-local relations. Thus, central government through its control of constitutional-legal
resources, is able to precisely determine its relations
with local authorities. Such a move can be described as
a strategy of 'authoritative allocation' (21) and the
reorganisation of local government provides a clear
example. The search for money from the European Community
by local authorities is an example of the use of a supra-
organisation. (22) Finally, appeals to legitimacy, or

claims that central government broke the rules of the game, can be found in the reactions of local authorities to the reorganisation of local government.

Neither central nor local government is wholly free of constraints in its choice of strategies. The amount of resources available to a local authority will affect its choice of strategies. Local authorities with considerable resources may well have more scope to choose amongst the available strategies than one with limited resources. Similarly, the more limited the opportunities for substituting one resource for another, the less the scope for choosing amongst available strategies. And both of these statements presuppose that the dominant coalition of the local authority perceives that the relationship is a problem and decides it can do something to influence the central department involved. Finally, it is possible that the variety of strategies employed will be affected by the nature of the problem. If there is little agreement between a central department and a local authority, relations could be both dynamic and conflictual with both sides employing a variety of strategies and expending a considerable amount of time and energy managing the relationship.

In brief, it is plausible to suggest that strategies are employed in central-local relations and that the existing literature can be used to provide a checklist of possible strategies. It is not possible, however, to document in any detail the process of exchange between central and local government.

Although strategies are the key feature of the process of exchange, they are not the sole feature. At least two others can be identified - namely personalities and the number of units.

'Personalities' is an elusive concept but it cannot be omitted from the analysis of central-local relations. Exchange is not just a question of available strategies but also of the details of their deployment. The timing of interventions and the ability to anticipate the moves of the other side will be influenced by the experience, skills and commitment of individuals. Individual appreciation of tactics can vary greatly. Accordingly, 'personalities' has been included in the analysis to stress that individual abilities influence the process of exchange between central and local government. (23)

It can also be argued that the relationship will be affected by the number of units involved. Thus, irrespective of resources, strategies or personalities, the larger the number of participants, the more complex the process of exchange, the greater the constraints on participants and the more difficult it will be for any participant to attain his desired outcome.

To this point it has been argued that the discretion of each level of government is influenced by the goals, decisions and relative power potential of the other. In turn, their relative power potential is a product of the resources, the rules of the game and the process of exchange. Finally, the process of exchange is influenced by the resources of the participants, strategies, personalities and the number of units. In brief, each level of government is constrained by the other and, consequently, discretion has to be negotiated. It now remains to consider the concept of discretion in more detail.

(e) Discretion

Studying the outcomes of the relationship between central and local government is important if anything is to be concluded about the relative power of the participants. The analysis of the bases, amount and scope of power-dependence tells us about the relative power potential of the participants. The analysis of the means for regulating power-dependence relations only tells us about the relative power of participants if we can infer something about the results of employing the resources. It is preferable, however, to explore directly whether differences in the bases or the means bring about different results. (24)

It is possible to identify a number of different types of outcome. For example, one could explore changes in the structure of interactions: that is, changes in their size, frequency, density, compactness and diversity. (25) However, this section focuses on the effects of variations in central-local relationships on policy-making or, more specifically, on changes in the degree of discretion in policy-making.

The concept of discretion has already been distinguished from the broader concept of local autonomy. It has also been limited to the interactions between public sector organisations. The concept can now be defined more precisely as 'the room for decisional manoeuvre possessed by a decision-maker' (26) in the context of interactions between public sector organisations. A local official or a civil servant has discretion, therefore, 'whenever the effective limits on his power leave him free to make a choice among possible courses of action or inaction'. (27) In this definition, discretion is a matter of degree and even a local authority subjected to the closest supervision by a central department will have some degree of discretion. Nor should it be thought that the limits on decision-makers are solely legal in origin. As the preceding analysis should have made clear, there are a range of constraints. Thus, a local authority is subject to <u>ultra vires</u> and this limits its discretion. It must have statutory authorisation for its actions. But even where its actions are <u>intra vires</u>, discretion will be limited by financial, hierarchical, political and informational constraints. Moreover, constraints can be self-imposed. The dominant coalition of the local authority may not realise it has room for manoeuvre or it may decide not to take advantage of whatever discretion it has.

There are further problems with the dependent variable of discretion in policy-making. The term 'policy-making' is an elusive one. It is possible to identify various stages in the policy-making process. For example, Herbert Simon distinguishes between the intelligence, design and choice stages, (28) and to this one could add, at a minimum, the stages of implementation and review. There is, however, no agreed characterisation of the stages of the policy process. (29) Once the various stages have been distinguished, there is the problem that, in practice, they tend to merge. The process of implementing a policy may elaborate and even reformulate the original policy design. It can be difficult to identify where design ends and implementation begins. (30) Finally, it is difficult to draw firm distinctions between a policy, a decision and a goal. Often no distinctions are drawn and there is a marked tendency to use the terms interchangeably. For Ira Sharkansky, policies are simply 'actions taken by governments'. (31) Raymond Bauer reserves the term policy for decisions 'which have the widest ramifications and the longest time perspective' and notes that the description of a particular course of action as a policy 'is somewhat dependent on the perspective of the individual who views the event'. (32) Moreover, many discussions of the policy process and of policies treat these terms as synonyms for goal-setting and goals. In fact, many discussions of policy-making adopt a 'goal model' of public sector organisations. (33)

In the absence of any agreed convention on the definition of policy and the stages of the policy process, each study adopts the definition best suited to its purposes. A distinction has already been drawn between goals and decisions. (34) For the purpose of this study, goals and policies can be treated as synonyms. Thus policies can be viewed as the claims a local authority or a central department makes for itself in terms of the services it intends to provide and the population it intends to serve. Decisions are choices between specific, alternative courses of actions.

It should now be clear that discretion in policy-making is a complex dependent variable. It involves the exploration of variations in the degree of discretion at the various stages (however delineated) of the policy-making and the decision-making processes. Attention cannot be limited to the initiation of major policies. For example, it is relevant to explore the degree of discretion of a local authority in the (ostensibly) routine decision-making associated with the implementation of a policy. A central department may severely limit the discretion of local authorities at the intelligence and choice stages of policy-making but local authorities may have considerably more discretion at the design, implementation and review stages. Nor should it be assumed that a local authority or a central department has discretion in decision-making simply because it seems to be a more detailed, or less controversial, process than that associated with setting goals/policies.

Although the literature on central-local relations provides examples of discretion (or the lack of it) at various stages of the policy-making and decision-making processes, these variations have not been systematically related to variations in the attributes of participants. Local authorities have considerable discretion in the implementation of some major policies but it is not clear why this is the case. Is it because they have a monopoly of the relevant expertise? There are also examples of the central control of local decisions but it is not always clear why such control should be exercised - e.g. tree inspection (35) - or even if it is exercised effectively. Unfortunately, therefore, the discussion has to remain at a general level.

Existing research may not suggest detailed explanations of how variations in central-local relations affect policy-making but it is possible to identify a number of questions which could be profitably explored in order to clarify the relationship, To begin with, many discussions of central-local relations adopt a 'top-down' model of policy-making - that is, goals are set up by a central department and implemented by a local authority. The above discussion suggests that it is equally important to explore the reverse situation - that is, the redefinition of a policy/goal in the process of implementation - if we are to perceive the full scope or limits of local discretion.

Second, it would appear to be important to explore in some detail the concept of 'policy' or 'goal'. It is possible that central-local relations are composed of a series of discrete policy areas each with its own distinctive characteristics. For example, the education policy area might have completely different characteristics to those of housing and, as a result, there may be marked differences in the degree of discretion available to the participants in the two areas. In such circumstances, it would not be possible to proceed on the assumption that central policies had similar characteristics and focus on variations in relationships and degrees of discretion. Rather, one would have to systematically compare both different policy areas and their respective relationships.

It is inadequate, of course, simply to describe the differences between the policy areas. It is also necessary to explore why these differences occur. For example, the differences between the education and housing policy areas may well stem from the greater professionalisation of the former. Because of the prominence of the professional in education, the link between centre and locality may be a functional one - i.e. between official counterparts in the two levels of government. If such a professional policy community exists, it may not be relevant to explore variations in discretion between the two levels of government. Rather the variations to be explored would be those between policy communities and between the professionals and the 'rest' irrespective of the level of government.

And this discussion of variations in the degrees of discretion of the two levels of government emphasises that the topic is not being explored solely because such variations are intrinsically interesting. The problem of central-local relations cannot be exclusively defined in terms of central control of local expenditure. It is more accurately described, to re-introduce Bell's terms, as the problem of the accountability of bureaucracy in post-industrial society. (36) In other words, the decisive power in modern society lies with bureaucracies and their managers, with political control becoming less and less effective. No-one regulates central-local relations except the participants. Thus, in French central-local relations, Crozier and Thoenig argue that the participants are primarily concerned to defend their interests and privileges in a closed and secret game. (37) In exploring discretion in British central-local relations, it is equally important to relate the analysis of interactions to the broader context of the power of bureaucracies. Are the participants in the policy communities accountable or, as in France, is the system closed with any constraints being self-imposed? An analysis of the 'ground' of central-local relations is essential for any attempt to explain the patterns of interaction.

GROUND: THE DISTRIBUTION OF POWER, RULES, INTERESTS AND VALUES

The framework for the analysis of interactions has been described as a power-dependence framework and, like many other approaches to interorganisational analysis, it focuses on power as resources. As argued earlier, such a focus begs certain key questions about the rules of the game, the distribution of resources and the interests and values sustaining the rules and the distribution of resources. Although the framework includes all these concepts, it does not explain the origin of the rules, it takes the distribution of resources as given and it treats values and interests as intra-organisational phenomena. It does not, therefore, explain changes in patterns of interaction. In order to provide such an explanation, it is necessary to link, explicitly, the micro-level analysis of interactions to a macro-level analysis of the changing role of government. Recent developments in the theory of corporatism, allied to the earlier discussion of organisational power, (38) suggest the form of such linkages.

There are two problems in applying the theory of corporatism to the study of central-local relations. First, the theory comes in a great many versions and much of the discussion is at a level of generality which does not suggest any immediate points of contact with the study of central-local relations. Second, in as far as the theory has been used to analyse governmental policy, it has been concerned with economic policy, industrial policy and industrial relations. When, as in Winkler's case, the theory is applied to British government and encompasses administrative changes, there are a number of fundamental weaknesses in the analysis. (39) This section raises a series of questions about central-local relations derived from the corporatism thesis. It does not present yet another revision of corporatist theory. Rather, the object is to specify in some detail the ways in which the power-dependence framework needs to be extended if it is to provide an explanation of changes in central-local relations.

For this purpose, Schmitter's 'ideal-type' definition of corporatism is particularly useful:

> 'Corporatism can be defined as a system of interest representation in which the constituent units organised into a limited number of singular, compulsory, non-competitive, hierarchically ordered and functionally differentiated categories, recognised or licensed (if not created) by the state and granted a deliberate representational monopoly within their respective categories in exchange for observing certain controls on their selection of leaders and articulation of demands and supports'. (40)

Schmitter is not suggesting that any governmental system possesses all these characteristics. He is concerned to establish the extent to which a system is developing these characteristics. And a number of the weaknesses found in

other variants of corporatism are avoided by the emphasis
on institutional and empirical characteristics in this
definition. He does not limit corporatism to a particular
ideology or set of values. He does not suggest 'that
corporatist associations will be the only constituent units
of the polity - completely displacing territorial
entities ...' (41) His distinction between 'societal' and
'state' corporatism avoids the problem of limiting
corporatism to the situation in which the various interests
are created by and dependent upon the state. In addition,
Schmitter's definition of pluralism is virtually the anti-
thesis of that for corporatism. Thus, in a pluralistic
system there is an unspecified number of competitive,
voluntary interests; they are not hierarchically ordered;
they are not licensed by the state; and they have no
monopoly of representation. (42) It is the comparison of
corporatism and pluralism which makes Schmitter's approach
particularly useful. (43) Some variant of pluralism is
commonly employed in the analysis of British government
and politics. In assessing the extent to which British
government is developing the institutional and empirical
characteristics of corporatism, one is assessing at one
and the same time, the extent to which the rules of the
game and the distribution of resources are changing.

Finally, in common with most corporatist theorists,
Schmitter relates corporatism to its social context:

> ' ... corporatization of interest representation
> is related to certain basic imperatives or needs
> of capitalism to reproduce the conditions for
> its existence and continually to accumulate
> further resources. Differences in the specific
> nature of these imperatives or needs at
> different stages in the institutional develop-
> ment and international context of capitalism,
> especially as they affect the pattern of con-
> flicting class interests, account for the
> difference in origins between the societal and
> state forms of corporatism'. (44)

To this 'macro-hypothesis', he adds a number of specific
imperatives - e.g. concentration of ownership, competition
between national economies, expansion of the role of
public policy. In brief, Schmitter's theory of societal
corporatism retains the virtues identified earlier - i.e.
the focus on the interdependence of organisations, the
power of the state and the broad socio-economic context -
but it avoids the problems arising from stressing a
particular ideology and the directive role of the state.

The next step is to apply the theory of societal corporatism to the study of central-local relations. The various
points are in the form of questions because the objective
is not to argue that Britain is a corporate state but to

compare the pluralistic, power-dependence framework with its emphasis on intergovernmental bargaining to the corporatist model and identify the ways in which the rules of the game and the distribution of resources might be changing.

(a) Pressure Group or Network?

The literature on central-local relations has tended to focus on the activities of either individual local authorities or local authority associations. But this ostensibly unexceptional focus requires some important assumptions. It implies that the pattern of interactions between central and local government involves an unspecified number of units; and that the behaviour of a unit can be explained solely in terms of its character- istics - e.g. membership, internal organisation. Although individual local authorities can act as 'institutionalised pressure groups' (45) it is possible that the above assumptions handicap any attempt to explain the behaviour of the various units of government. For example, only a limited number of units may be able to participate. Most important, the behaviour of any one unit may depend on its pattern of interactions with other units. The size, frequency, diversity and density of interactions with all other units, especially if there is any continuity in these characteristics, can affect interactions with any one unit. In other words, any unit of government is a member of a network and its behaviour is a product of both its own characteristics and the characteristics of the network. Such an argument may seem remarkably banal to anyone familiar with the literature on interorganisational analysis. However, a focus on the networks within which individual units of government are embedded is an essential first step if other aspects of the corporatist thesis are to be explored.

(b) Function or Community?

A common feature of definitions of corporatism is the emphasis on functionally differentiated interest repre- sentation or 'corporations'. The form of such functional differentiation in central-local relations is not, however, self-evident. The overwhelming bulk of the literature on corporatism focuses on economic and industrial policy and, in particular on the two corporations based respectively on capital and labour. Such a focus is unduly restrictive when discussing corporatist trends in central-local relations. A different and wider range of interests need to be considered. In this context, the distinctive features of a 'corporation' are shared interests and decision-making removed from the normal democratic/ institutional framework. Functional differentiation is not limited, therefore, to any particular interests. Two forms of differentiation need to be considered: policy communities and a national community of local government.

Interactions or the networks could be structured by
policy area or function and, consequently, it may be
possible to identify 'policy communities' or:

> ' ... personal relationships between major
> political and administrative actors - sometimes
> in conflict, often in agreement, but always in
> touch and operating within a shared framework.
> Community is the cohesive and orienting bond
> underlying any particular issue'. (46)

In other words, local authority departments providing a
particular service have regular contacts and a shared
framework with the corresponding central department or
section thereof. In all probability such policy
communities will not be limited to the relevant departments of government at the various levels of government.
They will also be composed of the affected professional
associations and other interest groups. As a result, a
comparison of the roles of units of government may be of
less importance than a comparison of 'public' and
'private' actors within a policy community.

An interest in a particular policy area is not, however,
the only shared interest of local governments. Each type
of local authority has some shared interests and all
types of local authority have an interest in the preser-
vation of local government. Accordingly, it is relevant
to ask if there is a 'national community' of local
government based on the local authority associations and
their various joint bodies: collectively referred to here
as public interest groups. (47)

The available evidence suggests that the networks are
structured as policy communities. (48) However, rather
than prejudging the issue, the emphasis should be placed
on comparing interactions within each policy community
between the constituent units; interactions between
policy communities; and interactions independent of, or
across, the policy communities. The objective is to
assess the relevance of the atomistic, pluralist model of
interactions rather than stipulate the form of networks.

(c) Fragmentation or Structure?

Pluralist theory tends to assume not only that there are
multiple participants in any issue but also that each
participant is competing with the others.If the pattern of
interactions is in the form of policy communities such
assumptions seem unwise. For example, it has been argued
that the local authority associations are key actors in
central-local relations. It has also been suggested that
large local authorities have more influence on central

departments than small local authorities. (4) However, such generalisations ignore the possibility that a local authority association or a large local authority may be peripheral to policy communities which are composed of a limited number of organisations. The importance of any particular unit of government could vary from policy community to policy community and the relative power potential of a unit of government may not be a product of its own characteristics but of network characteristics.

Corporatist theory also challenges the pluralist assumption of extensive competition whilst accepting the growing importance of some groups for policy-making. It suggests that, in place of fragmentation, there is an underlying structure of interactions based on policy communities. And it cannot be assumed that there is extensive competition within or between policy communities. Agreement can be negotiated within and between policy communities or it can be imposed by central departments. In fact, a broad consensus on policy objectives or goals can be a distinctive feature of policy communities (see below).

Nor can it be assumed that the participants in policy communities are local governments or central government. It may be more accurate to talk of the relevant functionally specialised section of these organisations. Thus, a local education department may have closer links with the relevant central department than with other departments in the same local authority. The bases of fragmentation is functional specialisation and not type of government organisations. The distinction between 'public' and 'private' collapses and the emphasis is switched to the interdependence of a variety of organisations. (50) The contribution of corporatist theory is to raise afresh questions about the ways in which this variety is structured. And policy communities are not the only possible structural form. Two counter trends can be identified. First, the introduction of corporate planning/management in local government can be seen as a means for countering the functional links between centre and locality. (51) Second, it is also possible to identify two conditions under which public interest groups can play a prominent role. First, where issues span policy communities (e.g. finance) the public interest groups could act as 'clearing houses' or 'sub-parliaments' for individual local authorities or, in the case of the local authority associations, for other public interest groups. (52) Second, the local authority associations could be of central importance when the interactions are limited to public interest groups; provided the contents of such interactions are complimentary to the immediate interests of the affected group and do not directly affect its pre-existing links with either central departments or local authorities.

Rather than viewing central-local relations as a complex

bargaining game involving many organisations, corporatist
theory raises the question of whether interactions are
based on policy communities or a national community. But
the analysis of the structure of networks has been
general and omits a number of key issues. Some of the
detailed features of these network structures are discussed below.

(d) Open or Closed?

The foregoing discussion assumes, for the most part, that
the most significant interactions are interactions at the
national level. Thus, policy communities have been discussed as if their members were the national professional
associations, national interest groups, central departments and public interest groups. However, any such
community will be composed of organisations which,
constitutionally are accountable to their members and in
some cases to elected representatives. Interactions are
not limited to the national level.

It could be argued that each participating organisation
has close contacts with its membership and that this contact takes the form of briefing and debriefing national
representatives. There are, of course, many forms of
reporting-back: e.g. annual conferences, 'house'
journals, regional committees. In such an 'open'
organisation, the more varied the interests of the membership, the greater the constraints on the leadership.
However, the inability of members to hold leaders to
account has been oft-documented. (53) Given the available
evidence on this topic in the study of central-local
relations, it is perhaps more plausible to argue that, for
example, the policy communities are 'closed': that is,
contact between leaders and membership is limited. (54)
And at least two reasons for this development can be
identified. First, the bureaucratisation of the internal
structures of organisations as they grow in size. Second,
the pressure upon an organisation from other participants
in the policy community to commit itself to an agreement
without continual reference back. As a consequence, the
organisations within a policy community are hierarchically
ordered or closed.

In the study of central-local relations, many of the
organisations differ from the interest groups which are
the focus of corporatist theory because they
are controlled by elected representatives. As a result,
the terms 'open' and 'closed' can have a distinct, second
meaning besides that of links with organisational members.
They also refer to the political accountability of
officials to elected members (and, of course, to the
accountability of elected members to the electorate). To
avoid any confusion, the accountability of officials and
of elected members is discussed separately, below.

(e) Representation or Intermediation?

The term 'interest group' suggests that the prime function
of such a group is to represent its members, articulating
their demands and protecting their interests. However,
an organisation - whether it be a professional association,
a public interest group or a trade union - may have its
own interests distinct from those of its members; may not
know or articulate members demands; and may attempt to
control members. In such circumstances, the term
'intermediation' (literally, 'coming between') seems more
appropriate. (55) Thus, a closed policy community comes
between local and central government: that is, the policy
community or network has its own interests and advances
its own proposals. Over time, each network has evolved
its own approach to problems: established routines of
contact, shared perceptions and values, and the stock of
tried knowledge and policies are brought to bear on new
problems. This shared 'appreciative system' of the network could differ markedly from that of members. (56) And
because the network or policy community contains
participants from central departments it can appear to
members that their organisation is representing the
interests of the central department rather than their
interests.

Not only can policy communities appear to be separated
from member interests but also they can have a monopoly
of representation. This access can be granted by central
departments or conceded by them but the effect on the
membership is the same: the channel for articulating their
demands is not carrying out this function, and it is the
only channel. The links between leaders and members
cannot be reduced to a question of frequency and form of
contact. Analysis must also include the content of interactions and explore the origins of a particular proposal,
the interest(s) it is designed to further and its consequences. In a different context, Heclo and Wildavsky have
argued that the consequences of community are delay,
ambiguity, contradiction and self-absorbtion whilst

> ' ... the citizens who are to be served and
> problems that must be met may slowly recede from
> view until they appear as if viewed from the
> small end of a telescope, distant, blurry and
> easily blinked away'. (57)

The extent to which local government has been or is being
absorbed into Whitehall's 'village community' is not only
pertinent in the era of the Consultative Council on Local
Government Finance but it also raises the question of
whether the much vaunted increase in central control is control by
statute and circular or indirect, social control of a more
pervasive nature. If the premises of decisions are shared
premises, removing the myriad of detailed controls will
change little.

(f)   Sectional or Public Interest?

At various junctures, reference has been made to the interests of policy communities. The concept of interests has a number of distinctive features when used in connection with public sector organisations. Many such organisations are perhaps best described as hybrid pressure groups because, in addition to their pressure group, bargaining activities on behalf of their members' or the policy communities' sectional interests, they are also part of the structure of government. Thus, one of their distinguishing features in pluralist theory is their integrative function or the need to accommodate a range of interests: to act both as broker and as arbiter of demands in the public interest. Accordingly, public sector organisations both represent their sectional interest and promote the public interest as they perceive it subject to the check of political accountability.

   Some support for this distinction can be found in a few studies of the local authority associations.   Cross suggests that:

> 'The broadness of (the AMC's) interest tends to
> make its wholly common interest less intense.
> It speaks for County Boroughs on the one hand
> and on the other for a large section of the
> population living largely under county govern-
> ment.   Perhaps this generality of interests
> adds to its responsibility'.

And the ability of the AMC to speak for a large section of the population rather than its own sectional interest is legitimated by its representative character:

> ' ... it is representation having its roots in
> the elective principle, with a line of accounta-
> bility, and having its ultimate source of
> authority in practically speaking the whole of
> the adult population of England and Wales'. (57)

In contrast to the pluralist view, corporatist theory does not define the role of government as that of broker. Rather the emphasis falls on the extension in the scope of government intervention;   the necessity of the state's regulatory and integrative tasks to sustain the conditions of capital accumulation;   and, in the process, the autonomy of the state to meet its own needs for growth and power. (59)   A detailed discussion of this conception of the role of government is less important at this particular point than the consequences which follow from the extension of government power.   At least three consequences can be identified.

First, with the extension of its tasks, government increasingly resorts to delegated and mediated enforcement. Thus, local government is by-passed by the allocation of functions to quangos: i.e. central government favours indirect, concealed forms of administration. In addition, potential dissent is forestalled by the co-option of the affected parties. (59) In other words, the legitimacy previously accorded to local authorities by the fact of their elected, representative nature no longer guarantees access to decision-making and, increasingly they have to take second place to the functionally differentiated, closed policy communities.

Second, public sector organisations are vulnerable to central intervention. It may be, as Shonfield has argued, that corporatism has developed more slowly in the United Kingdom because of 'the traditional British view of the proper relationship between public and private power (in which) the two ... are thought of as utterly distinct from one another'. But such attitudes offer little protection to local government. (60) As Sharpe has argued:

> 'Given the massive growth of government over the
> last half century or so, the reduction in the
> number of organisations with whom a central
> government has to deal is an important objective
> whether these organisations are 'private' pressure
> groups or 'public' local authorities. In this
> sense, all central governments have a very strong
> interest in the aggregation of groups and
> interests within the State and a particularly
> strong desire to aggregate the units of local
> government'. (61)

Finally, but closely related to the first two points, the political accountability of public sector organisations has declined. As noted earlier, the policy communities can be closed in the sense of not being accountable to the electorate. Not only are functions allocated to non-elected bodies but the sectional interests of policy communities dominate any attempts at defining a broader public interest. The responsibility for decisions now lies with the policy communities but they are not subject to the constraints of parliamentary accountability. The legitimacy of policy no longer resides in its approval by elected representatives but in its scientific, rational basis.

(g) Technocrat or Topocrat?

In theory at least the official at either the central or local level is accountable to the politician for his actions. It has been accepted that the official can play a major role in policy initiation but nonetheless his proposals must gain political approval and remain subject to political veto. With the growth in importance of policy communities, however, such checks are of decreasing relevance. Thus, Heclo and Wildavsky reject the distinction between Minister and civil servant preferring to describe both as 'political administrators' bound together by 'kinship' and 'culture'. (62) In other words, the participants within a policy community share a common 'appreciative system' which serves both to bind them together and to protect them from other policy communities and from the various mechanisms of political control. In Bell's terms, political conflict is now predominantly between the professional or political technocrat and the populace and the locus of this conflict is large-scale organisation. (63)

However, the rise of the technocrat has not necessarily been unchallenged. Beer has argued that the rise of the technocrat has promoted a new system of representation in the shape of topocrats. (64) To return to an earlier theme, therefore, it is necessary to ask whether there is a national community of public interest groups acting as a counterveiling power to the policy communities. And in applying these concepts to British central-local relations care has to be exercised in the use of the terms professional and technocrat. They are not synonyms. Although the term professional tends to imply sectional interests, it is worth emphasising that in British local government professional groups are centrally involved in the development of services and enjoy quasi-official status. They are not confined necessarily to a particular policy area. They can provide information and expertise to public interest groups and central departments. To employ a somewhat florid metaphor, they are one of the tentacles of leviathon.Of all the professional associations, it is not clear how many play a role spanning a number of policy areas. It is important, therefore, to determine the extent to which the roles of the professional associations are a product of differing definitions of the scope of their knowledge and interests. Are they limited to a particular policy community (technocrats) or do they span a number of such communities (topocrats)?

Finally, the rise of the technocrats raises a number of issues about the basis of legitimacy of policy decisions. Habermas has argued that:

> ' ... the development of the social system seems to be determined by the logic of scientific - technical progress. The immanent law of this progress seems to produce objective exigencies, which must be obeyed by any politics oriented toward functional needs. When this semblance has taken root effectively, then propaganda can refer to the role of technology and science in order to explain and legitimate why in modern societies the process of democratic decision-

making about practical problems loses its
function and 'must' be replaced by plebiscitary
decisions about alternative sets of leaders of
administrative personnel ... it can also become
a background ideology that penetrates into the
consequences of the depoliticised mass of the
population, where it can take on legitimating
power'. (65)

The notion of 'best professional practice' provides a
persuasive, acceptable rationale for policy decisions.
But to what extent is the power of the professional
limited by 'the cantankerousness of politics'? Certainly,
there have been examples where professional advice has
been effectively challenged, with high-rise building and
motorway construction providing the more spectacular
examples of recent years. The power of policy communities
may not lie, however, in their ability to influence the
outcomes of particular issues.

(h)   Issues or Agenda?

It is virtually axiomatic in pluralist theory that power
resides in the ability to determine the outcome of
particular issues. As argued in the discussion of
organisational power, (67) power can also reside in the
rules of the game which may favour one or more of the
participants. With the development of societal corporatism and the growing importance of policy communities,
there are a number of changes in the rules of the bargaining game.

First, recognition by the government, extending to the
licensing of participants, and the compulsory nature of
participation become features of the game. Obviously,
political necessity can dictate that a particular group or
organisation be accorded recognition but, and this is the
key point, participation itself ceases to be voluntary.
Whether because of the pressures of the situation, licensing, co-option, legislation or professional accreditation,
it is not possible to withdraw from the game. For
example, it is difficult to see how the local authority
associations could have refused to participate in the
Consultative Council on Local Government Finance.

Second, if each policy community has a distinct
appreciative system, it has, in fact, an agenda of 'relevant' issues and problems. Only some matters will be
deemed appropriate ones for decision and, to the extent
that domain consensus has been negotiated between policy
communities, the issue scope of the policy community will
be highly restrictive. It is perhaps too easily assumed
that organisations are continually negotiating with each
other. It is equally plausible to suggest that they are
primarily concerned to avoid each other. Such conflict

avoidance presupposes a restricted domain and a limited
agenda of issues simply because an extensive domain and a
broad issue scope increases the possibility of contact
with other organisations. (68) But irrespective of
whether an organisation avoids conflict or negotiation, it
is clear that power resides in the ability to control the
agenda and that such controls stem as much from the
expectations, interests and values of the participants as
from deliberate manipulation.

Finally, with the increasing scope of government intervention and the interpenetration of the public and private
sectors, there is a growing acceptance of the necessity of
such intervention in the interests of national economic
management. It is, therefore, no longer necessary to
justify state intervention itself. It is only necessary
to demonstrate that this particular intervention is
required in the interests of economic management. The
issue at stake concerns only the form of the intervention.
To the extent that local authorities accept the legitimacy
of such arguments by central government, they have
considerably limited their own room for maneouvre and
conceded considerable scope for policy initiatives to
central departments. The point emerged clearly in the
evidence given by the Society of Local Authority Chief
Executives (SOLACE) to the Expenditure Committee. Sir
Stanley Holmes, President of SOLACE, commented:

> ' ... accepting that the overall control is
> essential in the interests of the national
> economy, and accepting that, I suppose, Parlia-
> ment cannot bring itself in relation to many
> services to allow them to drop below a minimum
> level, having said that, one would have thought
> there was a case for greater liberation, greater
> freedom of decision, inside the broad framework;...'

However, later in their evidence, the Chairman of the
Expenditure Committee pointed out that this acceptance of
central government's responsibility for fixing the total
monies allocated to local government implied that they also
accepted 'how the money is rationed out, which means how
the rate support grant formula is fixed'. It may be
desirable for local government 'to make decisions on the
functions and the duties which Parliament has given them'
once 'the financial resources for local government have
been fixed' but, and this is the crucial point, any such
decisions only represent discretion at the margin: 'the
broad framework' could perhaps be best described as a
strait-jacket. (69)

(i) Resources or Control?

In pluralist theory, the resources of the participants are
of key importance in explaining their relative power
potential. However, corporatist theory suggests that the

relative power of central and local departments cannot be explained solely by reference to their respective resources. Power also lies in the rules of the game. At various points, it has also been suggested that legitimating ideologies or values are similarly important to understanding the relative power of participants in central-local relations. Three aspects of power as the 'mobilisation of bias' have been identified: the appreciative systems of policy communities, the scientific-rational ethos, and the inevitability of state intervention. Without repeating earlier discussions, a focus on power as mobilisation of bias suggests that control can reside not in the distribution of resources but in the prior acceptance that someone has the right to take that decision. Appeals to the scientific ethos, to best professional practice and to the imperatives of the economic management all serve to justify decisions whether or not those decisions are in the interests of affected parties. However, it cannot be assumed that the various aspects of values discussed above are complimentary, compatible or unchallenged. Belief in the value of local democracy still prevails. The values of policy communities may conflict with those of a national community. There is little or no evidence on this aspect of power in central-local relations. Corporatist theory does suggest, however, that the ever-growing state intervention is leading to ever-burgeoning state control. Central government increasingly selects the leaders and regulates the demands of groups. It could be argued that one of the major functions of the Consultative Council on Local Government Finance is precisely such social control. The basis of such control may lie in central government's organised monopoly of legitimate violence (70) or it may lie in the consensus on goals and procedures between central and local government in which the latter accepts that the control of local expenditure is an essential prerequisite of effective national economic management. Whatever explanation is preferred, corporatist theory highlights the importance of studying the ways in which legitimating ideologies are a source of power for some participants.

The discussion and comparisons of pluralist and corporatist theory was designed to identify the ways in which the power-dependence framework needed to be extended. Building upon the earlier discussion of organisational power, it has been argued that corporatist theory is an extremely useful tool for exploring changes in the rules of the game and in the distribution of resources. Although all the institutional and empirical characteristics of corporatism cannot be found in Britain, nonetheless the sharp, even exaggerated, contrast it provides with pluralist theory highlights the changes that could take place in central-local relations. In summary form, the major trends predicted by corporatist theory include the emergence of closed or hierarchical, non-competitive, compulsory, functionally differentiated policy communities with their own interests, expectations and values or legitimating ideologies. They have a concomitant ability to control the policy agenda and resist attempts to hold them to account by either members or constituent organisations. They have a monopoly of representation in the policy area and in exchange they are subject to controls in the selection of leaders and they are expected to regulate both their own demands and those of members or constituent organisations. Accordingly, the influence of individual local authorities and of public interest groups is severely constrained. Territorial politics are by-passed. The research task is clearly one of exploring the extent to which these characteristics are a feature of British central-local relations. To repeat a point made at the outset, the purpose of this section is not to argue that Britain is a corporatist state but to provide benchmarks against which to assess changes in central-local relation-ships. In the final section of this chapter, the pressures for change and the implications of these pressures for both the power-dependence framework and for future research will be assessed.

CONCLUDING DISCUSSION: the rationality of ambiguous confusion

The very sharpness of the contrasts between pluralist and corporatist theories, and the marked changes that the latter indicates for central-local relations, do not thereby render its various predictions implausible. As Schmitter points out there is considerable common ground between the two theories:

> ' ... (i) the growing importance of formal associational units of representation;   (2) the persistance and expansion of functionally differentiated and potentially conflicting interests;   (3) the burgeoning role of permanent administrative staffs, of specialised information, of technical expertise and, consequently of entrenched oligarchy;   (4) the decline in the importance of territorial and partisan represent-ation;   and (5) the secular trend toward expansion in the scope of public policy and (c) interpenetrat-ion of private and public decision arenas'. (71)

And drawing upon Shonfields work, Schmitter also suggests that the role of government in fostering full employment, promoting economic growth, controlling inflation, regulat-ing business cycles, regulating working conditions, resolving industrial disputes and protecting businessmen and organisations from the adverse consequences of econom-ic risk all serve to foster corporatist trends. (72)   That such trends can be identified in British government and that they are closely related to the economic context seem unexceptional conclusions. Of greater importance, is the precise form of the relationships between the economic context and the role(s) of government. Or, to rephrase the issue for the study of central-local relations, 'To what extent is the changing economic context of British government changing the relationship between central and local government?'

It is possible to identify some of the predicted changes in at least incipient form. The functional nature of the links between centre and locality has been noted on a number of occasions. (73) Conversely, the creation of the Consultative Council on Local Government Finance and the increase in the size of the local authority associations (74) can be viewed as a strengthening of the role of public interest groups and of the national community. More recently, the role of officials in, and the secrecy surrounding, the RSG negotiations has been described. (75) And, of course, the theme of the Layfield Report was the lack of accountability in the relationships between central and local government. (76) In other words, central-local relations could be said to display corporatist features. Within particular policy areas, the links between central and local government are rational in that actors at the two levels of government share common interests in the development of that policy area. However, the links between such policy communities are ambiguous and, when the system is viewed as a whole, as in the case of public expenditure decisions, the pattern of relationships is confused. There is competition not only between the various policy communities but also between the policy communities and both public interest groups (especially the local authority associations) and those central and local departments charged with responsibilities spanning policy areas. And paralleling Crozier's analysis of French central-local relations, the participants may have a vested interest in a system of confused and ambiguous relationships. (77) But to what extent is this system stable and what are the pressures for change?

The Layfield Report predicted a growth in central accountability if positive steps were not taken to strengthen local accountability. (78) Equally, corporatist theory would predict an intensification of corporatist features with ever-growing state intervention to manage the economy. The Conservative government's proposals to reform the grant system also suggest that central government is attempting to strengthen its ability to control local expenditure. (79) Assuming that the system of ambiguous confusion is transitional, two questions are of paramount importance. First, to what extent is the emergence of corporatist features in central-local relations a function of changes in the British economy? Second, what are the consequences of these changes for the power-dependence framework?

Unfortunately, current knowledge about central-local relations does not permit specific answers to the questions. There is an abundance of generalisations about the role of the state in capitalist society but few studies documenting the inter-relationship between economic change, state intervention and the consequences for particular policy areas and institutional arrangements. Unsatisfactory though the conclusion may be, it is only possible to urge that future studies of central-local relations should not focus on particular issues but explore the evolution of particular policy areas over a substantial period of time and attempt to determine the relationship between, and relative importance of, exogenous and endogenous change. Similarly, it is not possible to specify in detail the consequences of corporatist trends for the power-dependence framework. However, it is possible to identify, in general terms, two important consequences. The power-dependence framework focuses on the resources and strategies ignoring changes in the rules of the game and the distribution of resources. Corporatist theory, as argued in the previous section, points to important changes in the rules of the game and stresses the importance of legitimating ideologies in constraining the arenas within which resources can be deployed. In other words, by exploring the changing role of government, corporatist theory permits an analysis of other facets of power besides power as resources.

It was argued at the beginning of this chapter that the intention was to develop a systematic inventory or classification of elements to be explored in the study of central-local questions. Although the framework includes a number of suggestions which attempt to explain variations in the patterns of interactions and in the behaviour of actors, of its very nature it poses more questions than it answers. Accordingly, it is perhaps time to draw together the various questions and indicate which areas of research are of prime importance.

First, the framework directs attention to the question of why the relationship between central and local government varies through its focus on the bases of the power-dependence relationship. It asks whether financial resources are the crucial determinant in the relationship. Can the other resources compensate for financial weakness? How significant are the other resources in central-local relations? For example, although it is clear that there is contact between national and local politicians, we do not know how extensive it is or how important it is for policy decisions involving both levels of government. The same questions can be posed for each of the resources.

Second, the framework poses the question of how does the relationship vary. The agent and the partnership models answered the question virtually by definition. The framework admits that the relationship can vary from a high degree of discretion to a high degree of dependence and directs attention to the conditions underpinning these variations. It points to the variety of channels of communication between the two levels of government and raises questions about the relative importance and efficiency of these various channels. It also suggests that any satisfactory exploration of how the relationship varies must analyse the various stages of policy-making, the characteristics of different policy areas, and the differences between relationships involving policy/goals and those involving decisions.

Third, it raises a series of questions about how central departments and local authorities manage their relationships with each other. To what extent do participants recognise and work within agreed rules of the game? To what extent do public interest groups comprise a national local government community and provide individual local authorities with an effective central negotiating and bargaining capability? To what extent do participants employ strategies to manage their relationships? To what extent do participants compete for discretion in designing and implementing policies? In addition, within these general areas, a number of specific questions are raised. For example, on the rules of the game, attention is focused on identifying the rules and describing how they are applied in specific situations. A similar range of questions can be raised about the use of strategies.

Finally, the framework focuses on changes in the role of government and raises a series of questions about changes in the rules of the game and in legitimating ideologies. It also stresses the importance of a historical perspective relating changes in central-local relations to changes in the economic context of government.

Given the defects of the literature on central-local relations discussed earlier, it can be argued that the framework offers the opportunity to repair some of the more glaring omissions. The questions raised are in those areas not currently explored by the literature. Moreover, these questions are not a wholly idiosyncratic list of 'interesting' issues. The framework poses a series of related questions only some of which are specific to the study of central-local relations. Herein lies the rationale of the exercise and, hopefully, the claimed utility of the framework will be demonstrated by future research.

A major objective of this book has been to provide a framework for the analysis of central-local relations but it was not the only objective. It has also attempted to show that the subject can illuminate facets of British government of more general concern to social scientists.

More specifically, it has been argued that the study of central-local relations is a fruitful locus for the analysis of corporatism, of the power of the professional in government and for exploring the problems of accountability created by the interdependence of a multitude of complex governmental bureaucracies. Without repeating the earlier discussions of these topics, it is worth emphasising that these are not peculiar or unique features of central-local relationships but a widespread phenomenon in British government. Future research into central-local relations need not adopt a traditional legal-institutional approach and ignore these issues. In fact, to omit the power of professionals and the accountability of bureaucracies from the study of central-local relations would be to ignore two of its most important features. Bare-footed empiricism in whatever form will contribute little to our understanding of intergovernmental relations. The vocabulary on intergovernmental relations in Britain needs to be expanded and this book presents one attempt to develop a different vocabulary. Independently of any merits of the framework offered here, the need to ground the study of intergovernmental relations in a macro-perspective remains paramount.

NOTES AND REFERENCES

1. For a discussion of these problems and further references see: Ryan, A., The Philosophy of the Social Sciences. London: Macmillan, 1970 ch.4.
2. Glaser, B.G. and Strauss, A.L., The Discovery of Grounded Theory: Strategies for Qualitative Research Chicago: Aldine Pub. Co., 1967 p. 6.
3. Thompson, J.D., Organisations in Action New York: McGraw Hill, 1967 p. 30.
4. Parsons, T., 'On the Concept of Political Power' in Bell, R., Edwards, D.V. and Wagner, R.H., (eds.), Political Power: a reader in theory and research New York, The Free Press, 1969 p. 280.
5. Task and technological resources refer to the technology essential to tasks (e.g. computers) and task refers to the workflow activities of an organisation. Dependence arising from the need for task and technological resources can be found in local government - e.g. refuse collection and refuse disposal. However, examples in the area of central-local relations are difficult to identify. Physical resources refer to the land and buildings controlled by a local authority. Again, it is difficult to identify examples of how the control of such resources affects central-local relations. Both these resources seem relevant to county-district relations.
6. John Friend has suggested that a central department may treat local authorities as a class of similar organisations justifying its actions by referring to its general responsibility to a wider constituency than

129

individual local authorities. On the other hand, a local authority may resist being treated as part of a broad class of organisations and seek one-to-one links with the central department, justifying its actions by referring to its specific knowledge of, and responsibilities for, the local area. Letter to the author dated 4th September 1978. Quoted with permission.

7.   Layfield Report, Annex 9 and Annex 12.

8.   For a more detailed discussion and the appropriate references see ch. 3 above pp. 45-7 and notes 18-23.

9.   See: Thompson, op. cit., p. 26.

10.   Friend, J.K. 'The Dynamics of Policy Change', Long Range Planning Vol. 10 February 1977 p. 40.

11.   Vickers, Geoffrey Sir The Art of Judgement. London: Chapman and Hall, 1965 Ch.2 and passim; and Young, K., 'Values in the Policy Process' Policy and Politics Vol. 5 1977 pp. 1-22.

12.   On the 'departmental philosophies' of central departments see Lord Bridges, 'Portrait of a Profession' in Chapman, R.A. and Dunsire, A., (eds.), Style in Administration. London: Allen and Unwin, 1971 p.50.

13.   For a more detailed discussion of these concepts see the next section.

14.   For a constructive review of the difficulties see Young, K. and Mills, Liz, Understanding the Assumptive Worlds of Government Actors: issues and approaches. London: SSRC, 1980.

15.   See Ch. 4 above pp. 78-85.

16.   Truman, D.B., The Governmental Process New York: Alfred A. Knopf, 1951 pp. 343-4.

17.   Crozier, M. and Thoenig, J-C., 'The Regulation of Complex Organised Systems', Administrative Science Quarterly Vol. 21 1976 p. 551.

18.   Mackenzie, W.J.M., Theories of Local Government London: London School of Economics and Political Science, Greater London Papers No. 2, 1961 p. 5.

19.   Boyle, E. Crosland, A. and Kogan, M., The Politics of Education Harmondsworth: Penguin Books, 1971 p.171.

20.   See Ch. 3 above pp. 56-7.

21.   Benson, J.K., 'The Interorganisational Network as a Political Economy', Administrative Science Quarerly Vol. 20 1975 pp. 244-5.

22.   Hull, C., and Rhodes R.A.W., Intergovernmental Relations in the European Community Farnborough, Hampshire: Saxon House, 1977 pp. 49-52.

23.   On the influence of personalities in the politics of intergovernmental relations see Ch. 4 above p. 79 and p. 82.

24.   See Dahl, R.A., 'The Concept of Power' in Bell, R., Edwards, D.V. and Wagner, R.H., (eds.), Political Power: a reader in theory and research New York: The Free Press, 1969 pp. 83-4.

25. For a discussion of these characteristics of networks see Mitchell, J.C., 'The Concept and Use of Social Networks' in Mitchell, J.C., (ed.), Social Networks in Urban Situations. Manchester: Manchester University Press, 1969 pp. 1-29. For an illustrative application see Laumann, E.O., and Pappi, F.U., Networks of Collective Action New York: Academic Press, 1976.
26. Jowell, J., 'The Legal Control of Administrative Discretion', Public Law, Autumn 1973 p. 179.
27. Davis, K.C., Discretionary Justice Baton Rouge: Louisiana State University Press, 1969 p. 4.
28. Simon, H.A., The New Science of Management Decision New York: Harper and Row, 1960 p.2.
29. For an alternative conception see Agger, R.E., Goldrich, D., and Swanson, B.E., The Rulers and the Ruled New York: Wiley, 1964 p. 40.
30. For a detailed discussion see: School for Advanced Urban Studies, 'Implementation and the Central-Local Relationship' in Social Science Research Council, Central-Local Government Relationships London: SSRC, 1979 pp. 11-26.
31. Sharkansky, I., (ed.), Policy Analysis in Political Science Chicago: Markham, 1970 p. 1.
32. Bauer, R.A. and Gergen, K.J., The Study of Policy Formation New York: The Free Press, 1968 p. 2.
33. See for example: Quade, E.S., Analysis for Public Decisions New York: American Elsevier, 2nd edition, 1976 p. 20, pp. 33-4 and pp. 83-101.
34. See above p. 103
35. 'Supplementary Memorandum by the Society of Local Authority Chief Executives on Unnecessarily Detailed Control by Government Departments' in Eleventh Report from the Expenditure Committee, The Civil Service, Vol. II, Minutes of Evidence HC 535, London: HMSO, 1977 p. 1085.
36. See Ch. 1 above pp. 7-8.
37. Crozier and Thoenig op. cit., p. 556.
38. See: Ch. 3 above pp. 56-60.
39. See Ch. 1 above p. 6.
40. Schmitter, P.C., 'Still the Century of Corporatism?' in Schmitter, P.C. and Lehmbruch, G. (eds.), Trends Towards Corporatist Intermediation London: Sage, 1979 p. 13.
41. Schmitter, op. cit., p. 44.
42. Schmitter, op. cit., p. 15.
43. Other authors who make similar comparisons, many of whom also draw upon Schmitter's work, include: Crouch, C., Class Conflict and the Industrial Relations Crisis London: Heinemann, 1977; Crouch, C., The Politics of Industrial Relations Glasgow: Fontana/Collins, 1979; Beer, S., 'British Pressure Groups Revisted: Pluralistic Stagnation from the Fifties to the Seventies' Public Administration Bulletin No. 32 April 1980 pp. 5-16; McFarland, A.S. 'Recent Social Movements and Theories of Power in America' paper to the Annual Meeting of the American Political Science Association,

Washington, D.C., 31 August 1979; and Richardson, J.J. and Jordan, A.G., Governing Under Pressure Oxford: Martin Robertson, 1979.

44. Schmitter, op. cit., p. 24. See also: Schmitter, P.C., 'Modes of Interest Intermediation and Models of of Societal Change in Western Europe' in Schmitter and Lehmbruch, op. cit., pp. 63-94.

45. See: Scarrow, H., 'Policy Pressures by British Local Government: the case of regulation in the public interest' Comparative Politics Vol. 4 1971 pp. 1-28.

46. Heclo, H., and Wildavsky, A. The Private Government of Public Money London: Macmillan, 1974 p.XV. See also: Hogwood, B., 'Analysing Industrial Policy: a multiperspective approach' Public Administration Bulletin No. 29 April 1979 pp. 18-42.

47. See: Ch.4 above pp. 85-6.

48. Layfield Report, pp. 82-3.

49. Griffith, J.A.G., Central Departments and Local Authorities London: Allen and Unwin, 1966 p. 33 and p. 528.

50. In contrast to marxist theories of the state, corporatist theory recognises the variety of governmental institutions. See the literature cited in Ch. 1 above note 34.

51. For a more detailed discussion of this point see: Rhodes, R.A.W., 'Ordering Urban Change: corporate planning in the government of English cities' in Lagroye, J. and Wright, V. (eds.), Local Government in Britain and France London: Allen and Unwin, 1979 pp. 127-49.

52. See: Mackenzie, W.J.M., 'Pressure Groups in Britain' in Rose, R. (ed.), Studies in British Politics London: Macmillan, third edition, 1976 p. 354.

53. The classic analysis is: Michels, R., Political Parties New York: Collier Books, 1962. First published in 1915.

54. See for example: Isaac-Henry, K., The Association of Municipal Corporations and the County Councils Association - a study of influences and pressures on reorganisation 1945-72. Birmingham Polytechnic, mimeo 1978.

55. Schmitter, Modes of Interest Intermediation and Models of Societal Change in Western Europe', op. cit., p. 93.

56. Although it is an unusual useage, the term 'members' also encompasses individual local authority departments. Thus, the local department may participate in a policy community but it does not articulate or even share the interests, expectations and values of either fellow local departments or the elected council.

57. See: Cross, C.A., The AMC: a study of its structure Unpublished M.A. Thesis, University of Manchester, 1954. See also: Isaac-Henry, K., 'The English Local Authority Associations' Public Administration Bulletin No. 33 August 1980 (forthcoming).

58. For further discussion see: Winkler, J.T., 'Corporatism' European Journal of Sociology Vol. 17 1976 pp.134-36; Schmitter, 'Still the Century of Corporatism?' op. cit., pp. 22-40; and Jessop, R., 'Corporatism, Parliamentarism and Social Democracy' in Schmitter and Lehmbruch, op. cit., pp. 185-212.
59. See: Ch. 1 above pp. 4-5.
60. Shonfield, A., Modern Capitalism London: Oxford University Press, 1965, p. 99 quoted in Schmitter, 'Still the Century of Corporatism?' op. cit., p. 29.
61. Sharpe, L.J., 'Modernising the Localities: local government in Britain and some comparisons with France' in Lagroye and Wright, op. cit., pp. 42-3. Emphasis added.
62. Heclo, H. and Wildavsky, A., The Private Government of Public Money London: Macmillan 1974 p. 2.
63. Bell, D., The Coming of Post-Industrial Society Harmondsworth: Penguin Books, 1976 pp. 128-29.
64. See: Ch. 4 above pp. 85-6 and notes 51-54.
65. Habermas, J. Toward a Rational Society London: Heinemann, 1971 p. 105.
66. Bell, op. cit., p. 366.

67. See: Ch. 3 above pp. 56-7.
68. I am grateful to Renate Mayntz for drawing my attention to the importance of conflict avoidance. Personal communication.
69. Eleventh Report from the Expenditure Committee, op. cit., p. 737, p. 741 and p. 744.
70. Schmitter, 'Still the Century of Corporatism?' op. cit., p. 21.
71. Schmitter, 'Still the Century of Corporatism?' op. cit., p. 15.
72. Schmitter, 'Still the Century of Corporatism?' op. cit., pp. 28-9.
73. See for example: Sharpe, op. cit., p. 45-7.
74. On this last point see: Isaac-Henry, 'The English Local Authority Associations' op. cit.
75. See: Harris, R., and Shipp, P.J., Communications Between Central and Local Government in the Management of Local Authority Expenditure Coventry: 1OR, 1977; and Taylor, J.A., 'The Consultative Council on Local Government Finance: a critical analysis of its origins and development' Local Government Studies Vol. 5 No. 3 1979 pp. 7-36.
76. Layfield Report Chs. 4 and 5.
77. See for example: Hepworth, N.,'Local Government and Central Control' Public Administration Vol. 55 1977 p. 16.
78. Layfield Report, p. 74.
79. See: Society of Local Authority Chief Executives, The Local Government Bill: an appraisal prepared by SOLACE in collaboration with INLOGOV London: SOLACE, 1980.

Appendix: selected annotated bibliography

INTRODUCTION

Professor J.A.G. Griffith begins his 1966 study of central-local relations with the observation that:

> 'The working relationship between central
> departments and local authorities in England
> and Wales can be regarded in terms which are
> formal, informal, statutory, non-statutory,
> legal, extra-legal, financial, official,
> personal, political, functional, tragical,
> comical, historical, pastoral. Seneca
> cannot be too heavy nor Plautus too light'.

The central theme of this bibliography is based on an apparent paradox. Although there are a large number of studies of central-local relations in the United Kingdom, there are also too few, primarily because of the restricted focus of the existing material. The aim of this bibliography is to 'open up' the discussion of central-local relations and to identify themes in various disciplines which, although not commonly associated with the subject, nonetheless have a lot to offer in terms of theoretical and empirical insights. The comical and the pastoral may not figure prominently but many other facets of the relationship are covered.

Given its scope, it is obvious that the bibliography will be selective. Every effort has been made to include all the major items on central-local relations (narrowly defined) published in the post-war period but for many of the other topics a similar effort would have led to an appendix of inordinate length. For such topics as organisational power, games, intergovernmental relations and goals the emphasis has been placed on identifying a number of seminal texts. Assuming that this book has been successfull in its avowed intent of convincing readers of the merits of a broader approach to central-local relations, the interested individual should be able to rectify any omissions. Where possible, specialist bibliographies have been cited to assist in this process.

Finally, a number of detailed points should be drawn to the readers' attention. First, conference and occasional papers have been excluded unless they are known to be easily available. Second, the bibliography covers the period 1945-78. Where possible more recent items have been included but the inevitable delays in the arrival of journals and books in libraries mean that there will be gaps. Third, to guide the reader through a large number of items, the bibliography has been extensively sub-divided and a separate contents list has been compiled. A number of books and articles could easily have been included in more than one section. Only the most important items have been listed twice. Finally, the introductions to each section of the bibliography do not attempt to cover every item cited but to identify the most salient contributions.

CONTENTS

Section A

GENERAL

It has been argued that the study of central-local
relations can illuminate issues of more general concern
in the social sciences. It is virtually impossible to
provide a bibliography on these matters given the sheer
diversity of viewpoints encompassed by the constituent
disciplines. Accordingly, this section simply provides a
list of items which proved to be of particular use in
writing this book. As a result, there is a marked bias
in favour of the literature on corporatism (e.g. Winkler,
1976) and on post-industrial society (e.g. Bell, 1976).
The reader who does not find these interpretations
persuasive could consult Habermas (1971) and Pickvance
(1976) or Saunders (1980) for an excellent review of
'theories of the state'.

Given the amount of space devoted to interorganisational
analysis in particular and the sociology of organisations
in general, some readers may appreciate guidance on the
study of organisations. March (1965) is a compendious
review but it is now becoming dated. More recent, and
shorter, reviews are Perrow (1979) and Rose (1975). A
useful collection of articles can be found in Salaman
and Thompson (1973).

No references on the concept of power have been included
in this section. See Section D.4.

Albrow, M., (1973), 'The Study of Organisations:
    objectivity or bias?' in Salaman, G. and Thompson, K.
    (eds.) People and Organisations. London: Longmans.
Bell, D., (1976), The Coming of Post-Industrial
    Society. Harmondsworth: Penguin.
Benson, J.K., (1977), 'Organisations: a dialectical
    view', Administrative Science Quarterly (22): 1-21.
Birch, A. H., (1964), Representative and Responsible
    Government. London: Allen and Unwin.
Blackburn, R., (1972), 'The New Capitalism' in Blackburn
    R., (ed.) Ideology in Social Science. London:
    Fontana/Collins.
Brittan, S., (1975), 'The Economic Contradictions of
    Democracy', British Journal of Political Science (5):
    129-59.
Burns, T., (1974), 'On the rationale of the corporate
    system' in Marris, R. (ed.) The Corporate Society.
    London: Macmillan.
Cockburn, C., (1977), The Local State. London: Pluto
    Press.
Dearlove, J., (1979), The Reorganisation of British
    Local Government. London: Cambridge University Press.
Douglas, J., (1976), 'The Overloaded Crown', British
    Journal of Political Science (6) : 483-505.

Dunleavy, P., (1980) 'Theories of the State and Society
  and the Study of Central-Local Relations' in Jones, G.W.
  (ed.), Central-Local Relations in Britain Farnborough,
  Hants: Saxon House, 1980 (forthcoming).
Etzioni, A., (1968), The Active Society. New York:
  The Free Press.
Galbraith, J.K., (1972), The New Industrial State.
  London: Deutsch, second edn.
Galbraith, J.K., (1973), Economics and the Public Purpose
  Boston: Houghton Mifflin.
Grant, W.P. and Marsh, D., (1977), The C.B.I. London:
  Hodder and Stoughton.
Habermas, J., (1971), Towards a Rational Society.
  London: Heinemann.
Hague, D.C., Mackenzie, W.J.M., and Barker, A., (eds.),
  Public Policy and Private Interests: the Institutions
  of Compromise. London: Macmillan.
Hill, M.J., (1972), The Sociology of Public Admini-
  stration. London: Weidenfeld and Nicolson.
Jackson, J.A. (ed.), (1970), Professions and Profession-
  alisation. London: Cambridge University Press.
Jessop, R., (1979), 'Corporatism, Parliamentarism and
  Social Democracy' in Schmitter, P.C. and Lehmbruch, G.
  (eds.), Trends towards Corporatist Intermediation.
  London: Sage.
Jessop, R., (1980), 'The Transformation of the State in
  Postwar Britain' in Scase, R, (ed.), The State in
  Western Europe. London: Croom Helm.
Jones, G.W., (1977), Responsibility and Government.
  London: London School of Economics and Political
  Science.
King, A., (1975), 'Overload: Problems of Governing in
  the 1970s', Political Studies (23): 162-74.
La Porte, T.R., (ed.), (1974), Organised Social Complex-
  ity: challenge to Politics and Policy. Princeton. U.P.
March, J.G., (ed.), (1965), Handbook of Organisations.
  Chicago: Rand McNally.
Marris, R., (ed.), (1974), The Corporate Society London:
  Macmillan.
Marsh, D. and Grant, W.P., (1977), 'Tripartism: reality
  or myth?', Government and Opposition (12): 194-211.
Miliband, R., (1973), The State in Capitalist Society.
  London: Quartet.
Nichols, T., (1969), Ownership Control and Ideology.
  London: Allen and Unwin.
Perrow, C., (1979), Complex Organisations. Glenview,
  Ill.: Scott, Foresman, second edn.
Pickvance, C., (ed.), (1976), Urban Sociology: Critical
  Essays. London: Tavistock.
Poulantzas, N., (1973), Social Classes and Political
  Power. London: New Left Books.
Rose, M., (1975), Industrial Behaviour. Harmondsworth:
  Penguin.

Rose, R., (1978), 'Ungovernability: Is there Fire behind the Smoke?', Studies in Public Policy No. 16. Glasgow: University of Strathclyde.

Salaman, G. and Thompson, K. (eds.), (1973), People and Organisations. London: Longmans.

Sampson, A., (1974), The Sovereign State: the secret history of I.T.T. London: Coronet.

Saunders, P., (1980), Urban Politics: a sociological interpretation. Harmondsworth: Penguin Books.

Scase, R., (ed.), (1977), Industrial Society: Class, Cleavage, Control. London: Allen and Unwin.

Schmitter, P.C., (1974), 'Still the Century of Corporatism?', Review of Politics (36): 85-131.

Schmitter, P.C., and Lehmbruch, G. (eds.), (1979) Trends towards Corporatist Intermediation. London: Sage.

Smith, B.L.R., and Hague, D.C. (eds.), (1971), The Dilemma of Accountability in Modern Government. London: Macmillan.

Stanworth, P. and Giddens, A., (eds.), (1974), Elites and Power in British Society. London: Cambridge University Press.

Touraine, A., (1974), The Post-Industrial Society. London: Wildwood House.

Vickers, Sir G., (1972), Freedom in a Rocking Boat. Harmondsworth: Penguin.

Wilensky, H., (1964), 'The Professionalisation of Everyone', American Journal of Sociology (70): 137-58.

Winkler, J.T., (1976), 'Corporatism', European Journal of Sociology (17): 100-136.

Winkler, J.T., (1977), 'The Corporatist Economy: theory and administration', in Scase, R., (ed.), Industrial Society: Class, Cleavage Control. London: Allen and Unwin.

Winkler, J.T., (1975), 'Law, State, and Economy: The Industry Act 1975 in context', British Journal of Law and Society (2): 103-28.

Zeitlin, M., (1974), 'Corporate Ownership and Control: the large corporation and the capitalist class', American Journal of Sociology (79): 1073-1119.

Section B

METHODOLOGY

There is little point in providing yet another general
bibliography on methodology. This section has been
included to draw attention to two topics of particular
relevance to the argument of this book: the analysis of
networks and the study of values. On networks see
Mitchell (1969) and Laumann and Pappi (1976). For those
so inclined, a rigorous treatment of networks can be
found in Harray et al., (1965) and Doreian (1970), the
latter providing an introduction to the topic. Qualitative research methods are well described in Glaser and
Strauss (1967) and Bogdan and Taylor (1975). On the
specific topic of values or 'assumptive worlds' a number
of approaches are discussed in Young and Mills (1980) and
specific techniques are described in detail in Axelrod
(1976) and Putnam (1973). Finally, given that case
studies are frequently maligned, Geertz (1973) provides an
eloquent rationale for the 'theory-laden' case approach.

Axelrod, R., (ed.), (1976), Structure of Decision: the
   cognitive maps of political elites. Princeton N.J:
   Princeton University Press. esp. Chs. 3, 4, 10 and
   Appendix 1.
Barnes, J.A., (1969), 'Networks and Political Process'
   in Swartz, M.J. (ed.), Local-Level Politics. Chicago:
   Aldine-Atherton Publishing Co.
Boissevain, J. and Mitchell, J.C., (1973), Network
   Analysis: Studies in Human Interaction. The Hague:
   Mouton.
Bogdan, R. and Taylor, S. (1975), Introduction to
   Qualitative Research Methods. New York: Wiley.
Crozier, M., (1972), 'The Relationship Between Micro and
   Macro Sociology', Human Relations (25): 239-51.
Doreian, P., (1970), Mathematics and the Study of Social
   Relations. London: Weidenfeld and Nicolson.
Geertz, C., (1973), The Interpretation of Culture . New
   York: Basic Books.
Glaser, B.G. and Strauss, A.L., (1967), The Discovery of
   Grounded Theory: Strategies for Qualitative Research.
   Chicago: Aldine Pub. Co.
Harray, F., Norman, R., and Cartwright, D., (1965),
   Structural Models: an introduction to the theory of
   graphs. New York: J. Wiley & Sons.
Mitchell, J.C., (1969), 'The Concept and the Use of
   Social Networks', in Mitchell, J.C. (ed.), Social Net-
   works in Urban Situations. Manchester: Manchester
   University Press.
Laumann, E.O. and Pappi, F.U., (1976), Networks of
   Collective Action. New York: Academic Press.
Putnam, R.D., (1973), The Beliefs of Politicians:
   ideology, conflict and democracy in Britain and Italy.
   New Haven: Yale U.P.
Young, K. and Mills, L., (1980), Understanding the

'Assumptive Worlds' of Governmental Actors: Issues
and Approaches. London: SSRC.

Section C

INTERORGANISATIONAL ANALYSIS

Chapter 3 provides a detailed review of the literature on
interorganisational analysis. This section of the bibliography provides some additional references on the topic
but it will not repeat the earlier discussion. As noted
already, the seminal contribution is that of Thompson
(1967). The preoccupation with the measurement and
classification of exchanges is well illustrated in the
pages of the Administrative Science Quarterly. It is
probably still true to say that scarcely an issue goes
by without at least one article offering either a refinement of the theory or an empirical investigation of the
effect of the environment on organisations. Amidst the
welter of correlation coefficients, the work of Child
(1973), Crozier and Thoenig (1976) and Crozier and
Friedberg (1977) are important reminders that we are
making inferences about the way members of organisations
make choices. The past year has seen a number of
contributions which are critical of the deterministic
conception of the link between organisations and their
environment(s). An early, trenchant, critique was Benson
(1975) but he has now been joined by Aldrich (1979) Meyer
(1978) and Pfeffer and Salancik (1978). Due to their late
arrival on the scene, it has not been possible to discuss
these last three contributions in the text.

Aiken, M. and Hage, J., (1968), 'Organisational Inter-
    dependence and Intra-organisational structure',
    American Sociological Review (33): 912-30.
Aldrich, H.E., (1976), 'Resource Dependence and Inter-
    organisational Relations Between Local Employment
    Service Offices and Social Services Sector Organisations',
    Administration and Society (7): 419-54.
Aldrich, H.E. and Mindlin, S., (1978), 'Uncertainty and
    Dependence: two perspectives on environment', in
    Karpick, L., (ed.), Organisation and Environment:
    theory, issues and reality. London: Sage.
Aldrich,H.E., and Pfeffer, J., (1976), 'Environments of
    Organisations', in Inkeles, A., (ed.), Annual Review of
    Sociology, Vol.II. Palo Alto, California: Annual
    Reviews Inc.
Aldrich, H.E. (1979), Organisations and Environments.
    Englewood Cliff, N.J.: Prentice Hall.
Benson, J.K., (1975), 'The Interorganisational Network
    as a Political Economy', Administrative Science
    Quarterly (20): 229-49.
Blau, P.M. and Scott, W.R., (1963), Formal Organisations.
    London: Routledge and Kegan Paul.
Blau, P.M. and Schoenherr, R.A., (1971), The
    Structure of Organisations. New York: Basic Books.

Child, J., 'Organisational Structure, Environment and
  Performance: the role of strategic choice', in
  Salaman, G., and Thompson, K. (eds.), People and
  Organisations. London: Longmans.
Crozier, M., (1964), The Bureaucratic Phenomenon.
  Chicago: Chicago University Press.
Crozier, M., (1974), The Stalled Society. New York:
  Viking Press.
Crozier, M., and Friedberg, E., (1977), L'acteur et le
  système. Paris: Ed. du Seuil.
Crozier, M., and Thoenig, J-C, (1976), 'The Regulation
  of Complex Organised Systems', Administrative Science
  Quarterly (21): 547-70.
Elkin, S.L. (1975), 'Comparative Urban Politics and
  Interorganisational Networks', in Young, K. (ed.),
  Essays on the Study of Urban Politics. London:
  Macmillan.
Emery, F.E., and Trist, E.L., (1965), 'The Causal
  Texture of Organisational Environments', in Human
  Relations (18): 21-32.
Emery, F.E., and Trist, E.L., (1960), 'Socio-technical
  systems', in Churchman, C.W. and Verhulst, V., (eds.),
  Management Science: Models and Techniques. Oxford:
  Pergamon Press.
Etzioni, A., (ed.), (1969), A Sociological Reader on
  Complex Organisations. New York: Holt, Rinehart,
  second edn.
Evan, W.M., (1966), 'The Organisation-Set: toward a
  theory of interorganisational relations', in Thompson,
  J.D., (ed.), Approaches to Organisational Design.
  Pittsburgh: University of Pittsburgh Press.
Evan, W.M., (1972), 'An Organisation-set Model of
  Interorganisational Relations', in Tuite, M.F. et al.
  (eds.), Interorganisational Decision Making Chicago:
  Aldine Publishing Co.
Evan, W.M., (ed.), (1976), Interorganisational
  Relations. Harmondsworth: Penguin.
Friend, J.K., Power, J.M. and Yewlett, C.J.L., (1974)
  Public Planning: the intercorporate dimension. London:
  Tavistock.
Friend, J.K., (1976), 'Planners, Policies and Operation-
  al Boundaries: some recent developments in Britain',
  Policy and Politics (5): 25-44.
Friend, J.K., (1977), 'The Dynamics of Policy Change',
  Long Range Planning (10): 40-47.
Hanf, K. and Scharpf, F.W., (eds.), (1978), Inter-
  organisational Policy Making. London: Sage Publications
Harris, R.J.P. and Scott, D.J., (1974), 'Perspectives on
  Multi-Organisational Design', Local Government Studies
  No. 8 : 31-46.
Harris, R.J.P., (1976), 'Inter-Authority Decision Making:
  some implications for Local Government', Local Govern-
  ment Studies (2): No. 3. 17-26.
Hirsch, P., (1972), 'Processing Fads and Fashions: an
  organisation set analysis of cultural industry systems',
  American Journal of Sociology (77): 139-59.

Hirsch, P., (1975), 'Organisational Effectiveness and the Institutional Environment', <u>Administrative Science Quarterly</u> (20): 327-44.

Hood, C.C., (1976), <u>The Limits to Administration</u>. London: Wiley.

Jacobs, D. (1974), 'Dependency and Vulnerability: an exchange approach to the control of organisations', <u>Administrative Science Quarterly</u> (19): 45-59.

Jurkovich, R., (1974), 'A Core Typology of Organisation Environments', <u>Administrative Science Quarterly</u> (19): 380-394.

Karpik, L., (ed.), (1978), <u>Organisation and Environment: theory, issues and reality</u>. London: Sage.

Katz, D. and Kahn, R.L., (1966), <u>The Social Psychology of Organisations</u>. New York: Wiley.

Klonglan, G.E., Warren, R.D., Winkelpleck, J.M. and Paulson, S.K., (1976), 'Interorganisational Measurement in the Social Service Sector: differences by hierarchical level', <u>Administrative Science Quarterly</u> (21): 675-87.

Laumann, E.O., and Pappi, F.U., (1976), <u>Networks of Collective Action</u>. Academic Press.

Lawrence, P.R. and Lorsch, J.W., (1967), <u>Organisation and Environment</u>. Boston: Graduate School of Business Administration, Harvard University.

Levine, S. and White, P.E., (1961), 'Exchange as a Conceptual Framework for the Study of Interorganisational Relationships'. <u>Administrative Science Quarterly</u> (5): 583-601.

Litwak, W. and Hylton, L.F., (1962), 'Interorganisational Analysis: a hypothesis on coordinating agencies', <u>Administrative Science Quarterly</u> (6): 395-415.

Meyer, M, and associates, (1978), <u>Environment and Organisations: Theoretical and Empirical Perspectives</u>. San Francisco: Jossey-Bass.

Mindlin, S.E. and Aldrich, H., (1975), 'Interorganisational Dependence: a Review of the Concept and a Re-examination of the findings of the Aston Group', <u>Administrative Science Quarterly</u> (70): 382-92.

Neghandi, A.R., (ed.), (1972), <u>Organisation Theory in an Inter-organisational Perspective</u>. Ohio: Kent State University: Centre for Business and Economic Research.

Neghandi, A.R., (ed.), (1975), <u>Interorganisational Theory</u>. Ohio: Kent State University Press.

Perrow, C., (1970), <u>Organisational Analysis</u>. London: Tavistock.

Perrow, C., (1979), <u>Complex Organisations</u>. Glenview, Ill: Scott, Foresman, second edn.

Pfeffer, J. and Leblebici, H., (1973), 'Executive Recruitment and the Development of Interfirm Organisations', <u>Administrative Science Quarterly</u> (18): 449-61.

Peffer, J. and Salancik, G.R., (1978), <u>The External Control of Organisations</u>. London: Harper and Row.

Pondy, C.R., (1967), 'Organisational Conflict: Concepts and Models', Administrative Science Quarterly (12); 296-320.

Pugh, D.S. and Hickson, D.J., (1973), 'The Comparative Study of Organisations', in Salaman, G. and Thompson (eds.), People and Organisations. London: Longmans.

Pugh, D.S. and Hickson, D.J., (1976), Organisational Structure in its Context: the Aston Programme I. Farnborough, Hants: Saxon House.

Pugh, D.S. and Hinings, C.R., (1976), Organisational Structure: Extensions and Replications. The Aston Programme II. Farnborough, Hants.: Saxon House.

Pressman, J. and Wildavsky, A., (1973), Implementation. Berkeley, California: University of California Press.

Randall, R., (1973), 'Influence of Environmental Support and Policy Space on Organisational Behaviour', Administrative Science Quarterly (18): 236-47.

Rushing, W.A., and Zald, M.N., (eds.), (1976), Organisations and Beyond: selected essays of James D. Thompson. Lexington, Mass.: Lexington Books.

Samuels, R.J., (1978), 'Extra-Local Linkages and the Comparative Study of Local Politics", Comparative Urban Research (5): 24-43.

Scharpf, F.W., (1978), 'Intergovernmental Policy Studies: Isses, Concepts and Perspectives', in Hanf, K, and Scharpf, F.W., (eds.), Interorganisational Policy Making London: Sage.

Schon, D., (1971), Beyond the Stable State. London: Temple Smith.

Selznick, P., (1948), 'Foundations of the Theory of Organisations', American Sociological Review (13): 25-35.

Selznick, P., (1966), TVA and the Grass Roots. Berkeley and Los Angeles: University of California Press.

Stinchcombe, A.L., (1965), 'Social Structure and Organisations', in March, J.G., (ed.), Handbook of Organisations. Chicago: Rand McNally.

Stringer, J., (1967), 'Operational Research for Multi-Organisations', Operational Research Quarterly (18): 105-20.

Terreberry, S., (1968), 'The Evolution of Organisational Environments', Administrative Science Quarterly (12): 590-613.

Thompson, J.D. and McEwen, I., (1958), 'Organisational Goals and Environment: Goal-setting as an Interaction Process', American Sociological Review (23): 23-31.

Thompson, J.D., (1967), Organisations in Action. New York: McGraw Hill.

Tuite, M. Chisholm, R. and Radnor, M, (1972), Inter-organisational Decision Making. Chicago: Aldine Pub.Co.

Turk, H., (1970), 'Interorganisational Networks in Urban Society', American Sociological Review (35): 1-19.

Turk, H., (1973), 'Comparative Urban Structure from an Interorganisational perspective', Administrative Science Quarterly (18): 37-55.

Turk, H., (1977), Organisations in Modern Life. San Francisco: Jossey-Bass.

Wamsley, G. and Zald, M.N., (1973), 'The Political Economy of Public Organisations', Public Administration Review (33): 62-73.

Wamsley. G., and Zald, M.N., (1973), The Political Economy of Public Organisations. New York: Praeger.

Warren, R.L., (1967), 'The Interorganisational Field as a Focus for Investigation', Administrative Science Quarterly (12): 396-419.

Warren, R.L., Rose, S.M., and Bergunder, A.F., (1974), The Structure of Urban Reform: community decision organisations in stability and change. Lexington: D.C. Heath.

Section D

ORGANISATIONAL POLITICS

This section of the bibliography covers organisational politics in general as well as specific concepts important in the analysis of this aspect of organisations: namely, games, goals and power.

The study of organisational politics has been fragment-ary. Although there have been a number of reseach reports over the years, they have not been seen as a body of literature and, until recently, there have been no attempts to develop systematic analyses of the phenomenon. Some of the earlier contributions are reviewed in Rhodes (1980) and the work of Burns (1961, 1966) and Crozier (1963) remains amongst the best available. More recent work is critically reviewed in Clegg (1975) and Fox (1973). A number of studies by political scientists have covered the same kind of ground, although not in all cases with any awareness of the work on organisations. The examples include Allison (1971), Danziger (1978), Kaufman (1960), Meltsner (1976), Seidman (1970), and Wildavsky (1964 and 1975). A conscious attempt to blend the two disciplines is made in Greenwood et al., (1977) and Ranson et al., (1980).

Although the 'Introduction' to this bibliography promised no comic relief, some amusement can be found in the literature on 'games'. Berne (1968), Cornford (1949) and Potter (1947) both instruct and entertain. Drama is provided by Snow (1972 and 1977). In a more analytical vein, Crozier and Friedberg (1977), Crozier (1976), Bailey (1969) and Bardach (1977) all use the 'game' analogy to describe and analyse political processes. Finally, and most rigorously, there is the extensive literature on game theory. A good introduction is provided by Luce and Raiffa (1958) and the application of game theory to the sociology of organisations is discussed in Peaucelle (1969).

Given the central importance of 'goals' to the analysis of organisations, the literature on the topic is disa-ppointing. Good reviews of the field, such as it is, can be found in Etzioni (1960), Gross (1969) and Mohr (1973). The 'Carnegie School' approach to goals, with its emphasis on coalition behaviour, can be best approached by reading the originals: Cyert and March (1963), Simon (1964) and Thompson (1967). The organisational goals literature needs to be supplemented by an examination of 'action theory'. See for example: Silverman (1970). This perspective has found a toehold in political science and useful contributions have been made by Vickers (1969) and Young (1977).

The literature on 'power' is voluminous. A useful collection of papers on power in Britain (along with additional references) can be found in Urry and Wakeford (1973) and a selection of theoretical papers can be found in Bell et al., (1969). The references provided here include the 'classics' - e.g. Dahl (1957), Blau (1964), Parsons (1967);and a sample of the literature on power in organisations - e.g. Cartwright (1959), French and Raven (1968), Kahn and Boulding (1964) and Perrow (1970). Of particular importance, however, are those papers which focus on the mobilisation of bias. See: Bachrach and Baratz (1962, 1963 and 1970). Their contribution has been criticised from a variety of standpoints and a comparison of the arguments in Clegg (1975), Lukes (1974), Parry and Morriss (1974) and Polsby (1979) is instructive. Finally, there has been a marked resurgence of interest in organisational power and the nature of this revival can be judged from a reading of Blau (1974), Clegg (1979), and McNeil (1978).

Section D.1

GENERAL

Albrow, M., (1970), Bureaucracy. London: Macmillan.
Allison, G., (1971), Essence of Decision. Boston.
Little, Brown.
Bailey, F.G., (1977), Morality and Expediency. Oxford:
Blackwell.
Burns, T., and Stalker, G.M., (1961), The Management of
Innovation. London: Tavistock.
Burns, T., (1961-2), 'Micropolitics: Mechanisms of
Institutional Change', Administrative Science Quarterly
(6): 257-81.
Burns, T., (1966), 'On the Plurality of Social Systems'
in Lawrence, J.R. (ed.), Operational Research and the
Social Sciences. London: Tavistock.
Burns, T., (1967), 'The Comparative Study of Organis-
ations' in Vroom, V.H., (ed.), Methods of Organis-
ational Research. Pittsburgh: University of
Pittsburgh Press.
Burns, T., (1969), (ed.), Industrial Man.
Harmondsworth: Penguin.
Burns, T., (1977), The B.B.C.: Public Institution and
Private World. London: Macmillan.
Chandler, A., (1962), Strategy and Structure. Cambridge,
Mass.: The MIT Press.
Child, J., (1973), 'Organisation Structure, Environment
and Performance: the role of strategic choice', in
Salaman, G., and Thompson, K., (eds.), People and
Organisations. London: Allen and Unwin.
Cohen, M.D., March, J.G. and Olsen, J.P., (1972), 'A
G. ʳ ɪge Can Model of Organisational Choice',
Administrative Science Quarterly (17): 1-25.
Crozier, M., (1964), The Bureaucratic Phenomenon.
Chicago: University of Chicago Press.
Cyert, R.M. and March, J.G., (1963), A Behavioural
Theory of the Firm. Englewood Cliff, N.J.: Prentice
Hall.
Dalton, M., (1959), Men Who Manage. New York: J. Wiley
and Sons.
Danziger, J.N., (1978), Making Budgets. London: Sage.
Etzioni, A., (1975), A Comparative Analysis of Complex
Organisations. New York: Free Press, second edn.
Fox, A., (1973), 'Industrial Relations: a social
critique of pluralist ideology', in Child, J. (ed.)
Man and Organisation. London: Allen and Unwin.
Gawthrop, L.C., (1969), Bureaucratic Behaviour in the
Executive Branch. New York: Free Press.
Gouldner, A., (1954), Patterns of Industrial Bureau-
cracy. New York: Free Press.
Gouldner, A.W., (1955), 'Metaphysical Pathos and the
Theory of Bureaucracy', American Political Science
Review (49): 496-507.

Greenwood, R., Hinings, C.R. and Ranson, S., (1977), 'The Politics of the Budgetary Process in English Local Government', Political Studies (25): 25-47.

Hickson, D.J.,Hinings,C.R., Lee, C.A., Schneck, R.E., and Pennings, J.M., (1971), 'A Strategic Contingencies' Theory of Intraorganisational Power', Administrative Science Quarterly (16): 216-29.

Hinings, C.R., Hickson, D.J., Pennings, J.M. and Schneck, R.E., (1974), 'Structural Conditions of Intra-organisational Power', Administrative Science Quarterly (19): 22-44.

Hofstede, G. and Kassem, M.S. (eds.), (1976), European Contribution to Organisation Theory. Assen/Amsterdam. Van Gorcum.

Kaufman, H., (1960), The Forest Ranger. Baltimore, Maryland: The John Hopkins Press.

Lawrence, P.R. and Lorsch, J.W., (1967), Organisation and Environment. Boston: Graduate School of Business, Harvard University.

March, J.G., (1962), 'The Business Firm as a Political Coalition', Journal of Politics (24): 662-78.

March, J.G. and Simon, H.A. (1958), Organizations. New York: Wiley.

Mechanic, D., (1962), 'Sources of Power of Lower Participants in Complex Organisations', Administrative Science Quarterly (7): 349-364.

Meltsner, A., (1976), Policy Analysts in the Bureaucracy. Los Angeles and Berkeley: University of California Press.

Perrow, C., (1972), Complex Organisations. Glenview, Ill.: Scott, Foresman, first edn.

Pettigrew, A.M., (1973), The Politics of Organisational Decision-making. London: Tavistock.

Pettigrew, A.M., (1975), 'Towards a Political Theory of Organisational Intervention', Human Relations (28): 191-208.

Ranson, S., Hinings, C.R. and Greenwood, R., (1980), 'The Structuring of Organisational Structures' Administrative Science Quarterly (25): 1-17.

Rhodes, R.A.W., (1980), 'Organisational Politics' in Brown, M. and Muir, L., (eds.), Social Work: a theory and practice text. London: Macdonald and Evans, forthcoming.

Seidman, H., (1970), Politics, Position and Power. London: Oxford University Press.

Self, P., (1972), Administrative Theories and Politics London: Allen and Unwin.

Selznick, P., (1966), TVA and Grass Roots. Berkeley and Los Angeles: University of California Press.

Silverman, D., (1970), The Theory of Organisations. London: Heinemann.

Silverman, D. and Jones, J., (1976), Organisational Work London: Macmillan.

Simon, H.A., (1957), Administrative Behaviour. New York: Free Press, 2nd edn.

Simon, H.A., (1960), The New Science of Management Decision. New York: Harper and Row.

Strauss, A., Schatzmman, L., et al., (1963), 'The Hospital and its Negotiated Order', in Friedson, E., (ed.), The Hospital in Modern Society. New York: Macmillan.

Tivey, L., (1978), The Politics of the Firm. London: Martin Robertson.

Weick, K.E., (1979), The Social Psychology of Organising Reading, Mass.: Addison-Wesley, second edn.

Wildavsky, A., (1964), The Politics of the Budgetary Process. Boston: Little, Brown.

Wildavsky, A., (1975), Budgeting. Boston: Little, Brown.

Section D.2.

GAMES

Bailey, F.G., (1965), 'Decisions by Consensus in Councils and Committees' in Barton, M. (ed.), Political Systems and the Distribution of Power. London: Tavistock, ASA Monographs, No. 2.

Bailey, F.G., (1969), Strategems and Spoils. Oxford: Blackwell.

Bardach, E., (1977), The Implementation Game. Cambridge, Mass.: The MIT Press.

Bennet, J.W., (1967), 'Microcosm-Macrocosm Relationships in North American Agrarian Society', American Anthropologist (69): 441-454.

Berne, E., (1968), Games People Play. Harmondsworth: Penguin Books.

Cornford, F.M., (1949), Microscosmographica Academica. Cambridge: Bowes and Bowes.

Crozier, M., (1976), 'Comparing Structures and Comparing Games', in Hofstede, G. and Kassem, M.S. (eds.), European Contributions to Organisation Theory. Assen/Amsterdam: Van Gorcum.

Crozier, M., and Friedberg, E., (1977), L'Acteur et le Système. Paris: Ed. du Seuil.

Goffman, E., (1970), Strategic Interaction. Oxford: Blackwell.

Huizinga, J.H., (1970), Homo Ludens: a study of the play element in Culture. London: M.T. Smith.

Long, N.E., (1958), 'The Local Community as an Ecology of Games', American Journal of Sociology (64): 251-261.

Luce, R.D., and Raiffa, H., (1958), Games and Decisions. New York: Wiley.

Mackenzie, W.J.M., (1967), Politics and Social Science Harmondsworth: Penguin.

Peaucelle, J.L., (1969), 'Théories des jeux et sociologie des organisations', Sociologie du Travail (49): 22-43.

Potter, S., (1947), Theory and Practice of Gamesmanship. London: Rupert Hart Davies.

Rapoport, A., (1961), Fights Games and Debates. Ann
Arbour: The University of Michigan Press.
Schelling, T.C., (1960), The Strategy of Conflict.
Cambridge, Mass.: Harvard University Press.
Snow, C.P., (1972), The Corridors of Power.
Harmondsworth: Penguin.
Snow, C.P., (1977), The Masters. Harmondsworth:
Penguin.

Section D.3.

GOALS

Cyert, R.M., and March, J.G. (1963), A Behavioural
Theory of the Firm. Englewood Cliffs, N.J.: Prentice
Hall.
Etzioni, A., (1964), Modern Organisations. Englewood
Cliffs, N.J.: Prentice Hall.
Etzioni, A., (1960), 'Two approaches to Organisational
Analysis: a critique and a suggestion',
Administrative Science Quarterly (5): 257-78.
Gross, E., (1969), 'The Definition of Organisational
Goals', British Journal of Sociology (20): 277-94.
Mohr, L.B., (1973), 'The Concept of Organisational Goal',
American Political Science Review (67): 470-81.
Perrow, C., (1961), 'The Analysis of Goals in Complex
Organisations', American Sociological Review (26):
854-66.
Perrow, C., (1970), Organisational Analysis. London:
Tavistock.
Simon, H.A., (1964), 'On the Concept of Organisational
Goal', Administrative Science Quarterly (9): 1-22.
Silverman, D., (1970), The Theory of Organisations.
London: Heinemann.
Thompson, J.D., (1967), Organisations in Action. New
York: McGraw Hill.
Vickers, G. Sir, (1969), The Art of Judgement. London:
Methuen.
Vickers, G. Sir, (1970), Value Systems and Social
Processes. Harmondsworth: Penguin.
Young, K., (1977), 'Values in the Policy Process',
Policy and Politics (5): 1-22.
Yuchtman, E., and Seashore, S.E., (1967), 'A System
Resource Approach to Organisational Effectiveness',
American Sociological Review (32): 891-903.

Section D.4

POWER

Bachrach, P. and Baratz, M.S., (1962), 'Two Faces of
Power', American Political Science Review (56): 947-52.
Bachrach, P. and Baratz, M.S., (1963), 'Decisions and Non-
Decisions: An Analytical framework', American Politi-
cal Science Review (57): 632-42.

Bachrach, P. and Baratz, M.S., (1970), Power and Poverty: Theory and Practice. New York: Oxford University Press.

Barry, B.M., (ed.), (1976), Power and Political Theory. New York: Wiley.

Bell, R., Edwards, D.V. and Wagner, R.H., (eds.), (1969), Political Power: a reader in theory and research. New York: The Free Press.

Birnbaum, P., (1976), 'Power Divorced from its sources: a critique of the exchange theory of power', in Barry, B., (ed.), Power and Political Theory. London: Wiley.

Blau, P.M., (1964), Exchange and Power in Social Life. New York: Wiley.

Blau, P.M., (1974), 'Parameters of Social Structure', American Sociological Review (39): 615-35.

Cartwright, D., (ed.), (1959), Studies in Social Power. Ann Arbor: University of Michigan.

Clegg, S., (1975), Power, Rule and Domination. London: Routledge and Kegan Paul.

Clegg, S., (1979), The Theory of Power and Organisation. Routledge and Kegan Paul.

Crenson, M.A., (1971), The Un-Politics of Air Pollution: A Study of Non-Decision Making in the Cities. Baltimore: John Hopkins Press.

Crozier, M., (1973), 'The Problem of Power', Social Research (40): 211-28.

Dahl, R.A., (1957), 'The Concept of Power', Behavioural Science (2): 201-15.

Emerson, R.M., (1962), 'Power-Dependence Relations', American Sociological Review (27): 31-41.

French, J.R.P. and Raven, B., (1968), 'The Bases of Social Power' in Cartwright, D. and Zander, A., (eds.), Group Dynamics. London: Tavistock.

Galbraith, J.K., (1963), American Capitalism: the concept of counterveiling power. Harmondsworth: Penguin.

Kahn, R.L., and Boulding, K., (1964), Power and Conflict in Organisations. London: Tavistock.

Lukes, S., (1974), Power, A Radical View. London: Macmillan.

McCoy, C.A., and Playford, J., (eds.), (1967), Apolitical Politics. New York: Thomas Y. Crowell.

McNeil, K., (1978), 'Understanding Organisational Power: Building on the Weberian Legacy', Administrative Science Quarterly (23): 65-90.

Martin, R., (1977), The Sociology of Power. London: Routledge and Kegan Paul.

Parry, G. and Morriss, P., (1974), 'When is a Decision not a Decision?' in Crewe, I., (ed.), British Political Sociology Yearbook, Vol. I, Elites in Western Democracy. London: Croom Helm.

Parsons, T., (1967), 'On the Concept of Political Power', in Parsons, T., Sociological Theory and Modern Society. New York: The Free Press.

Perrow, C., (1970), 'Departmental Power and Perspectives in Industrial Firms', in Zald, M.N., (ed.), Power in Organisations. Nashville: Vandebilt University Press.

Pettigrew, A.M., (1972), 'Information Control as a Power Resource', Sociology (6): 187-204.

Polsby, N., (1979), 'Empirical Investigations of Mobilisation of Bias in Community Power Research', Political Studies (37): 527-41.

Urry, J., and Wakeford, J. (eds.), (1973), Power in Britain. London: Heinemann.

Section E

INTERGOVERNMENTAL RELATIONS

The review of the literature on intergovernmental
relations (IGR) in Chapter 4 only covered developed
countries and focused primarily on the Federal Republic
of Germany, France and the United States of America.
This section of the bibliography is similarly confined in
scope.

The general section focuses on the concepts of federalism, decentralisation and IGR. The concept of federalism
is reviewed in Birch (1966), Sawyer (1969) and Vile (1973).
The concept of decentralisation is reviewed in Fesler
(1949 and 1965), Maass (1959) and Dupré (1969). The concept of intergovernmental relations is reviewed in
Wright (1974) and Anderson (1960). All of these books
and articles provide a wealth of additional citations.
In addition, this section includes comparative studies of
the various types of IGR - see for example: Birch (1955),
Carnell (1961), May (1969) and Wheare (1946) - as well as
descriptions of systems not covered in the following
sections - see for example: Sbragia (1979) and Simeon
(1972). The problems of comparison are discussed in
Clark (1974), Daland (1969) and Ashford (1976). Finally,
the comparative study of local government (especially the
use of financial indicators) is discussed in Ashford
(1975), Davey (1971), IULA (1955), Marshall (1969),
Sherwood (1969) and Walsh (1969). Additional citations can
be found in Rhodes (1980) and Walsh (1969).

The section of this bibliography on the Federal Republic
of Germany overlaps with the discussion of Scharpf's work
in Chapter 3 and the citations in section D.1. A detailed
commentary is not necessary, therefore. Those readers unfamiliar with the Federal Republic of Germany will find
Johnson (1973b) an excellent introduction. The
administrative problems of the Federal Republic are discussed in Mayntz and Scharpf (1975).

The discussion of intergovernmental relations in France
in Chapter 3 focused on the work of Crozier and Thoenig.
This section of the bibliography provides a number of
additional references, most notably Gremion (1969 and
1970), Gremion and Worms (1970), Worms (1966) and
Kesselman (1967). For the reader unfamiliar with French
local government a useful, but out-of-date, introduction
is Chapman (1953). This account will need to be read in
conjunction with Machin (1977) and Wright (1978). The
sections of the bibliography on France and the Federal
Republic of Germany both emphasise the parallels between
the interorganisational analysis and the intergovernmental relations literatures.

As many readers will realise, the discussion of IGR in
this book draws heavily on American experience. The
amount of work on American federalism is of truly
terrifying proportions. An invaluable bibliography is
provided by Wright and Peddicord (1975) and the publications of the Advisory Commission on Intergovernmental
Relations are an excellent source of statistical data.
The journal Publius reviews most publications on
federalism when they appear as well as providing many useful articles. Perhaps the best introduction is Wright
(1978): it is certainly one of the most up-to-date. In
the remainder of this section, I have simply listed those
items which were of the greatest help in writing Chapter
4. Of these books and articles, Beer (1978), Reagan
(1972), Landau (1969) and Sundquist (1969) are especially
noteworthy.

Finally, the European Communities have prompted much
theorising about the processes of integration and bargaining. These theories are reviewed in Pentland (1973) and
Hodges (1972) contains a useful selection of articles and
extracts from books. The policy-making processes of the
European Communities, and the consequent interactions of
national governments and of national governments and
supra-national institutions are analysed in Coombes (1970),
Lindberg (1963),Lindberg and Scheingold (1970) and
Wallace et al., (1977). For British readers Cosgrove
(1970) provides a useful bibliography.

Section E.1

GENERAL

Ashford, D.E., (1975), 'Theories of Local Government: some comparative considerations', Comparative Political Studies (8): 90-107.

Ashford, D.E., (1976), Democracy, Decentralisation and Decisions in Subnational Politics, Sage Professional Papers in Comparative Politics Vol. 5, Series No. 01-059, London: Sage.

Ashford, D.E., (1978), 'Territorial Politics and Resource Allocation: The Politics of Transfers or While You Are Up Get Me a Grant', European Studies Newsletter (8) No. 2 November: 1-10.

Ashford, D.E., (1979), 'Territorial Politics and Equality: Decentralisation in the Modern State', Political Studies (27): 71-83.

Anderson, W., (1960), Intergovernmental Relations in Review. Minneapolis: University of Minnesota Press.

Birch, A.H., (1955), Federalism, Finance and Social Legislation. Oxford: The Clarendon Press.

Birch, A.H., (1966), 'Approaches to the Study of Federalism', Political Studies (14): 15-33.

Carnell, F.G., (1961), 'Political Implications of Federalism in New States', in Hicks, U.K. et al., Federalism and Economic Growth in Undeveloped Countries. London: Allen and Unwin.

Clark, T.N., (1974), 'Community Autonomy in the National System: Federalism, Localism and Decentralization' in Clark, T.N. (ed.), Comparative Community Politics. New York: Halsted Press.

Daland, R.T., (1969), 'Comparative Perspectives and Urban Systems', in Daland, R.T., (ed.), Comparative Urban Research. Beverley Hills, California: Sage Publications.

Davey, F.J., (1971), 'Local Autonomy and Independent Revenue', Public Administration (49): 45-50.

Dupré, J. Stefan, (1969), 'Intergovernmental Relations and the Metropolitan Area' in Feldman, L.D. and Goldrick, M.D. (eds.), The Politics and Government of Urban Canada. London: Methuen.

Fesler, J.W., (1949), Area and Administration. Alabama: University of Alabama Press.

Fesler, J.W., (1965), 'Approaches to the understanding of decentralisation', Journal of Politics (27): 536-566.

Fried, R.C., (1963), The Italian Prefects. New Haven: Yale University Press.

International Union of Local Authorities, (1955), Local Government Finance and its Importance for Local Autonomy. The Hague: IULA.

Livingston , W.S., (1956), Federalism and Constitutional Change. London: Oxford University Press.

Maass, A., (ed.), (1959), Area and Power. Glencoe, Ill.: Free Press.

Marshall, A.H., (1969), Local Government Finance.
  The Hague: I.U.L.A.
May, R.J., (1973), 'Decision-Making and Stability in
  Federal Systems', Canadian Journal of Political Science
  (3): 73-87.
May, R.J., (1969), Federalism and Fiscal Adjustment.
  London: Oxford University Press.
Rhodes, R.A.W., (1980), 'Developing Countries', in
  Rowat, D.C., (ed.), International Handbook on Local
  Government Organisation. Westport: Greenwood Press.
Riker, W., (1969), 'Six Books in Search of a Subject or
  Does Federalism Exist and Does It Matter?', Comparative
  Politics (2): 135-46.
Sawyer, G., (1969), Modern Federalism. London: C.A.
  Watts.
Sbragia, A., (1979), 'Not All Roads Lead to Rome: Local
  Housing Policy in the Unitary Italian State',
  British Journal of Political Science (9): 315-39.
Sherwood, F.P., (1969), 'Devolution as a Problem of
  Organisation Strategy', in Daland, R.T., (ed.),
  Comparative Urban Research. Beverley Hills, California:
  Sage Publications.
Simeon, R., (1972), Federal-Provincial Diplomacy:
  the making of recent policy in Canada. Toronto:
  University of Toronto Press.
Vile, M.J.C., (1973), Federalism in the United States,
  Canada and Australia. London: H.M.S.O. (Research
  Paper No. 2 to the Commission on the Constitution
  (Kilbrandon)).
Walsh, A.H., (1969), The Urban Challenge to Government.
  New York: Praeger.
Wheare, K.C., (1946), Federal Government. London:
  Oxford University Press.
Wright, D.S. (1974), 'Intergovernmental Relations: an
  analytical overview', Annals of the American Academy
  of Political and Social Science (416): 1-16.

Section E.2.

FEDERAL REPUBLIC OF GERMANY

Hanf, K. and Scharpf, F.W., (eds.), (1978), Inter-
  organisational Policy Making. London: Sage Publi-
  cations.
Johnson, N., (1973a), Federalism and Decentralisation
  in the Federal Republic of Germany. London: H.M.S.O.
  (Research Report No. 1 to the Commission on the
  Constitution (Kilbrandon)).
Johnson, N., (1973b), Government in the Federal
  Republic of Germany. Oxford: Pergamon Press.
Mayntz, R., and Scharpf, F.W., (1975), Policy-Making in
  the German Federal Bureaucracy. Amsterdam: Elsevier.

158

Merkl, P.H., (1959), 'Executive- Legislative Federalism in West Germany', American Political Science Review (53) 732-41.

Scharpf, F.W., (1977), 'Public Organisation and the Waning of the Welfare State', European Journal of Political Research (5): 339-62.

Scharpf, F.W., Reissert, B., and Schnabel, F., (1976), Politikverflechtung. Kronberg: Scriptor.

Scharpf, F.W., Reissert, B. and Schnabel, F., (1978), 'Policy Effectiveness and Conflict Avoidance in Inter-governmental Policy Formation', in Hanf, K. and Scharpf, F.W., (eds.), Interorganisational Policy Making. London: Sage.

Section E.3.

FRANCE

Becquart-Leclerq, J., (1978), 'Relational Power and Systemic Articulation in French Local Polity', in Karpik, L. (ed.), Organisation and Environment: theory, issues and reality. London: Sage.

Chapman, B., (1953), Introduction to French Local Government. London: Allen and Unwin.

Crozier, M., and Thoenig, J-C., (1976), 'The Regulation of Complex Organised Systems', Administrative Science Quarterly (21): 547-70.

Crozier, M. and Friedberg, E., (1977), L'Acteur et Le Système. Paris: Ed. du Seuil.

Dupuy, F., and Thoenig, J.C., (1979), 'Public Trans-portation Policy Making in France as an Implementation Problem', Policy Sciences (11): 1-18.

Grémion, P., (1969), La Structure du pouvoir au niveau départmental. Paris: Groupe de Sociologie des Organisations.

Grémion, P., (1970), 'Introduction à une étude du système politico-administratif local', Sociologie du Travail (1): 51-73,

Grémion, P. and Worms, J.P., (1970), Les Institutions Régionales et la Société Locale. Paris: Groupe de Sociologie des Organisations.

Grémion, P., (1976), Le Pouvoir Periphique. Paris: Ed. du Seuil.

Kesselman, M., (1967), The Ambiguous Consensus. New York: Alfred A. Knopf.

Kesselman, M., (1970), 'Overinstitutionalisation and Political Constraint: the case of France', Comparative Politics (3): 21-44.

Machin, H., (1977), Prefect in French Public Admini-stration. London: Croom Helm.

Machin, H., (1974), 'The French Prefects and Local Administration', Parliamentary Affairs (27): 237-50.

Milch, J., (1974), 'Influence as Power: French Local Government Reconsidered', British Journal of Political Science (4): 139-62.

Sulieman, E., (1974), Politics Power and Bureaucracy in
France. Princeton: Princeton University Press.
Thoenig, J-C. and Friedberg, E., (1969), 'Politiques
Urbaines et stratégies corporatives', Sociologie du
Travail (4): 387-412.
Thoenig, J-C., (1978), 'State Bureaucracies and Local
Government in France' in Hanf, K., and Sharpf, F.W.,
(eds.), Interorganisational Policy Making. London: Sage.
Thoenig, J-C., (1978), 'Pouvoir d 'Etat et Pouvoirs
locaux', Pouvoirs (4): 25-37.
Worms, J., (1966), 'Le préfet et ses notables',
Sociologie du Travail (3): 249-75.
Wright, V., (1974), 'Politics and Administration under
the Fifth French Republic', Political Studies (22):
44-65.
Wright, V., (1978), The Government and Politics of
France. London: Hutchinson.

Section E.4.

UNITED STATES OF AMERICA

Anderson, W., (1960), Intergovernmental Relations in
Review. Minneapolis: University of Minnesota Press.
Beer, S.H., (1973), 'The Modernisation of American
Federalism', Publius (3): 49-95.
Beer, S.H., (1976), 'The Adoption of General Revenue
Sharing: a case study in public sector politics',
Public Policy (24): 127-96.
Beer, S.H., (1978), 'Federalism, Nationalism and
Democracy in America', American Political Science
Review (72): 9-21.
Caputo, D.A., (ed.), (1975), 'General Revenue Sharing
and Federalism', special issue of the Annals of the
American Academy of Political and Social Science (419).
Carroll, J.D. and Campbell, R.W., (eds.), (1976),
Intergovernmental Administration 1976. Syracuse, N.Y.:
Maxwell School.
Derthick, M., (1974), Between State and Nation
Washington: The Brookings Institution.
Elazar, D. et al., (eds.), (1969), Cooperation and Con-
flict in American Federalism. Itasca, Illinois:
Peacock.
Elazar, D., (1972), American Federalism: A View From
the States. New York: Crowell.
Landau, M., (1969), 'Redundancy, Rationality and the
Problem of Duplication and Overlap', Public Admini-
stration Review (39): 346-58.
Leach, R., (ed.), (1974), 'Intergovernmental Relations
in America Today', Special issue of the Annals of the
American Academy of Political and Social Science (416).
Lowi, T.J., and Stone, A., (ed.), (1978), Nationalising
Government: Public Policies in America. London: Sage.
Lowi, T.J., (1978), 'Europeanization of America: From
United States to United State', in Lowi, T.J., and
Stone. A., (eds.), Nationalizing Public Policies in

America. London: Sage.
McKay, D., (1979), 'The Rise of the Subventionary State:
US. Intergovernmental Relations in the 1970's', Paper
prepared for the Meeting of the Council of European
Studies Research Group on Territorial Politics and
Resource Allocation. Paris.
Martin, R.C., (1965), The Cities and the Federal System.
London: Athlone Press.
Pressman, J., (1975), Federal Programs and City
Politics. Berkeley: University of California Press.
Reagan, M.D., (1972), The New Federalism. New York:
Oxford University Press.
Reynolds, H.W., (ed.), (1965), 'Intergovernmental
Relations in the United States', Special Issue of the
Annals of the American Academy of Political and Social
Science (359).
Riker, W., (1964), Federalism: Origin Operation
Significance. Boston: Little, Brown.
Sundquist, J.L., (1969), Making Federalism Work.
Washington, D.C.: The Brookings Institution.
Vile, M.J.C., (1961), The Structure of American
Federalism. London: Oxford University Press.
Wildavsky, A., (1967), American Federalism in Perspect-
ive. Boston: Little, Brown.
Wildavsky, A., (1975), 'A Bias Toward Federalism',
Graduate School of Public Policy Working Paper No.40.
Berkeley: University of California.
Wright, D.S., (1975), 'Intergovernmental Relations and
Policy Choice', Publius (5): 1-24.
Wright, D.S., (1978), Understanding Inter-Governmental
Relations. North Scituate, Massachusetts: Duxbury Press.
Wright, D.S. and Peddicord, T.E., (1975), Inter-
governmental Relations in the United States: selected
books and documents on Federalism and National-State-
Local Relations. Philadelphia, Pa.: Centre for Study
of Federalism, Temple University.

Section E.5.

EUROPEAN COMMUNITIES

Coombes, D., (1970), Politics and Bureaucracy in the
European Community. London: Allen and Unwin.
Cosgrove, C.A., (1970), A Readers' Guide to Britain and
the European Communities. London: Chatham House/PEP
European Series No. 14.
Deutsch, K.W. et al., (1957), Political Community and the
North Atlantic Area. Princeton: Princeton University
Press.
Haas, E.B., (1964), Beyond the Nation State. Stanford:
Stanford University Press.
Hodges, M., (ed.), (1972), European Integration.
Harmondsworth: Penguin.
Hoffmann, S., (1966), 'The Fate of the Nation State',
Daedalus (95): 862-915.
Hull, C. and Rhodes, R.A.W., (1977), Intergovernmental

Relations in the European Community: the case of sub-national government. Farnborough, Hants.: Saxon House.

Lindberg, L.N. (1963), The Political Dynamics of European Economic Integration. Stanford: Stanford University Press.

Lindberg, L.N. and Scheingold, S.A., (1970), Europe's Would-Be Polity. Englewood Cliffs, N.J.: Prentice Hall.

Lindberg, L.N. and Scheingold, S.A., (eds.), (1971), Regional Integration: theory and research. Cambridge, Mass: Harvard University Press.

Pentland, C., (1973), International Theory and European Integration. London: Faber and Faber.

Wallace, W., Wallace, H., and Webb, C., (1977), Policy-Making in the European Communities. London: Wiley.

Section F

INTERGOVERNMENTAL RELATIONS IN BRITAIN

This section of the bibliography is far and away the longest and it attempts to provide a detailed bibliography on
central-local relations. Other facets of intergovernmental relations in Britain are covered in the next
section. In spite of its length, there are a number of
omissions. First, it does not include every official
publication concerning intergovernmental relations in the
post-war period. Only the major reports have been
included. Each of these reports - e.g. Layfield,
Kilbrandon, Redcliffe-Maud - was published along with
its minutes of evidence (written and oral). This
supporting material has not been listed, primarily because
it is so extensive. Nonetheless, it constitutes an invaluable source of opinion and data for the researcher.
Second, a considerable amount of useful but ephemeral
material appears in the local government press, notably:
Local Government Chronicle, Municipal Journal, Municipal
Review, and County Councils Gazette. With very few
exceptions, articles in these journals have not been
cited. Given the changes occurring in central-local
relations at the time of writing, however, these journals
are an essential component of any bibliography simply
to keep up-to-date with current events. Finally, to avoid
undue repetition, relevant work cited elsewhere in the
bibliography is not repeated in this section unless it is
particularly important.

Among the large number of studies listed under· the head-
ing 'Central-Local Relations: general' the major
attempts to describe and analyse the system are Chester
(1951), Griffith (1966) West Midlands Study Group (1956)
and Sharp (1969). More recent attempts to provide an all-
round appraisal of the system are to be found in the
Committee of Inquiry into Local Government Finance (1976)
and Central Policy Review Staff (1977).

Moving beyond the general studies, there are a variety
of approaches each concerned with different aspects of the
relationship between central and local government. One
prominent strand is concerned with the effects on local
authorities of financial dependence. See: Alt (1971),
Boaden (1970, 1971a and 1971b), Ashford (1974) and
Oliver and Stanyer (1969). A second, and somewhat
unexpected, strand focuses on the links between M.P.s and
local government. See: Butler (1953), Keith-Lucas (1955)
Mackenzie (1954) and Mellors (1974). Third, and in
addition to the case studies of particular services
listed in Section 1 F (e), there are a variety of case
studies of the influence of central government on either
particular local authorities or on specific decisions.
For the former see Green (1959), Dearlove (1973), Lee

(1963), Lee et al., (1974), Minns (1974), Mitchell (1974)
and Skinner and Langdon (1974). For the latter see: Brier
(1970), Gregory (1971), Jones (1966), Scarrow (1971) and
Swann (1972). Fourth, there are a number of commentaries
on the state of central-local relations. Their usual
pessimistic tone is clearly illustrated by Dell (1960),
Hill (1966), Robson (1954, 1966a and 1966b). A more
balanced view can be found in Jones (1975 and 1979) and
Rhodes (1976 and 1979). Finally, and perhaps most
typically, there are a large number of legal and historical commentaries on the relationship. See for example:
Cross (1974), Fox (1956), Garner (1973), Keith-Lucas and
Richards (1978) and Smellie (1969).

Many of the items cited above discuss the financial
aspects of central-local relations but Section F.1 (b)
identifies the most important contributions to this topic.
Perhaps the best introduction is Hepworth (1976) although
the Committee of Inquiry into Local Government Finance
(1976) is a goldmine of information. The development of
the system is admirably described in Rhodes, G. (1976).
The (recurring) debate about new sources of local revenue
can be traced through Hanson (1956), R.I.P.A. (1956),
Marshall (1971) and the arguments surrounding the
recommendations of the Layfield Report. On the latter
see: Cripps and Godley (1976), Jones (1977), Johnson
(1977) and Stewart (1977). Finally, the 'problem' of controlling local expenditure can be explored by looking at
Wright (1977), Taylor, (1979), Else and Marshall (1979)
and Society of Local Authority Chief Executives (1979).

The reorganisation of local government raises the key
issue of the relative power of the two levels of
government. The ease with which reorganisation was
affected is the central theme of Ashford's (1976 and 1978)
analysis. The reorganisation is described in Wood (1976)
and Richards (1976) and critically evaluated in Jones
(1973), Rhodes (1974 and 1980), Sharpe (1978 and 1979)
and Stanyer (1973). The issue of whose interests were
served by reorganisation is approached tangentially in
Brand (1974) and directly by Dearlove (1979).

In spite of their obvious importance, very little
information is available on the attitudes and roles of
central departments in their relationships with local
authorities. Apart from general descriptions of the civil
service (e.g. Bridges 1971, Heclo and Wildavsky 1974 and
Clarke 1971), the reader is reduced to culling tit-bits
of information from a variety of sources. Griffith (1966)
and Regan (1977) offer helpful analyses but Draper is
disappointing as are most contributions to the New
Whitehall Series (e.g. Newsom (1954) and Pile (1979)).
The exception is Sharp (1969) although this is now dated.
Some useful information is available from memoirs and
interviews. The best amongst these sources is Crossman

(1975) but he is hotly pursued by Boyle et al (1971). This section also includes a number of items on the regional organisation of central departments. For the most part, they describe the organisation and do not explore relationships with local authorities. Painter (1972) and Smith (1969) present some information on this aspect of central-local relations. (See also the work of Friend et. al., cited in Section C).

The selection of material on central-local relations includes items on specific services. Given the wealth of material available on the individual services, this list is necessarily selective. As noted in the text, books and articles lacking the phrase 'central-local relations' in their title tend to be seen as irrelevant. This tendency is most marked in the case of books and articles on specific services. They are mentioned but rarely. In spite of its many failings, therefore, this sub-section of the bibliography goes some way towards repairing a long standing omission. It is organised by major service and every effort has been made to ensure that all the items cited contain at least some reference to central-local relations. Without commenting on each service in detail a number of items are particularly noteworthy. On education see: Birley (1970), Blackstone (1971), Byrne (1974), Kogan and van der Eyken (1973) and Regan (1977). On housing see: Cullingworth (1966) and Murie et. al., (1976). On industrial relations see: Coates (1972) and Thomson and Beaumont (1979). On the police see: Marshall (1965) and Regan (1966). On social work see Hall et. al., (1975) and Glennester (1975). Finally, Griffith (1966) provides detailed information on education, highways, housing, planning, children's services and health and welfare services but it has only been listed under education.

Section F.1(a)

CENTRAL-LOCAL RELATIONS: GENERAL

Alt, J.E., (1971), 'Some Social and Political Correlates of County Borough Expenditures', British Journal of Political Science (1): 49-62.
Ashford, D.E., (1974), 'The Effects of Central Finance on the British Local Government System', British Journal of Political Science (4): 305-322.
Ashford, D.E., (1977), 'Are Britain and France "Unitary"?', Comparative Politics (9): 483-99.
Ashford, D.E., (1975), 'Resources, Spending and Party Politics in British Local Government', Administration and Society (7) No.3: 286-311.
Association of County Councils et. al., (1979), Review of Government Controls over Local Authorities. London: ACC.

Association of Municipal Corporations (1972), AMC 1873-1973. London: A.M.C.

Banwell, H., (1959), 'The New Relations Between Central and Local Government', Public Administration (37): 201-12.

Barker, A., (1979), Central-Local Government Relationships in Britain as a Field Study: A Commentary and Research Register. London: SSRC.

Boaden, N., and Alford, R., (1969), 'Some Sources of Diversity in English Local Government Decisions', Public Administration (47): 203-23.

Boaden, N., (1970), 'Central Departments and Local Authorities: the relationship examined', Political Studies (28): 175-86.

Boaden, N., (1971a), 'Innovation and Change in English Local Government', Political Studies (19): 416-29.

Boaden, N., (1971b), Urban Policy Making. London: Cambridge University Press.

Brier, A.P., (1970), 'The Decision Process in Local Government: A Case Study of Fluoridation in Hull', Public Administration (48): 153-68.

Briggs, E. and Deacon, A., (1974), 'The Creation of the Unemployment Assistance Board', Policy and Politics (2): 43-68.

Burkhead, J., (1974), 'Federalism in a Unitary State: Regional Economic Planning in England', Publius (4): No. 2 39-61.

Butler, D.E., (1953), 'Local Government in Parliament', Public Administration (31): 46-7.

Buxton, R., (1970), Local Government. Harmondsworth: Penguin.

Central Government Controls Over Local Authorities (1979), Cmnd. 7634. London: H.M.S.O.

Central Policy Review Staff, (1977), Relations Between Central Government and Local Authorities. London: H.M.S.O.

Chester, D.N., (1951), Central and Local Government. London: Macmillan.

Cohen, E.W., (1951), 'Aspects of Local Government in England and Wales', Public Administration Review (11): 253-59.

Cohen, L.H., (1973), 'Local Government Complaints: the M.P.'s Viewpoint', Public Administration (51): 175-83.

Commission on the Constitution 1969-73 (Kilbrandon), (1973), Vol. 1, Report Cmnd. 5460. London: H.M.S.O.

Committee of Inquiry into Local Government Finance (Layfield), (1976), Report Cmnd. 6453. London: H.M.S.O.

Committee on the Management of Local Government (Maud) (1967), Vol. 1, Report London: H.M.S.O.

Cross, C.A., (1974), The Principles of Local Government Law. London: Sweet and Maxwell.

Crouch, W.W., (1950), 'Local Government under the British Labour Government', Journal of Politics (12): 232-59.

Deacon, A., and Briggs, E., (1974), 'Local Democracy and Central Policy: the issue of paupers votes in the 1920's', Policy and Politics (2): 347-64.

Dearlove, J., (1973), The Politics of Policy in Local Government. London: Cambridge University Press.

Dell, E., (1960), 'Labour and Local Government', Political Quarterly (31): 333-347.

Donnison, D.V., (1962), Health, Welfare and Democracy in Greater London. London: London School of Economics and Political Science, Greater London Papers No.5.

Finer, S.E., (1957), The Life and Times of Sir Edwin Chadwick. London: Methuen.

Fox, H.M., (1956), 'Judicial Control of the Spending Powers of Authorities', Law Quarterly Review (72): 237-59.

Garner, J.F., (1973), 'The Ultra Vires Doctrine and the Local Government Act', Local Government Studies No.4: 17-25.

Gill, A.M., (1972), 'The Relationship Between Central and Local Authorities', letter to Public Administration (50): 215-6.

Green, L.P., (1959), Provincial Metropolis. London: Allen and Unwin.

Gregory, R., (1971), The Price of Amenity. London: Macmillan.

Griffith, J.A.G., (1966), Central Departments and Local Authorities. London: Allen and Unwin.

Griffith, J.A.G., (1969), 'Maud- off the Target', New Statesman, 20th June 1969: 866-7.

Griffith, J.A.G. (1974), Local Authorities and Central Control. London: Barry Rose Publications.

Gutchen, R.M., (1961), 'Local Improvements and Centralisation in Nineteenth Century England', Historical Journal (4): 85-96.

Hambleton, R., (1977), 'A Guideline is a Trap', New Society, 24th March 1977. 601-2.

Harris, J.S., (1955), British Government Inspection as a Dynamic Process: the local services and central departments. New York: Praeger.

Harris, J.S., (1955), 'Central Government Inspection of Local Services in Britain', Public Administration Review (15): 26-34.

Harris, R. and Shipp, P.J., (1977), Communications Between Central and Local Government in the Management of Local Authority Expenditure. Coventry: Institute for Operational Research.

Hartley, O.A., (1971), 'The Relationship Between Central and Local Authorities', Public Administration (49): 439-56.

Hartley, O.A., (1972), 'Inspectorates in British Central Government', Public Administration (50): 447-66.

Hartley, O.A., (1973), 'The Functions of Local Government: a study in theory and practice', Local Government Studies No.4: 27-40.

Hepworth, N.P., (1977), 'Local Government and Central
Control', Public Administration (55): 11-16.
Hill, F., (1966), 'The Partnership in Theory and Practice'
Political Quarterly (37): 169-79.
Institute of Public Administration, (1947), 'The Position
of the Regional and Local Authorities in Relation to the
Central Authority', Public Administration (25): 189-95.
Institute of Public Administration (1948), 'Central Con-
trol of Local Authorities', Public Administration (26):
118-22.
Jones, G.W., (1966), 'A Forgotten Right Discovered',
Parliamentary Affairs (19): 363-72.
Jones, G.W., (1973), 'Herbert Morrison and Poplarism',
Public Law. Spring: 11-31.
Jones, G.W., (1974), 'Intergovernmental Relations in
Britain', Annals of the American Academy of Political
and Social Science (416): 181-93.
Jones, G.W., (1975), 'Varieties of Local Politics',
Local Government Studies (1) No.2: 17-32.
Jones, G.W., (1979), 'Central-Local Relations, Finance
and the Law', Urban Law and Policy (2): 25-46.
Jones, G.W., (ed.), (1980), Central-Local Relations in
Britain. Farnborough, Hants.: Saxon House.
Jowell, J., (1973), 'The Legal Control of Administrative
Discretion', Public Law. Autumn: 178-220.
Keith-Lucas, B., (1955), 'Local Government in Parliament'
Public Administration (33): 207-10.
Keith-Lucas, B., (1957), 'Three White Papers on Local
Government', Political Quarterly (28): 328-38.
Keith-Lucas, B., (1962), 'Poplarism', Public Law. Spring:
52-80.
Keith-Lucas, B., and Richards, P.G., (1978), A History
of Local Government in the Twentieth Century. London:
Allen and Unwin.
Leach, S, and Moore, N., (1979), 'County/District Relations
in Shire and Metropolitan Counties in the Field of Town
and Country Planning: a Comparison', Policy and Politics
(7): 165-79.
Lee, J.M., (1963), Social Leaders and Public Persons,
Oxford: The Clarendon Press.
Lee, J.M. and Wood, B. with Solomon, B.W., and Walters, P.,
(1974), The Scope of Local Initiative. London:
Martin Robertson.
Mackenzie, W.J.M., (1954), 'Local Government in
Parliament', Public Administration (32): 409-23.
Mackenzie, W.J.M., (1961), Theories of Local Government.
London: London School of Economics and Political
Science, Greater London Papers No.2.
Mellors, C., (1974), 'Local Government in Parliament',
Public Administration (52): 223-9.
Minns, R., (1974), 'The Significance of Clay Cross:
Another Look at District Audit', Policy and Politics (2)
No.4: 309-24.
Mitchell, A., (1974), 'Clay Cross', Political Quarterly
(45); 165-79.

Newton, K, and Sharpe, L.J., (1977), 'Local Outputs Research: Some Reflections and Proposals', Policy and Politics (5): 61-82.

Newton, K., (1979), 'Ninety Thousand million Pounds: Central Government Grants, Territorial Justice and Local Democracy in Post-War Britain', Paper for a meeting of a Council of European Studies Research Group on Territorial Politics and Resource Allocation, Paris.

Oliver, F.R., and Stanyer, J., (1969), 'Some Aspects of the Financial Behaviour of County Boroughs', Public Administration (47): 169-84.

Parkinson, M., (1971), 'Central-Local Relations in British Parties: a local view', Political Studies (19): 440-46.

Poole, K.P., (1978), The Local Government Service. London: Allen and Unwin.

Rees, I.B., (1971), Government and Community. London: Charles Knight.

Rhodes, G., (1965), Administrators in Action Vol. 2. London: Allen and Unwin.

Rhodes, G., (1972), The New Government of London: the first five years. London: Allen and Unwin.

Rhodes, R.A.W., (1975), 'The Lost World of British Local Politics?', Local Government Studies (1) No.3: 39-60.

Rhodes, R.A.W., (1976), 'Centre-Local Relations', in Committee of Inquiry into Local Government Finance, Appendix 6, The Relationship Between Central and Local Government. London: H.M.S.O.

Rhodes, R.A.W., (1979a), 'Ordering Urban Change: corporate planning in the government of English Cities', in Lagroye, J., and Wright, V., (eds.), Local Government in Britain and France. London: Allen and Unwin.

Rhodes, R.A.W., (1979b), 'Future Research into Central-Local Relations: a framework for analysis', in Social Science Research Council, Central-Local Government Relationships. London: SSRC.

Robson, W.A., (1954), The Development of Local Government. London: Allen and Unwin.

Robson, W.A., (1966a), 'Local Government in the Welfare State', Political Quarterly (37): 121-7.

Robson, W.A., (1966b), Local Government in Crisis. London: Allen and Unwin.

Robson, W.A., (1967), Politics and Government at Home and Abroad. London: Allen and Unwin.

Royal Commission on Local Government in England 1966-69. (Redcliffe-Maud) (1969), Vol. 1. Report. Cmnd. 4040 London: H.M.S.O.

Royal Commission on Local Government in Scotland 1966-69 (Wheatley) (1969), Vol. 1. Report Cmnd. 4150 Edinburgh: H.M.S.O.

Scarrow, H.A., (1971), 'Policy Pressures by British Local Government: The Case of Regulation in the "Public Interest"', Comparative Politics (4): 1-28.

Scarrow, H.A., (1972), 'The Impact of British Domestic Air Pollution Legislation', British Journal of Political Science (2): 261-82.

Scarrow, H.A., (1973), 'New Perspectives on British Local Government', World Politics (26): 126-38.

School of Advanced Urban Studies, (1978), 'Implementation and the Central-Local Relationship', in Social Science Research Council, Central-Local Government Relationships London: SSRC.

Self, P., (1976), 'Rational Decentralisation', in Griffith, J.A.G., (ed.), From Policy to Administration London: Allen and Unwin.

Sharp, Dame, E., (1962), 'The Future of Local Government', Public Administration (40): 375-86.

Sharp, Dame, E., (1969), The Ministry of Housing and Local Government. London: Allen and Unwin.

Sharpe, L.J., (1970), 'Theories and Values of Local Government', Political Studies (18): 153-74.

Sharpe, L.J., (1975), 'Innovation and Change in British Land-use planning', in Hayward, J., and Watson, M., (ed.), Planning Politics and Public Policy: the British, French, and Italian Experience. London: Cambridge University Press.

Skinner, D., and Langdon, J., (1974), The Story of Clay Cross. Nottingham: Spokesman Books.

Smellie, K.B., (1960), A History of Local Government. London: Allen and Unwin, fourth edition.

Smith, B.C., (1976), Policy Making in British Government London: Martin Robertson.

Smith, B.C., and Stanyer, J., (1976), Administering Britain. Glasgow: Fontana/Collins.

Society of Local Authority Chief Executives (1977), 'Supplementary Memorandum by the Society of Local Authority Chief Executives on Unnecessarily Detailed Control by Government Departments', in Eleventh Report of the Expenditure Committee, The Civil Service, Vol.2, Minutes of Evidence. H.C. 535 London: H.M.S.O.

Stanyer, J., (1976), Understanding Local Government. Glasgow: Fontana/Collins.

Stewart, J.D., (1977), Management in an Era of Restraint and Central and Local Government Relationships. London: The Municipal Group.

Swaffield, J.C., (1970), 'Local Government in the National Setting', Public Administration (48): 307-15.

Swann, B., (1972), 'Local Initiative and Central Control: the Insulin Decision', Policy and Politics (1): 55-63.

Taverne, D., (1976), 'The Story of Clay Cross', Local Government Studies (2) No.1: 57-61.

Toulmin-Smith, J., (1951), Local Self-Government and Centralisation. London: Chapman.

Warren, J.H., (1952), The Local Government Service. Allen and Unwin.

West Midlands Study Group, (1956), Local Government and Central Control. London: Routledge and Kegan Paul.

Willson, F.M.G., (1961), <u>Administrators in Action Vol.I.</u>
London: Allen and Unwin.

Section F.1(b)

FINANCE

Ashford, D.E., (1979), 'A Victorian Drama: the
financial subordination of British local government',
Paper for a meeting of the <u>Council of European Studies</u>
<u>Research Group</u> on Territorial Politics and Resource
<u>Allocation, Paris.</u>
Blackburn, J.S., (1979), <u>Presentation and Interpretation</u>
<u>by Local Government of White Papers on Public Expendi-</u>
<u>ture.</u> Birmingham: Inlogov.
Boyle, L., (1966), <u>Equalisation and the Future of Local</u>
<u>Government Finance.</u> Edinburgh: Oliver and Boyd.
Chester, D.N., (1966), 'Local Finance', <u>Political</u>
<u>Quarterly</u> (37): 180-91.
Committee of Inquiry into Local Government Finance,
(Layfield) (1976), <u>Report.</u> Cmnd. 6453 London: H.M.S.O.
Cripps, F., and Godley, W., (1976), <u>Local Government</u>
<u>Finance and Its Reform.</u> Cambridge: University of
Cambridge, Department of Applied Economics.
Crispin, A., (1976), 'Local Government Finance:
assessing the central government's contribution',
<u>Public Administration</u> (54): 45-61.
Department of the Environment, (1977), <u>Local Government</u>
<u>Finance.</u> Cmnd. 6813 London: H.M.S.O.
Department of the Environment, (1973), <u>Local Government</u>
<u>Finance in England and Wales.</u> London: H.M.S.O.
Drummond, J.M., (1952), <u>The Finance of Local Government.</u>
London: Allen and Unwin.
Drummond, J.M., and Kitching, W.A.C., (1962), <u>The</u>
<u>Finance of Local Government.</u> London: Allen and Unwin.
Else, P.K., and Marshall, G.P., (1979), <u>The Management</u>
<u>of Public Expenditure.</u> London: Policy Studies Institute.
Hanson, A.H., (1956), <u>Financing Local Government.</u>
London: Fabian Research Series No. 178.
Helmore, L.M., (1961), <u>The District Auditor.</u> London:
Macdonald and Evans.
Hepworth, N.P., (1976), <u>The Finance of Local Government.</u>
London: Allen and Unwin, third edn.
Hepworth, N.P., (1976), 'Public Expenditure Controls
and Local Government', <u>Local Government Studies</u> (2):
1-14.
Hepworth, N.P., (1976), 'The Real Issues Facing Layfield'
<u>Local Government Studies</u> (2) No.2: 1-14.
Institute of Municipal Treasurers and Accountants, (1956),
<u>Local Expenditure and Exchequer Grants.</u> London: IMTA.
Johnson, N., (1977), 'Editorial: the Layfield Report',
<u>Public Administration</u> (55): 1-9.
Jones, G.W., (1977), <u>Responsibility and Government.</u>
London: London School of Economics and Political
Science.

Lees, D.S. et. al., (1965), Local Expenditure and
Exchequer Grants. London: IMTA.
Local Government Studies (1976), (2) No.4: 59-69,
'Reviews of the Layfield Report by Norman Chester and
Hedley Marshall'.
Marshall, A.H., (1960), Financial Administration in
Local Government. London: Allen and Unwin.
Marshall, A.H., (1971), New Revenues for Local Govern-
ment. London: Fabian Research Series No. 295.
National Community Development Project, (1975), Rates of
Decline: an unacceptable base of public finance.
(Submission to the Layfield Committee on Local
Government Finance). London: NCDP.
Nicholson, F.J., and Topham, N., (1972), 'Investment
Decisions and the size of Local Authorities', Policy
and Politics (1): 23-44.
Rhodes, G., (1976), 'Local Government Finance 1918-1966',
in Committee of Inquiry into Local Government Finance,
Appendix 6. The Relationship Between Central and
Local Government. London: H.M.S.O.
Rose, M., (1978), Rate Support Grant: Needs Element,
Rate Equalisation and London's Inner Urban Areas.
London: G.L.C. Research Memorandum, RM.47.
Royal Institute of Public Administration, (1956), New
Sources of Local Revenue. London: Allen and Unwin.
Society of Local Authority Chief Executives (1980), The
Local Government Bill: an appraisal prepared by SOLACE
in collaboration with INLOGOV. London: SOLACE.
Steer, W.S., (1956), 'The Financing of Local Government',
Political Quarterly (27): 423-33.
Stewart, J.D., (1977), 'The Green Paper on Local
Government Finance - A Viewpoint', Local Government
Studies (3) No. 4: 9-15.
Taylor, J.A., (1979), 'The Consultative Council on Local
Government Finance: a critical analysis of its
origins and development', Local Government Studies (5)
No.3: 7-36.
Wright, M., (1977), 'Public Expenditure in Britain:
the crisis of control', Public Administration (55):
143-69.

Section F.1(c)

THE REORGANISATION OF LOCAL GOVERNMENT

Ashford, D.E., (1976), The Limits to Consensus: the
reorganisation of British local government and the
French contrast. Ithaca, New York: Western Societies
Program for International Studies, Paper No. 6
Cornell University.
Ashford, D.E., (1978), 'French Pragmatism and British
Idealism: Financial Aspects of Local Reorganisation',
Comparative Political Studies (11) No.2: 231-54.
Ashford, D.E., (1976), 'Reorganising British Local
Government: a policy problem', Local Government
Studies (2) No. 4: 1-18.

Brand, J.A., (1974), Local Government Reform in England. London: Croom Helm.

Bristow, S.L., (1972), 'The Criteria for Local Government Reorganisation and Local Authority Autonomy', Policy and Politics (1): 143-62.

Craven, E., (ed.), (1975), Regional Devolution and Social Policy. London: Macmillan.

Davies, C.J., (1973), 'The Reform of Local Government with Special reference to England', Studies in Comparative Local Government (7): 35-45.

Dearlove, J., (1979), The Reorganisation of British Local Government. London: Cambridge University Press.

Isaac-Henry, K., (1975), 'Local Authority Associations and Local Government Reform', Local Government Studies (1) No. 3: 1-12.

Isaac-Henry, K., (1978), The Association of Municipal Corporations and the County Councils Association - a study of influences and pressures on reorganisation of local government 1945-72. Birmingham Polytechnic, mimeo.

Jones, G.W., (1966-67), 'Mr. Crossman and the Reform of Local Government 1964-1966', Parliamentary Affairs (20): 77-89.

Jones, G.W., (1973), 'The Local Government Act 1972 and the Redcliffe-Maud Commission', Political Quarterly (44): 154-66.

Local Government in England: Government Proposals for Reorganisation. Cmnd. 4584. London: H.M.S.O.

Redcliffe-Maud, Lord and Wood, B., (1974), English Local Government Reformed. London: Oxford University Press.

Rhodes, R.A.W., (1974), 'Local Government Reform: three questions', Social and Economic Administration (8): 6-21.

Rhodes, R.A.W., (1980), 'The Changing Pattern of Local Government in England: reform or reorganisation?', in Gunlicks, A.B., (ed.), Local Government Reform and Reorganisation: an international Perspective. New York: Kennikat Press.

Richards, P.G., (1975), The Local Government Act 1972: Problems of Implementation. London: PEP and Allen and Unwin.

Richards, P.G., (1975), The Reformed Local Government System. London: Allen and Unwin, second edn.

Sharpe, L.J., (1978), 'Reforming' the Grass Roots: an alternative analysis', in Butler, D., and Halsey, A.H., (eds.), Policy and Politics: essays in honour of Norman Chester. London: Macmillan.

Sharpe, L.J., (1979), 'Modernising the Localities; Local Government in Britain and some comparisons with France', in Lagroye, J., and Wright, V., (eds.), Local Government in Britain and France. London: Allen and Unwin.

Stanyer, J., (1973), 'The Redcliffe-Maud Royal Commission on Local Government', in Chapman, R.A. (ed.), The Role of Commissions in Policy Making. London: Allen and Unwin.

Wood, B.,   (1976),   The Process of Local Government
   Reform. London: Allen and Unwin.

Section F.1(d)

THE ROLE OF CENTRAL DEPARTMENTS

Boyle, E., Crosland, A., and Kogan, M.,   (1971), The
   Politics of Education. Harmondsworth: Penguin.
Bridges, E.,   (1971),   'Portrait of a Profession', in
   Chapman, R.A. and Dunsire, A., (eds.), Style in
   Administration. London: Allen and Unwin.
Chapman, L.,   (1978), Your Disobedient Servant. London:
   Chatto and Windus.
Clare, J.,   (1972),   'Inside the monolith responsible for
   our environment',
   'Who makes the decisions that change our environment?'
   'Peter Walker: Minister of Hope and Glory'.
   The Times 8, 9 and 10 May.
Clark, A.,   (1977),   'Ministerial Supervision and the
   Size of the Department of the Environment', Public
   Administration (55): 197-204.
Clarke, Sir R.,   (1971),   New Trends in Government.
   London: H.M.S.O.
Committee on the Civil Service,   (1968),
   Report. Cmnd. 3638 London: H.M.S.O.
Cross, J.A.,   (1970),   'The Regional Decentralisation of
   British Government Departments', Public Administration
   (48): 423-41.
Crossman, R.H.S.,   (1975),   Diaries of a Cabinet Minister,
   Vol. 1, Minister of Housing. London: Cape/Hamilton.
Draper, P.,   (1977),   Creation of the D.O.E. London:
   H.M.S.O.
Eleventh Report from the Expenditure Committee, (1977),
   The Civil Service. HC 535 London: H.M.S.O.
Griffith, J.A.G.   (1966),   Central Departments and Local
   Authorities. London: Allen and Unwin.
Harris, J.S.,   (1958),   'Regional Decentralisation of
   Government Departments in Britain', Canadian Journal of
   Economics and Political Science (24): 57-69.
Heclo, H., and Wildavsky, A.,   (1974), The Private
   Government of Public Money. London: Macmillan.
Hood, C., Dunsire, A., and Thompson, K.S.,   (1978), 'So
   You Think You Know What Government Departments Are...?',
   Public Administration Bulletin, No. 27 August: 20-32.
Hood, C., Dunsire, A., and Thompson, S.K.,   (1979a),'Com-
   paring the Scottish Office with Whitehall: a
   quantitative approach', British Journal of Political
   Science (9): 257-80.
Hood, C., Dunsire, A., and Thompson, S.K.,   (1979b),'Des-
   cribing the Status Quo in Whitehall: a prerequisite for
   the analysis of change', Public Administration Bulletin
   No. 31 December: 20-36.

Jenkins, R., (1971), 'A Study in Whitehall Style:
R. Jenkins Compares the Workings and the Atmosphere of
the Home Office and Treasury', Sunday Times Weekly
Review 17 January.
Johnson, N., (1971), 'The Reorganisation of Central
Government', Public Administration (49): 1-12.
Macmillan, Sir H., (1966), Winds of Change. London:
Macmillan.
Macmillan, Sir H., (1969), Tides of Fortune. London:
Macmillan.
Newsom, Sir F., (1954), The Home Office. London:
Allen and Unwin.
Painter, C., (1972), 'The Repercussions of Admini-
strative Innovation: the West Midlands Economic
Planning Council', Public Administration (50): 467-84.
Pile, Sir W., (1979), The Department of Education and
Science. London: Allen and Unwin.
Plowden, W., (1970), 'Riding Two Horses: the Crosland
Ministry' New Society. 1 January: 7-10.
The Reorganisation of Central Government (1970), Cmnd.
4506. London: H.M.S.O.
Regan, D.E., (1977), Local Government and Education.
London: Allen and Unwin.
Self, P., (1967), 'Regional Planning in Britain:
analysis and evaluation', Regional Studies (1): 3-10.
Sharp, Dame E., (1969), The Ministry of Housing and
Local Government. London: George Allen and Unwin.
Sharpe, L.J., (1977), 'Whitehall-Structures and People',
in Kavanagh, D., and Rose, R., (eds.), New Trends in
British Politics. London: Sage.
Smith, B.C., (1964), Regionalism in England, Vol.1,
Regional Institutions - a guide. London: Acton
Society Trust.
Smith, B.C., (1965), Regionalism in England, Vol.2. Its
Nature and Purpose 1905-65. London: Acton Society
Trust.
Smith, B.C., (1965), Regionalism in England, Vol. 3,
The New Regional Machinery. London: Acton Society
Trust.
Smith, B.C., (1967), Field Administration. London:
Routledge and Kegan Paul.
Smith, B.C., (1969), Advising Ministers. London:
Routledge and Kegan Paul.
Willson, F.M.G., and Chester, D.N., (1968), The
Organisation of British Central Government. London:
Allen and Unwin, second edn.
Wilson, H., (1971), The Labour Government 1964-70.
London: Weidenfeld and Nicolson/Michael Joseph.

Section F.1.(c)

FUNCTIONS

(i) Education

Armytage, W.H.G., (1964), Four Hundred Years of English
   Education. London: Cambridge University Press.
Baron, G., and Howell, D.A., (1974), The Government and
   Management of Schools. London: The Athlone Press.
Batley, R., et. al., (1970), Going Comprehensive. London:
   Routledge and Kegan Paul.
Birley, D., (1970), The Education Officer and his World.
   London: Routledge and Kegan Paul.
Blackie, J., (1970), Inspecting and the Inspectorate.
   London: Routledge and Kegan Paul.
Blackstone, T., (1971), A Fair Start: the Provision of
   Pre-School Education. Harmondsworth: Allen Lane,
   Penguin Press.
Brand, J.A., (1965), 'Ministry Control and Local Auton-
   omy in Education', Political Quarterly (36): 154-63.
Byrne, E., (1974), Planning and Educational Inequality:
   a study of the rationale of resource allocation.
   Windsor: National Foundation for Educational Research.
Dent, H.C., (1971), The Educational System of England
   and Wales. London: London University Press.
Edmonds, E.L., (1962), The School Inspector. London:
   Routledge and Kegan Paul.
Gosden, P.H., (1972), The Evolution of a Profession: a
   study of the contribution of teachers' associations to
   the development of school teaching as a professional
   occupation. Oxford: Blackwell.
Griffith, J.A.G., (1966), Central Departments and Local
   Authorities. London: George Allen and Unwin.
Isaac-Henry, K., (1970), The Politics of Comprehensive
   Education in Birmingham 1957-1967. University of
   Birmingham: Unpublished M.Soc.Sc. Thesis.
Jennings, R.E., (1977), Education and Politics: Policy-
   making in local education authorities. London:
   Batsford.
Kogan, M., (1975), Educational Policy Making: a study
   of interest groups and parliament. London: Allen
   and Unwin.
Kogan, M., (1978), The Politics of Educational Change.
   Glasgow: Fontana/Collins.
Kogan, M., and Van der Eyken, W., (1973), County Hall.
   Harmondsworth: Penguin Books.
Kogan, M., Boyle, E., and Crosland, A., (1971), The
   Politics of Education. Harmondsworth: Penguin.
Parry, J.P., (1971), The Provision of Education in
   England and Wales. London: Allen and Unwin.
Peschek, D., and Brand, J., (1966), Policies and
   Politics in Secondary Education. London: London School
   of Economics and Political Science, Greater London
   Paper No. 11.

Regan, D.E., (1977), Local Government and Education. London: Allen and Unwin.

Ribbins, P.M., and Brown, R.J., (1979), 'Policy Making in English Local Government: the case of secondary school reorganisation', Public Administration (57): 187-202.

Saran, R., (1967), 'Decision-Making by a Local Education Authority', Public Administration (45): 387-40.

Saran, R., (1973), Policy Making in Secondary Education. London: Oxford University Press.

Vaizey, J., (1958), 'Block Grants and the Control of Education', Political Quarterly (29): 155-65.

Vaizey, J., (1963), The Control of Education. London: Faber and Faber.

Vaizey, J., and Sheehan, J., (1968), Resources for Education. London: Allen and Unwin.

(ii) Housing

Barnett, M.J., (1969), The Politics of Legislation: the Rent Act 1957. London: Weidenfeld and Nicolson.

Craven, E., (1975), 'Housing', in Klein, R., (ed.), Inflation and Priorities. London: Centre for Studies in Social Policy.

Cullingworth, J.B., (1979), Essays on Housing Policy. London: Allen and Unwin.

Cullingworth, J.B., (1966), Housing and Local Government in England and Wales. London: Allen and Unwin.

Donnison, D.V., (1967), The Government of Housing. Harmondsworth: Penguin.

Murie, A., Niner, P., and Watson, C., (1976), Housing and the Housing System. London: Allen and Unwin.

Young, K., and Kramer, J., (1978), Strategy and Conflict in Metropolitan Housing. London: Heinemann.

(iii) Industrial Relations

Balfour, C., (1972), Incomes Policy and the Public Sector. London: Routledge and Kegan Paul.

Beaumont, P.B., (1977), 'Incomes Policy, Productivity and Manual Workers Earnings in the Local Government Sector', Local Government Studies (3) No. 1: 17-29.

Bocock, J., (1973), 'The Politics of White Collar Unionisation', Political Quarterly (44): 294-303.

Clegg, H., (1978), The System of Industrial Relations in Great Britain. Oxford: Blackwell.

Coates, R.D., (1972), Teachers' Unions and Interest Group Politics. London: Cambridge University Press.

Cunningham, I., and Fahey, U., (1976), 'Administrators and Professionals in Local Government', Local Government Studies (2) No.4: 19-29.

Deem, R., (1976), 'Profesionalism, unity and militant action: the case of teachers', Sociological Review (24): 43-61.

Jackson, M., (1977), Industrial Relations. London: Croom Helm.

177

Levinson, H.M., (1972), Collective Bargaining by British Local Government Employees. Ann Arbor: Michigan: Institute of Industrial and Labor Relations.

Manzer, R.A., (1970), Teachers and Politics: the role of the N.U.T. in the making of national education policy in England and Wales since 1944. Manchester: Manchester University Press.

Medlicott, P., (1974), 'What the N.U.T. Does', New Society 19 December 754-5.

Perkin, H., (1969), Key Profession: the history of the Association of University Teachers. London: Routledge and Kegan Paul.

Spoor, A., (1967), White Collar Union: sixty years of NALGO. London: Heinemann.

Thomson, A.W.J., and Beaumont, P.B., (1979), Public Sector Bargaining: a study of relative gain. Farnborough, Hants.: Saxon House.

(iv) Planning

Cullingworth, J.B., (1974), Town and Country Planning in Britain. London: Allen and Unwin, fifth edn.

Dobry, Sir G., (1975), Review of the Development Control System: Final Report. London: H.M.S.O.

Donnison, D.V., (1973), 'Planning and Government' in Cowen, P., (ed.), The Future of Planning. London: Heinemann.

Friend, J.K., and Jessop, W.N., (1969), Local Government and Strategic Choice. London: Tavistock.

Friend, J.K., Power, J.M., and Yewlett, C.J.L., (1974), Public Planning: the intercorporate dimension. London: Tavistock.

Friend, J.K., (1976), 'Planners, Policies and Organisational Boundaries: some recent developments', Policy and Politics (5): 25-44.

Hart, D., Skelcher, C., and Wedgewood-Oppenheim, F., (1978) Goals and Objectives in Planning: the regional dimension. Birmingham: Institute of Local Government Studies.

Jowell, J., (1977), 'Bargaining in Development Control', Journal of Planning and Environment Law July: 414-33.

Long, J., Self, P., and Eversley, D., (1961), The Wythall Inquiry: a planning test case. London: London Estates Gazette.

McKay, D., and Cox, A., (1979), The Politics of Urban Change. London: Croom Helm.

Planning Advisory Group (1965), The Future of Development Plans. London: H.M.S.O.

School for Advanced Urban Studies (1977), Planning Systems Research Project: final report. Bristol: SAUS.

Solesbury, W., (1974), Policy in Urban Planning. Oxford. Pergamon.

(v) Police and Fire

Banton, M., (1964), The Police in the Community. London:
  Tavistock.
Cain, M., (1973), Society and the Policeman's Role.
  London: Routledge and Kegan Paul.
Critchley, J.A., (1967), A History of the Police in
  England and Wales, 1900-1966. London: Constable.
Keith-Lucas, B., (1960), 'The Independence of Chief
  Constables', Public Administration (38): 1-11.
Marshall, G., (1965), Police and Government. London:
  Methuen.
Raison, T., and Connelly, N., (1975), 'Law and Order'
  in Klein, R., (ed.), Inflation and Priorities. London:
  Centre for Studies in Social Policy.
Regan, D.E., (1966), 'The Police Service: an extreme
  example of central control over local authority staff',
  Public Law Spring: 3-34.
Royal Commission on the Police, (1962), Final Report.
  Cmnd. 1728 London: H.M.S.O.
Schofield, J.A., (1978), 'Determinants of Urban Services
  Expenditure - Fire and Social Services', Local Govern-
  ment Studies (4) No.2: 65-80.
Thomas, M., (1969), The Fire Service and its Personnel.
  London: H.M.S.O.

(vi) Social Work

Davies, B., (1968), Social Needs and Resources in Local
  Services. London: Michael Joseph.
Davies, B., Barton, A., McMillan, I.S., and Williamson, V.,
  (1972), Variations in Services for the Aged. London:
  Bell.
Davies, B., Barton, A., and McMillan, I.S., (1972),
  Variations in Children's Services Among British Urban
  Authorities. London: Bell.
Donnison, D.V., (1962), Health, Welfare and Democracy
  in Greater London. London: London School of Economics
  and Political Science, Greater London Papers, No.5.
Donnison, D.V., and Chapman, V., et.al., (1965), Social
  Policy and Administration. London: Allen and Unwin.
Glennester, H., (1975), Social Service Budgets and
  Social Policy. London: Allen and Unwin.
Hall, P., Land, H., Parker, R., and Webb, R., (1975),
  Change Choice and Conflict in Social Policy. London:
  Heinemann.
Hall, P., (1976), Reforming the Welfare: the politics
  of change in the personal social services. London:
  Heinemann.
Jeffreys, M., (1965), An Anatomy of Social Welfare
  Services. A Survey of Social Welfare Staff and their
  Clients in the County of Buckinghamshire. London:
  Michael Joseph.
McCreadie, C., (1975), 'Personal Social Services', in
  Klein, R., (ed.), Inflation and Priorities. London:
  Centre for Studies in Social Policy.

Parker, J., (1967), Local Health and Welfare Services.
London: Allen and Unwin.
Powell, J.E., (1966), Medicine and Politics. London:
Pitman Medical.

(vii) Transport

Buxton, M., (1975), 'Transport', in Klein, R., (ed.),
Inflation and Priorities. London: Centre for Studies
in Social Policy.
Dunnett, J., (1962), 'The Relationship Between Central
and Local Government in Planning and Execution of Road
Schemes', Public Administration (40): 253-65.
Gregory, R., (1967), 'The Minister's Line: or the M4
comes to Berkshire: Parts I and II', Public
Administration (45): 113-28; 269-86.
Hart, D., (1976), Strategic Planning in London: the
rise and fall of the primary road network. Oxford:
Pergamon.
Rhodes, G., (1965), Administrators in Action Vol. 2.
London: Allen and Unwin.

Section F.2

OTHER SUB-NATIONAL INSTITUTIONS

In keeping with one of the main themes of this book, the
bibliography covers intergovernmental relations in
Britain and not just central-local relations. Moreover,
this section is able to focus on intergovernmental
relations exclusively because an excellent bibliography
has just been published covering many aspects of the
peripheral regions and there is little point in dupli-
cating its contents. See: Pollock and McAllister (1980).
Accordingly, items on nationalism, devolution and
historical accounts of the relationship between the
English and the peripheral regions have been excluded.

One of the first political scientists to explore the
plural nature of British government was Richard Rose.
See: Rose (1976 originally published 1970). Subsequently Hechter's (1975) 'internal colonialism' thesis
has provoked much discussion. See: Page (1978) and Birch
(1977). However, the focus of debate has been 'devolution'. The Commission on the Constitution (1973), and
especially its many volumes of written and oral evidence,
is an important source of both fact and (contentious)
opinion on devolution. A wealth of references are
available in Pollock and McAllister (1980) and some recent
publications are discussed in McLean (1977).

Intergovernmental relations are not limited, however, to
devolution. 'The rise and rise' of quangos is a distinctive feature of the post-war period in Britain. The
pioneering studies are Smith and Hague (1971), Smith (1974)
and Hague et al., (1973). However, the various commentaries by Hood are particularly valuable. The National
Health Service is one group that has attracted a lot of
attention and the series of studies by Brown cover many
aspects of the service including links with other public
sector organisations. Brown (1975) is a useful introduction and the links between the national health service
and local government are discussed in Norton and Rogers
(1977) and Thomas and Stoten (1975).

Of the various peripheral regions, the Isle of Man and
the Channel Islands have attracted least comment. The
Commission on the Constitution (1973) provides a useful
introduction to the islands and this account can be
followed with Home Office (1969) and Kermode (1979).
There is no similar paucity of literature on Northern
Ireland although the vast majority of books and articles
are not concerned with intergovernmental relations. Of
particular use are Lawrence (1965), The Review Body on
Local Government in Northern Ireland (1970) and Birrell
(1978). There is more material specifically on inter-

governmental relations in Scotland. Page (1978) provides
an introduction to the system of central-local relations
in Scotland and Kellas (1975) covers Scottish government
as a whole. The remaining items on Scotland cover more
detailed aspects of the local government system. The
items by Midwinter and Page form part of a continuing
project and further publications on Scottish central-
local relations can be expected. Finally, Madgwick and
James (1980) is probably the first attempt to describe
central-local relations in Wales although Randall (1972)
and Rowlands (1972) both provide accounts of the origins
and development of the Welsh Office. However, as this
section of the bibliography should make clear, there may
be a wealth of material on the peripheral regions but only
a minute proportion of it is concerned with intergovernmental relations.

Section F.2.(a)

OTHER SUB-NATIONAL INSTITUTIONS: GENERAL

Birch, A.H.,   (1977),   Political Integration and Dis-
    integration in the British Isles.   London: Allen and
    Unwin.
Commission on the Constitution 1969-73 (Kilbrandon),
    (1973), Vol. 1, Report. Cmnd. 5460 Vol. 2 Memorandum
    of Dissent by Lord Crowther-Hunt and Professor A.T.
    Peacock. Cmnd. 5460-1 London: H.M.S.O.
Hechter, M.,   (1975),   Internal Colonialism: the Celtic
    Fringe in British National Development 1536-1966.
    London: Routledge and Kegan Paul.
Ionescu, G.,   (1975),   Centripetal Politics: Government
    and the New Centres of Power. London: Hart-Davis,
    MacGibbon.
McLean, I.,   (1977),   'The Politics of Nationalism and
    Devolution', Political Studies (25):   425-30.
Page, E.,   (1978),   'Michael Hechter's Internal Colonial
    Thesis: theoretical and methodological problems',
    European Journal of Political Research (6):   295-317.
Pollock, L., and McAllister, I.   (1980), A Bibliography of
    United Kingdom Politics: Scotland, Wales and Northern
    Ireland. University of Strathclyde, Glasgow: Studies
    in Public Policy Volume III.
Rose, R.,   (1976),   'The United Kingdom As a Multi-Nation-
    al State', in Rose, R., (ed.), Studies in British
    Politics. London: Macmillan, third edn.
Rose, R.,   (1977),   'The United Kingdom as an Intellectual
    Puzzle', Glasgow: University of Strathclyde, Studies in
    Public Policy No.7.
Smith, B.C., and Stanyer, J.,   (1976),   Administering
    Britain. London: Fontana/Collins.
Stanyer, J.,   (1974),   'Nationalism, Regionalism and the
    British System of Government', Social and Economic
    Administration (8): 136-57.

Section F.2.(b)

QUANGOS

(i) <u>General</u>

Beesley, M.E., (1973), 'The Industrial Reorganisation
   Corporation: a study in choice of public management',
   <u>Public Administration</u> (51): 61-89.
Bowen, G., (1978), <u>Survey of Fringe Bodies: a report</u>.
   London: Civil Service Department.
Hague, D.C., Mackenzie, W.J.M., and Barker, A., (eds.),
   (1973), <u>Public Policy and Private Interests</u>. London:
   Macmillan.
Hogwood, B., (1979), 'The Tartan Fringe: Quangos and
   Other Assorted Animals in Scotland', <u>Studies in Public</u>
   <u>Policy</u> No. 34. Glasgow: University of Strathclyde.
Hood, C.C., (1973), 'The Rise and Rise of the British
   Quango', <u>New Society</u> 16 August 1973: 386-8.
Hood, C.C., (1975), 'Government by Other Means', in
   Chapman, B.C., and Potter, A.M., (eds.), <u>WJMM: Political</u>
   <u>Questions</u>. Manchester: Manchester University Press.
Hood, C.C., (1978), 'Keeping the Centre Small:
   explanations of agency type', <u>Political Studies</u> (26):
   30-46.
Hood, C.C., (1979), 'The World of Quasi-government',
   Paper presented to the <u>Annual Conference of the Public</u>
   <u>Administration Committee</u>, University of York.
Hood, C.C., and Bradshaw, J.R., (1977), 'The Family
   Fund: implications of an unorthodox agency', <u>Public</u>
   <u>Administration</u> (55): 447-64.
Jordon, G., (1976), 'Hiving-off and Departmental
   Agencies', <u>Public Administration Bulletin</u> No. 21 August:
   37-51.
National Economic Development Office (1976), <u>A Study of</u>
   <u>UK Nationalised Industries</u>. London: H.M.S.O.
Smith, B.L.R., (ed.), (1974), <u>The New Political Economy:</u>
   <u>the Public use of the private Sector</u>. London:
   Macmillan.
Smith, B.L.R. and Hague, D.C., (eds.), (1971), <u>The</u>
   <u>Dilemma of Accountability in Modern Government</u>. London:
   Macmillan.

Section F.2.(b)

(ii) <u>National Health Service</u>

Brown, R.G.S., (1979), <u>Reorganising the National Health</u>
   <u>Service</u>. Oxford: Basil Blackwell and Martin Robertson.
Brown, R.G.S., Griffin, S., and Haywood, S.C.,
   <u>Preparations for Change</u>; (1973),
   <u>Waiting for Guidance</u>; (1974),
   <u>The Shadow and the Substance</u>; (1975),
   <u>New Bottles: Old Wine</u>. Hull: University of Hull,
   Institute of Health Studies.
Brown, R.G.S., (1975), <u>The Management of Welfare</u>.Glasgow:

183

Fontana/Collins.

Brown, R.G.S., (1976), 'Collaboration Between the N.H.S. and Local Government', Local Government Studies (2) No. 2: 15-25.

Kogan, M., (1976), 'Reorganisation of the National Health Service on Humberside', Local Government Studies (2) No.3: 71-75.

Norton, A., and Rogers, S., (1977), Collaboration Between Health Authorities and Local Authorities. Birmingham: Institute of Local Government Studies.

Norton, A., (1978), 'Implementation of Policies with Special Reference to the field of Socio-Medical Care in Britain'. Paper presented to the European Consortium for Political Research, joint sessions, Grenoble.

Thomas, N., and Stoten,B.,(1974), 'The N.H.S. and Local Government', in Jones, K., (ed.), The Year Book of Social Policy 1973. London: Routledge and Kegan Paul.

Section F.2.(c)

THE PERIPHERY

(i) Channel Islands and the Isle of Man

Commission on the Constitution 1969-1973 (Kilbrandon), (1973), Vol. 1., Report. Cmnd. 4040 London: H.M.S.O.

Gladden, E.N., (1967), Civil Services of the United Kingdom 1855-1970. London: Frank Cass.

Le Herissier, P., (1971), The Development of the Government of Jersey. Unpublished Ph.D. thesis, University of Kent.

Home Office (1969), Report on the Joint Working Party on the Constitutional Relationship between the Isle of Man and the United Kingdom. London: H.M.S.O.

Kermode, D.G., (1968), 'Legislative - Executive Relationships in the Isle of Man', Political Studies (16): 18-42.

Kermode, D.G., (1974), 'Regional Self-Government: A Case Study of the Isle of Man', Public Administration (52): 161-77.

Kermode, D.G., (1973/4), 'Legislation without Representation: the Application of U.K. Legislation to the Isle of Man', Parliamentary Affairs (27): 67-81.

Kermode, D.G., (1979), Devolution at Work: a case-study of the Isle of Man. Farnborough, Hants.: Saxon House.

Political and Economic Planning, (1960), 'Local Self-Government. The Experience of the U.K., the Isle of Man and the Channel Islands', Planning (26) No. 444: 231-78.

Section F.2.(c)

(ii) Northern Ireland

Birrell, D., (1978), 'The Centralisation of Local
   Government Functions in Northern Ireland - an Appraisal',
   Local Government Studies (4) No. 4: 23-37.
Busteed, M.A., and Mason, H., (1971), 'Local Government
   Reform in Northern Ireland', Irish Geographer (6):
   315-322.
Commission on the Constitution 1969-1973 (Kilbrandon),
   (1973), Vol. 1, Report. Cmnd. 5460 London: H.M.S.O.
Johnston, J.H., (1970), 'Reorganisation of Local
   Government in Northern Ireland', Area (4): 17-21.
Lawrence, R.J., (1965), The Government of Northern
   Ireland: Public Finance and Public Services 1921-64.
   Oxford: Clarendon Press.
Mackintosh, J.P., (1971), 'The Report of the Review Body
   on Local Government in Northern Ireland: the Macrory
   Report', Public Administration (49): 13-23.
The Review Body on Local Government in Northern Ireland
   (1970), Report. Cmnd. 546. Belfast: H.M.S.O.

Section F.2.(c)

(iii) Scotland

Clarke, M.G., and Drucker, H.M., (1976), Our Changing
   Scotland: A Yearbook of Scottish Government 1976-77.
   Edinburgh: EUSPB.
Committee of Inquiry into Local Government Finance
   (Layfield), (1976), Report. Cmnd. 6453 London:
   H.M.S.O.
Currie, A., (1957), 'Valuation and Rating in Scotland',
   Public Administration (35): 187-91.
Commission on the Constitution 1969-1973 (Kilbrandon),
   (1973), Vol. 1, Report. Cmnd. 5460 London: H.M.S.O.
Drucker, H.M., and Clarke, M.G., (1978), The Scottish
   Government Yearbook 1978. Edinburgh: Paul Harris.
Duff, R.R., (undated), Patterns of Expenditure and
   Financial Control in Scottish Government/Administration.
   Edinburgh: Department of Politics, Edinburgh University.
Heald, D., (1979), 'The Scottish Rate Support Grant:
   How Different from the English and Welsh?' Paper
   presented to the Joint Conference of the Local Politics
   and United Kingdom Politics Groups of the Political
   Studies Association, University of Strathclyde, March
   1979.
Howat, B., (1976), Policy Planning and the First
   Regional Reports in Scotland. Glasgow: The Planning
   Exchange. Occasional Paper No. 2.
Keating, M.J., (1973), 'The Scottish Local Government
   Bill', Local Government Studies (1) No.1: 49-61.
Keating, M.J., (1976), 'Administrative Devolution in
   Practice: the Secretary of State for Scotland and the

Scottish Office', Public Administration (54): 133-45.
Kellas, J.G., (1975), The Scottish Political System.
London: Cambridge University Press, second edn.
Lipman, V.D., (1949), 'Some Contrasts Between English
and Scottish Local Government', Public Administration
(27): 168-80.
Local Government (Scotland) Act 1973, London: H.M.S.O.
Local Government Finance in Scotland, (1977), Cmnd. 6811,
Edinburgh: H.M.S.O.
McDonald, S.T., (1977), 'The Regional Report in Scotland:
A Study of Change in the Planning Process', Town
Planning Review (48): 215-32.
Mackintosh, J.P., (1964), 'Regional Administration: Has
it Worked in Scotland?', Public Administration (42):
253-75.
Mackintosh, J.P., (1964), 'Devolution, Regionalism and
the Reform of Local Government: the Scottish Case',
Public Law Spring: 19-32.
Mackintosh, J.P., (1968), The Devolution of Power.
Harmondsworth: Penguin Books.
Mackintosh, J.P., (1970), 'The Royal Commission on Local
Government in Scotland', Public Administration (48):
49-56.
Midwinter, A.F., (1979), 'Local Authority Financial
Planning in a Turbulent Environment', Glasgow:
University of Strathclyde, Studies in Public Policy No.
46.
Midwinter, A.F., and Page, E., (1979), 'Remote
Bureaucracy or Administrative Efficiency: Scotland's
New Local Government System', Glasgow: University of
Strathclyde, Studies in Public Policy No. 38.
Milne, Sir D., (1957), The Scottish Office. London:
Allen and Unwin.
Page, E., (1978), 'Why Should Central-Local Relations in
Scotland be Different to Those in England?', Public
Administration Bulletin No. 28 December: 51-72.
Reform of Local Government in Scotland. Cmnd. 4583.
Edinburgh: H.M.S.O.
Royal Commission on Local Government in Scotland 1966-1969
(Wheatley), (1969), Report. Cmnd. 4150 London:
H.M.S.O.
Stonefrost, M.F., (1976), 'Local Government and Devo-
lution after Layfield', Paper to the Annual Conference
of the Society of Local Authority Chief Executives,
Brighton, 2 June.
Wilkinson, M., and Howat, B., (1977), Regional Reports
and Structure Plans in Scotland. Glasgow: The Planning
Exchange, Occasional Paper No. 3.
Young, R., (1977), The Search for Democracy: a guide to
and polemic about Scottish local government. Glasgow:
Heatherbank Press.

Section F.2.(c)

(iv) <u>Wales</u>

Commission on the Constitution 1969-73 (Kilbrandon),
    (1973), Vol. 1, <u>Report</u>. Cmnd. 5460 London: H.M.S.O.
Madgwick, P.J., and James, M., (1980), 'The Network of
    Consultative Government in Wales', in Jones, G.W., (ed.)
    <u>Central-Local Relations in Britain.</u> Farnborough, Hants:
    Saxon House.
Randall, P.J., (1972), 'Wales in the Structure of
    Central Government', <u>Public Administration</u> (50): 353-72.
Rowlands, E., (1972), 'The Politics of Regional
    Administration: the Establishment of the Welsh Office',
    <u>Public Administration</u> (50): 333-51.
Trice, J.E., (1970), 'Welsh Local Government Reform: an
    assessment of ad hoc administrative reform', <u>Public Law</u>
    Autumn: 277-47.
Welsh Office (1971), <u>The Reform of Local Government in</u>
    <u>Wales</u>. Cardiff: H.M.S.O.
A.B. Phillip, <u>The Welsh Question</u> (Cardiff: University of
    Wales Press, 1975).

Author index

189

Subject index